The Word of the Light

Thomas Dexter Lynch
and
Cynthia Elizabeth Lynch

◆

Hara Publishing

Scott Balsdon Company
Baton Rouge, LA
–preparation and development–

DEDICATION

This book is dedicated to Sri Chinmoy — spiritual master, Guru, and friend. With his gentle love to guide me, I have come so far — I know I have still so much farther to go.

The discerning reader will easily note the influence my Guru, Sri Chinmoy, has had on the preparation of this book. As my teacher for more than fifteen years, he has taught me so much. I am forever in his debt.

All my heart's infinite love. All my soul's eternal gratitude.

Faithfully,

Varayuvati

Cynthia E. Lynch

Baton Rouge, Louisiana, 1998

ACKNOWLEDGEMENTS

Preparing a book is rarely the work of one person. Interestingly, getting reactions to the early versions of this work was difficult and we acknowledge the reactions especially of Ann Allen, Roli Balsdon, Darly S. DeArmond, Richard Omdal,Gary Duty, and Kenneth S. Zagacki. Max Davis offered useful practical publishing suggestions. John Larkin volunteered his professional skills to do the composition. John Protevi was the manuscript copy editor. Vicki McCown was the final copy editor. Sheryn Hara was the marketing and distribution agent. Judy Johnson and Pam McLaughlin did the cover design. Indexing was done by Nancy Ball. Secretarial assistance was provided by Shirley Dejean and Elizabeth Russ.

Although the selection of quotes and the transitional sentences are the work of these authors, we must recognize this book is really over 900 quotes from what we believe is the heart of the holy scriptures of five religious traditions. More will be said in the introduction, but in this acknowledgement we felt the need to recognize that this work is really our attempt to properly reflect the combined wisdom of many traditions.

TABLE OF CONTENTS

ACQUIRING SPIRITUAL WISDOM

THE KINGDOM OF
GOD APPRENTICESHIP

FEW WILL SUCCEED BUT ALL CAN

BRINGING FORTH THE FRUIT

JOIN GOD

WARNINGS

CLARIFICATIONS

WHAT IS NEXT?

REFERENCES

INDEX

Foreword

◆

I can see now why my grandfather, Mohandas Karamchand Gandhi, was so perturbed by the religious differences around the world. Civilization, to him and to most reasonable people, means progressing, improving, rising above the level at which we are. In other words, it means progressing from a state of being uneducated to being educated; from backward to being forward; from ignorance to being wise.

Yet, ironically, the more "civilized" we become the more violent and intolerant we are becoming. Obviously, something is seriously wrong. Gandhi recognized the fault of modern civilization when he said "there is an inverse relationship between materialism and morality. When one increases the other decreases." Our incessant pursuit of materialism has corrupted our morals, ethics, values and beliefs.

He was pained that religion, which is the universal quest for peace and salvation, was being misused to divide and destroy humanity. How can we find peace, if we hate so much? How can we value life, if we are willing to kill?

How can we carry a gun in one hand and the Bible in the other and with a heart full of malice seek redemption and salvation? Why do we turn religion into everything that it should not be? So divisive? So competitive? So totally devoid of Truth?

As children growing in the ashram commune, we often listened to Grandfather tell us that religion must be seen as a huge tree. The trunk of the tree represented spirituality, the branches represented the various religions and the leaves the various denominations. All the religions derived their nourishment from the same source, "spirituality." In its totality the tree looks beautiful and serves humanity positively. However, when dismembered it loses its beauty and usefulness.

At other times he used the analogy of a mountain. If the objective is to get to the summit, why should it matter to anyone from which side one gets there? It is the same with religion. If the summit we are trying to reach is salvation, why should it matter which religion one chooses to follow to attain peace and salvation? This should be an individual choice and must be respected by all.

Gandhi never said anything he could not first put into practice. His daily prayers, known widely as the Gandhi Prayer and attended by hundreds every morning and evening, incorporated hymns from every major religion of the world.

A friendly study of all scriptures, he said, is the sacred duty of every individual. He encouraged everyone to undertake this "friendly" study with an open mind so that we could take from each all that is important and relevant.

No religion is perfect, he said, and none possesses the TRUTH. All religions are trying their best to seek answers to such vexing questions as: The meaning of life. Instead of beating each other on the heads we ought to be helping in this quest. Is it not ironical that humankind has killed and maimed more people in the name of Love, Peace, God and Salvation than ever before?

As we approach the twenty-first century and a new millennium, the questions that inevitably assail one's mind are: Should we carry the garbage of the twentieth century into the next one? Do we really have to? Can we not change our ways? Will change come only after total annihilation of human life?

Dr. Thomas D. and Cynthia E. Lynch have endeavored to show humankind the "oneness" of all religions of the world. I know this scholarship will not be wasted. It will take us a step nearer the realization that faith, like the sun enlightens and enriches everyone equally.

Arun Gandhi

Introduction

<hr />

This book is titled *The Word of the Light* because it is about God's spiritual wisdom found in the fundamental writings of every religion. In those writings, "light" and "word of the light" are common metaphors for spiritual wisdom. The assertion that spiritual wisdom is the permanent universal truth of God raises some problems. One is that many people and groups claim to know **the** spiritual wisdom on virtually every subject. Conversely, many others claim that spiritual wisdom does not exist.

Given these conflicting claims about spiritual wisdom, how can we decide what spiritual wisdom is? The sciences use the Scientific Method to define "acceptable knowledge or truths," but postmodernist philosophers argue that realistically there cannot be any universal truths about God or anything else (Grenz: 1996). Although we understand that philosophy has not developed any totally accepted proof for the acceptance or the denial of God's existence, we wrote this book under the assumption that God does exist, simply based on our faith. We also believe He has been communicating His spiritual wisdom to humankind continually throughout time and that we can read that wisdom in the most sacred books of the world's religious traditions. To isolate the spiritual wisdom used in this book, we applied the simple method of consensus. If a given spiritual wisdom is common to the five major current religious traditions (i.e., Hinduism, Judaism, Buddhism, Christianity, and Islam), we consider the spiritual wisdom as universal and authentic.

FUNDAMENTAL QUESTION AND BOOK THEME

This book addresses the fundamental question: What is the purpose of our individual and collective existence? Our answer uses, literally, the word of God as articulated in the holy scriptures of today's five largest religious traditions. Thus, regardless of the tradition to which you might belong, the answer to the fundamental question is the same because the message is the same from each tradition. There is no more important question to the inquiring mind than: "Why do I exist?" People who have struggled with this fundamental question know that they are dealing with a mystery of remarkable complexity. Some have concluded that there is no purpose to our individual or collective existence, only that there is such an existence. Others have chosen to impose their own reason, such as the continual accumulation of knowledge so as to leave an increasingly better inheritance for our descendants. Some have decided that God has nothing to do with the answer, whereas others, including these authors, believe God is essentially the answer.

The answer presented here centers on God's existence and each person's relationship to God because our answer is derived by citing over nine hundred scripture quotes from the five traditions. Except for this introduction, the authors of this book limited their own thoughts to providing transitions and attempting to add clarity to the quotes throughout the book. The fundamental question is answered in each section of this book simply by using the words of the combined holy scriptures. Because this work is rooted firmly in the combined spiritual wisdom literature of humankind, it represents a unified answer of almost all those who have faith in God. One of the subtleties of spiritual wisdom is that it is best understood by looking at the entirety but can only be grasped individually. For all of us, spiritual wisdom is a series of mysteries. Although we have to solve them with our own efforts, we are continually given clues that allow us to discover them.

Spiritual wisdom is also one whole with many interdependent parts that work together as a single system. As we examine each part, we need to understand it both in terms of each separate concept but also in terms of how that concept interrelates with the other parts. Thus, to solve the mysteries we need to examine each new concept within the context of what we have already learned. Solving these mysteries appears to be similar to a building process or like moving down a path where we slowly add one additional concept at a time but always reflecting on how it interrelates with what we have already learned. What might seem like repetition in later sections is really a reexamination of earlier concepts with an awareness that is much deeper, thanks to our accumulated knowledge.

After this introduction, this book is divided into 11 parts with 114 sections that progressively add the additional clues or concepts we eventually use to solve the mysteries of spiritual wisdom, thus answering this book's fundamental question. Each section has at least one holy scripture quote from each of the five major religious traditions and each section averages about eight quotes per section. Each part has several sections with some having as few as three but most having 12. The first part, SEEK AND YOU WILL FIND, begins our learning process with twelve essential concepts. For example, our attitude must be one of discovery and we must seek until we successfully solve the mysteries. The second part, UNDERSTANDING GOD, explains (1) that we must perceive that we are not yet capable of fully understanding God, (2) that He wants our commitment, and not mere gestures, to learning His mysteries, and (3) that we must stop trying to understand God by redefining Him into our own image. The third part, THE PATH CALLED LIFE, addresses directly why God gave us life. The fourth part, ACQUIRING SPIRITUAL WISDOM, explains why spiritual wisdom is central to our quest and how we should go about acquiring it.

The fifth part, THE KINGDOM OF GOD APPRENTICESHIP, explains more advanced lessons such as the source of spiritual wisdom and the significance of having a righteous heart. The sixth part, FEW WILL

SUCCEED BUT ALL CAN, presents an explanation of why so few will solve the mysteries in spite of the fact that all can be successful. The seventh part, BRING FORTH THE FRUIT, helps us to realize that solving the mysteries is not sufficient because we must also internalize what we have learned. The eighth part, JOIN GOD, tells us bluntly that we can, should, and will be God's treasure if we both embrace and join Him. The ninth part, WARN-INGS, points out the difficulties that make joining God a constant challenge. The tenth part, CLARIFICATIONS, helps the seeker who has gained some spiritual wisdom to understand more complex considerations such as the likely condemnation from others concerning their new spirituality. The eleventh part, WHAT IS NEXT, presents the conclusions of this book, including the importance of honoring God's wish that we all must have the free choice to believe or not to believe in God.

Many readers will find this book an excellent tool for self-help or personal motivation. However, upon further examination of this book, the reader will soon discover that an implicit irony exists. We need to seek God, the Kingdom of God, and Oneness with God not because of self-help reasons but because it is the correct thing to do. If we do that, remarkable improvements will be made in oneself and even collectively in humankind, but the individual's motivation needs to be something larger — namely, love of God. The irony is that we get what we truly want by not wanting it. We get what we truly want by loving God and all of God's creation.

THE GOSPEL OF THOMAS

The challenge for us was to find how to look for a common spiritual wisdom message. Given the remarkable volume of written material on the five major religious traditions, how can one proceed? One advantage the authors had is that all the scriptures are translated into English. Although the translations can and do present some problems, at least the significant scriptures exist in English. The initial research challenge was to identify a key so that we could focus on our inquiry in a manageable manner. The key we selected was the text called the **Gospel of Thomas,** or sometimes, the *fifth gospel* (Winterhalter: 1988).

The existing organized Christian faiths do not yet recognize the **Gospel of Thomas** as holy scripture, as the world of the twentieth century only redis-covered it a few decades ago (Winterhalter: 1988, 1 & 5). Given the fact that church "authorities" take centuries to debate and decide such issues, we felt its delayed inclusion was not significant for our inquiry. In addition, we rather liked its separation from the existing Christian version of the *Bible* as we want-ed to show a little less bias on our part in terms of favoring current tradition-al Christian texts.

We selected the **Gospel of Thomas** as the key analytical tool in this inquiry for several reasons. Firstly, it is a short collection of 114 sayings that are mostly direct quotes of Jesus Christ. Given that Christianity is currently the largest religion, we felt His sayings were an appropriate focus of inquiry. Secondly, many early Christians, in the first centuries of the religion, consid-ered these quotes central to the understanding of their Christian faith (Layton: 1987, xvi). Thirdly, the sayings correspond closely to the accepted Christian scriptures but are much more manageable for purposes of our analysis. Fourthly, Apostle Thomas or someone using his name compiled these sayings about the same time and possibly even earlier than the existing accepted Christian scriptures (Layton: 1987, 377; Bloom: 1992). Because they remained buried for centuries, there was less opportunity for alteration by later religious editors for church or political reasons. And fifthly, since the say-ings are apparently randomly ordered, someone is not likely to have written or edited them to advance some special cause (Layton: 1987, 376).

The latter is an important consideration because both religious and secular leaders have used religious works over the centuries for various political pur-poses (Freidman: 1987 & 1989). Finding an ancient document that had little likelihood of being revised for political purposes at some point in history is dif-ficult and speaks to the significance of the **Gospel of Thomas**.

THE DISCOVERY

The scientific community only recently discovered and brought to the attention of the public the full text of the **Gospel of Thomas.**   It was buried in Egypt for over a thousand years until a remarkable discovery shortly after World War II (Robinson: 1987, x). Ancient prophecies foretold that the Gnostic books would again see the light of day when the world arrived at a state of readiness to hear the messages (Singer: 1995, 54-69).   The Hermetists, associated with the Platonic Academy, were also known for unearthing books hidden away in Egypt's remote past (Conze: 1995, 138-139). Until the gospel was systematically destroyed by Imperial Rome, early Christians used it for several centuries and at least one copy was buried to save it for later generations.

Fragments of the gospel written in the ancient Greek language existed prior to the Egyptian discovery of the buried text (Layton: 1987, 378). Indeed the differences in translations between those few Greek fragments and the later ones found in the Coptic language text are of interest and are noted later in this book. The first international language that early Christians used was ancient Greek. It was a rich and even in some ways superior language to modern English. As Christianity spread to the Gentile communities, Greek became the important language (Layton: 1987, xxiii).

Early Christian thought was not limited, though, to any particular languages; the language of Egypt, for instance, was Coptic. The important city of Alexandria and the nation of Egypt were significant centers of culture (Layton: 1987, xxiv). Naturally, the Egyptian religious community translated almost all Christian written materials into the Coptic language (Robinson: 1987, 2). With the establishment of monasteries as centers of learning, the major and even minor monasteries had collections of the major religious writings that were central to their faith (Meinardus: 1989; Robinson: 1987, 19).

In December 1945, Muhammad 'Ali al-Sammān Muhammad Khalifah discovered what is now called the *Nag Hammadi Library.* This collection of writings included the **Gospel of Thomas** (Robinson: 1987, ix). The date marked not only the end of World War II but also the Christmas season. The discoverer of the library compounds the oddity of the discovery. He was not a noted researcher or archeologist but a camel driver from the Egyptian village of El Gasr. He found the collection of Coptic books in a large clay jar in a cave near Hamra Dom and the larger Nag Hammadi. He was digging for fertilizer. Within four weeks of the discovery, there was another bizarre twist of circumstances. In an act of vengeance, he killed his father's murderer and never returned to Nag Hammadi for fear of further retaliation. Interestingly, the Arabic meaning of the discovery site is "highly commendable place" (Rudolph: 1987, 41-42).

Henri-Charles Puech, an early French researcher on the *Nag Hammadi Library*, described the place of discovery as "a high cliff of chalk whose southern slope faced the bend formed by the Nile some 60 miles downstream from Luxor" (Rudolph: 1987, 39). Moses most likely knew the area many years earlier. The cliffs were quite near the ancient Shenesit-Chenoboskion, where St. Pachomius founded his first monasteries in the fourth century. In the binding of one book were two receipts for grain from the district of Dispolis and Dendera. The receipts bear the dates 333, 341, 346, and 348. Academics date the discovery from about 350 A.D. and the Coptic text confirms the time. Fragments of letters in the binding that mention a Father Pachom imply a monastic environment (Rudolph: 1987, 43).

Although the reason for the burial of the texts is impossible to learn, Rome considered the Gnostic texts, including the **Gospel of Thomas,** to be heretical at the time of their burial. Surprisingly, a letter from that time did survive to our era. It was the 39th Festal Letter of Athanasius of Alexandria, which was written against "heretical books." The letter says that false books were being circulated under the names of the Apostles (Rudolph: 1987). Could the Apostles and their associates have written the *Nag Hammadi Library?* Has a more complete version of the New Testament emerged after centuries? The contemporary academic community believes that most "books" of the library were written many years after the New Testament scriptures. Nevertheless, such noted people as Apostles John, James, and Andrew, and even Mary, the closest friend of Jesus Christ, are the authors according to the documents themselves (Robinson: 1987).

As a set of documents, they often address the myths of Christianity using a Gnostic theme (Robinson: 1987; Layton: 1987, xxiv & xxvi). The Gnostic movement in early Christianity was significant. The movement may date from the time of Christ Himself but scholars know the movement was active as early as 180 A.D. (Layton:1987, 8). As a school of thought, it was often inconsistent and highly imaginative, with its own dualistic version of the creation story contrary to that of the Old Testament (Layton: 1987, 12-17). The purpose of this book does not include a description of the Gnostic movement except to note its relationship to the **Gospel of Thomas**. For a comprehensive presentation of the Gnostic works discovered in 1948, the reader should refer to the *Nag Hammadi Library* itself (Robinson: 1987).

The Christian faith became *the state faith* of the Roman Empire after Constantine became the undisputed emperor of the Roman Empire in 325 A.D. (deHaven-Smith: 1994, 47; Layton: 1987, xvii; Mack: 1994, 287-288). One year later the emperor called the first council of Christian bishops to meet in Nicae. The Emperor wanted a religion with standards and regular-ized procedures as a practical necessity for his empire (Mack: 1994, 287-289). Possibly as an indirect result of the wishes of the emperor, someone, perhaps a monk, buried the *Nag Hammadi Library* in order, presumably, to save it for future generations. In this same era, Jerome prepared the first *Bible* in Latin using about one-third of the Christian material then available, excluding the Gnostic gospels and the **Gospel of Thomas** (Rudolph: 1987, 41-42). The established church, working through the state, exterminated the heretical groups, as has been the practice at other times in Christian history. Given the message of Jesus Christ, such actions seem wrong, but the facts are well estab-lished by history and do reflect the all-too-common character of humankind. The Roman Christian genocide applied to both the Christian Gnostics them-selves and all of their written tradition. The execution of the policy was remarkably efficient. Ironically, for centuries the only trace of Gnostic thought that existed were the writings of the church leaders who argued that the Gnostics were heretics: a very one-sided but accepted argument (Robinson: 1987, 5; Layton: 1987, xxiv & xxvi). Eventually, after the enlight-enment period, some adventurers discovered a few Gnostic works (Layton: 1987, xxvii; Mead: not dated). The contemporary academic community had to wait until the Nag Hammadi discovery before there was a reasonable cumulative understanding of the Gnostic version of Christianity (Kloppenborg, et al.:1990, 91). One book in that so-called library collection is the **Gospel of Thomas**.

THE TEXT ITSELF

The **Gospel of Thomas** begins, "These are the hidden sayings that the living Jesus uttered and which Jude, who is called Thomas, wrote down." *Didymos Judas Thomas* compiled the 114 sayings of Jesus Christ that compose the **Gospel of Thomas**. According to the academic community, the purported authors of many of the books in the library and even the *Bible* are incorrect (Bloom: 1992; Mack: 1994). In the case of the **Gospel of Thomas**, the possibility exists that the Apostle Thomas did write it (Mack: 1993 and 1994). Even if the Apostle Thomas did not write the exact words in the gospel, it is likely to reflect his view because in that era schools were associated with major teachers. They used the name of their master and wrote as if their master were writing the document (Kloppenborg, et al.:1990, 91).

The Syrian church in the area of Edessa with which Thomas is associated is the likely original source of this gospel. Current scholars doubt if the compiler composed the entire gospel in Aramaic, the language of Christ, and then translated it into Greek. However, they do believe that many sayings were first circulated in Aramaic, and there may be a very close relationship between the **Gospel of Thomas** and the so-called **Q** (from the German word "Quelle," meaning "source") (Mack: 1993, 181). The academic community believes that the authors of the canonical gospels used the Q in preparing what we call the New Testament. The Q was a collection of Jesus' sayings and the canonical gospels added information to make a literary story from the sayings (Mack: 1993, 183).

Although a part of the Gnostic *Nag Hammadi Library* collection, the **Gospel of Thomas** lacks the reference to the typical dualistic concept of the creation of humankind associated with most Gnostic materials (Layton: 1987, 12 & xvi). Jesus and others called Didymos Judas Thomas the **twin** of Jesus Christ and James the **brother** of Christ. Both terms suggested not a family tie but a description of the closeness of the two Apostles to Christ's consciousness and viewpoint (Layton: 1987, 359). Both the Aramaic "thomas" and the Greek "didymos" mean "twin" (Koester: 1978).

The Apostle Thomas was the one apostle who was most similar to Jesus Christ (Meyer: 1992, 67-68). Thomas is not only associated with the church at Edessa but some claim he brought Christianity to India (Layton: 1987, 359

& 361; Kersten:1986, 1994; Prophet: 1984, 1987). Scholars believe that the **Gospel of Thomas** preserved a more original form of the actual sayings of Christ than the New Testament (Mack: 1993, 181 & 183; Layton: 1987, 377; Koester: 1978, 125; Mack: 1994, 61). The **Gospel of Thomas** was likely written about the same time as the Q — about 50 to 90 years after the birth of Christ — and thus written before the synoptic gospels (Layton: 1987, 377; Robinson: 1987, 194; Mack: 1994, 60). The synoptic **Gospels of Matthew, Mark, and Luke** may have influenced the Coptic *translators* of the **Gospel of Thomas** but not the original writer (Koster: 1978, 125). In this book, we sometimes used the Greek rather than the Coptic version when fragments existed, as we felt that the Greek might be more accurate. Our assumption was that there are fewer translation mistakes in the Greek version (Winterholster: 1988, 4).

When the translation might make a difference to our understanding, both Greek and Coptic versions are presented in this book. Certainly there may have been some word changes that took place in the **Gospel of Thomas** as monks and others translated it from language to language in the early Christian era, but we also assume that great care was taken to record the information correctly, as this was before Christianity became the Roman state religion. The gospel was frozen (literally buried) in time since the middle of the fourth century. This suggests that it may have suffered less corruption due to scribe and translation changes than the New Testament itself.

We referred to two translations of the **Gospel of Thomas** in this book. We used the Marvin Meyer translation as the primary one. At this writing, Dr. Meyer is a professor of religion at Chapman University. His translation appears in his 1992 book *The Gospel of Thomas*. We also employed the translations of Bentley Layton, a professor of ancient Christian history at Yale University, which appeared in his 1987 book *The Gnostic Scriptures*. Professor Layton makes reference to the Greek fragments. We used several of those Greek fragments in this book as noted in the actual presentations of the sayings. If Professor Layton's name is not cited next to the **Gospel of Thomas** quote in this book, the Meyer translation was used. In some quotes we used the symbols < >. This is part of the quoted translation and it means the translator is adding the words between the symbols. In some cases, the symbols <...> and [ ] are used to indicate missing material. The use of ( ) within quoted material means the translator supplied text for the sake of clarity.

In his book Professor Layton notes that the **Gospel of Thomas** is a concentration of sayings *focusing on the theme of salvation.* Eschatological sayings are conspicuously absent. Stress is placed on the role of the individual in reaching salvation, the importance of the Grace of God, and responsibility of the person who accepts this message (Layton: 1987, 377).

The authority and authenticity of the sayings are strong. The use of the disconnected sayings of the wise is traditionally reserved for authoritative wisdom of a wise sage in this era. Thus, the format suggests that these are the true sayings of Jesus Christ. The **Gospel of Thomas** often quotes Jesus directly. These epithets and the lack of any historical framework reinforce the implication that the quotes reflect the heavenly wisdom of Jesus. The fact that the **twin** of Christ is the author of the gospel also adds to the authentication of the document. People in this region had an especially high regard for Thomas's personal authority. He not only presents the sayings but implies that the sayings constitute the hidden message of Jesus Christ. He suggests that the reader can discover the meaning of the saying. The use of the term "gospel" adds to the authority and authenticity as the term is reserved for uniquely important religious documents (Layton: 1987, 377 & 378).

BOOK ORGANIZATION

The **Gospel of Thomas** is the linchpin of this book, as it is our primary source to organize the universal spiritual wisdom found in the five religious traditions. Each of the 114 sayings of the gospel constitutes the topic for the sections of this book. We believe that shared wisdom is **all-important**. Spiritual wisdom teaches us that God has loved us and continues to love everyone of us throughout time. This belief led us to conclude that true spiritual wisdom must be present in the holy scriptures of at least the five current major religious traditions. We selected quotes from the major scriptures from each tradition. For example, we used the *Koran* for the Islam tradition. We recognized that Arabic is the correct language to read the *Koran*, but our inability to read Arabic led us to use the *Koran* translated by N. J. Dawood and published in 1993 by Penguin Books of New York. We used the King James version for both the *Hebrew Bible* and New Testament quotes. The italics in the King James quotes are special emphases placed there by the preparers of the *Bible* and not the authors of this book. For the Hindu tradition, we used the book *Hindu Scriptures* translated by R. C. Zaehner and published in 1992 by J. M. Dent and Sons Ltd. of London, England. For the Buddhist tradition, we selected four books: (1) *Dhammapada*, translated by Thomas Cleary and published in 1994 by Bantam Books of New York; (2) *The Diamond Sutra and The Sutra of Hui-neng*, translated by A. F. Price and Wong Mou-lam and published in 1990 by Shambhala of Boston; (3) *What The Buddha Taught*, written and translated by Walpola Rahula and published in 1974 by Grove Weidenfeld of New York; and (4) *The Sutra on the Eight Realizations of the Great Being*, written and translated by Thich Nhat Hanh and published in in 1987 by Parallax Press of Berkeley, California.

The form of citation after each quote requires clarification. For the *Koran* the first number represented the chapter and the second represented the approximate paragraph of the English version using the translator's method. For the *Hebrew Bible* and the New Testament, we cited the book name, chapter number, and verse number used in the King James version of the *Bible*. For the Hindu scriptures, we cited specific books by chapter and approximate paragraph number in our English version. For the Buddhist scriptures, we cited a book or well known work with the approximate paragraph number from our English version. We used boldface type to enable the reader to more easily identify the source religious document.

We suggest this book be read deliberately from the first saying to the last. As one section is finished, we suggest that you meditate and reflect on what you have read. We hope you enjoy this introduction to spiritual wisdom as much as we have enjoyed and grown from researching and writing this book. As the **Gospel of Thomas** says, *"Whoever has ears to hear should hear."*

Seek
and You Shall Find

DISCOVER THE INTERPRETATION

Question:

How can we reach God and His salvation?

Brief Answer:

We can reach God by discovering and solving
for ourselves God's mysteries.

from the *Gospel of Thomas*

1. And He said, "Whoever discovers the interpretation of these sayings will not
   taste death."

Longer Answer:

This **Gospel of Thomas** saying communicates two important lessons about spiritual wisdom: (1) the eternal character of spiritual wisdom and (2) the need to constantly search for it.

First, the permanence of spiritual wisdom. This is expressed by using the metaphor "will not taste death." In a similar manner, the **New Testament** says, "Abraham is dead, and the prophets; and thou sayest, If man keep my saying, he shall never taste of death" (John 8:52). Spiritual wisdom is about the universal and the permanent.

Spiritual wisdom commonly uses metaphors to explain important truths. For example, the **New Testament** uses the expressions "Kingdom of Heaven" or "Kingdom of God." These two metaphors represent the "ideal" and "reality" expressing the permanent truth of God. They contrast with the alternative "ideal" or "reality" called the Kingdom of Man. In this situation, the difference between the human and divine kingdoms means one is temporary and includes death and the other is permanent and does not know death. Throughout this book, we refer to one as the Kingdom of Man and the other as the Kingdom of God.

The second lesson from this saying invites each individual, as a seeker, to discover God's mysteries. In the **Gospel of Thomas**, Jesus continually confronts us with mysteries in these sayings, just as God presents us with mysteries as we proceed through our lives. In the **Gospel of Thomas**, the metaphor for spiritual mysteries is a complex word puzzle that each of us must solve in our own way. Spiritual wisdom tells us that simply *trying* is the key to successfully reaching the goal of salvation and full understanding. As noted in the introduction, we use the 114 sayings of the **Gospel of Thomas** to understand the larger spiritual wisdom recorded throughout history.

In this book, we look not only at the **New Testament**, but also examine the **Hebrew Bible** (also called the Old Testament) and the spiritual wisdom found in three other traditions: Hinduism, Buddhism, and Islam. The quotes from all the traditions help us grow in our comprehension and appreciation of God's love for all of us and His spiritual wisdom that is found in every place and time. The **Hebrew Bible** describes how to achieve true happiness and understanding through spiritual wisdom as follows:

Happy *is* the man *that* findeth wisdom,
and the man *that* getteth understanding.
For the merchandise of it *is* better than the merchandise of silver,
and the gain thereof than fine gold.
She *is* more precious than rubies:
and all the things thou canst desire are not to be compared unto her.
Length of days *is* in her right hand;
and in her left hand riches and honour.
Her ways *are* ways of pleasantness,
and all her paths *are* peace.
She *is* a tree of life to them that lay hold upon her;
and happy *is every one* that retaineth her.
(Proverbs 3:13-18)

The **Koran** also helps our understanding of spiritual wisdom by using the metaphor "blind." Parables and stories are also common means used to uncover spiritual wisdom in all of the religious traditions. The term "blind" is not used in the sense of *unsighted* but rather to mean *not being able to comprehend* God's mysteries. God places the truth in front of us, but we can not or will not see it. We are not able to transcend our normal human perspective to comprehend the larger perspective of God. The **Koran** says, "Momentous signs have come to you from your Lord. He that sees them shall himself have much to gain, but he who is blind to them shall lose much indeed. I (Muhammad) am not your keeper" (Koran 6:104). God communicates with us freely and frequently, but we sometimes just do not understand.

As we venture into the world of spiritual wisdom, another difficult concept to understand is the limited and illusory nature of the language we use. Although language must be used to communicate ideas and present the holy scriptures, real lasting truth cannot be contained in expressions of any language, fathomed by its definitions, or revealed by persons of title or position. Everything—the very character "life" or "reality"—is limited and impermanent, including language. The Buddhist Sutra says that no language can communicate fully the mysteries of God. Hence, the need for the use of the metaphor, parable, and story. Each of us is a finite being with a finite mind. Nevertheless, we must try to understand the infinite when we think about God and His wisdom.

The following quote from the **Diamond Sutra** presents a conversation between Subhuti, who is a student, and the Tathagata, who has already mastered spiritual wisdom:

> "Subhuti, what do you think? Has the Tathagata attained the consummation of incomparable enlightenment? Has the Tathagata a teaching to enunciate?"
>
> Subhuti answered: "As I understand Buddha's meaning there is no formulation of truth called consummation of incomparable enlightenment. Moreover, the Tathagata has no formulated teaching to enunciate. Wherefore? Because the Tathagata has said **that truth is incontainable and inexpressible. It neither is nor is not** (emphasis added). Thus it is that this unformulated principle is the foundation of the different system of all the sages." (The Diamond Sutra 7)

God's truth is not containable or even totally expressible by our language and our mind.

Spiritual wisdom says the soul's immortality is achieved only when it becomes fully aware of and understands the mysteries of God. Without that awareness, there can be no lasting reality. Thus language becomes a serious obstacle for understanding spiritual wisdom. Accepting this dilemma can be very difficult. After all, how else are we to communicate our thoughts? Fortunately, in spite of the human inability to communicate adequately with language, God's mysteries can be discovered. The question is, How? The Hindu scriptures say that trying to understand spiritual wisdom must be done through the heart. The Hindu writings help us appreciate that our inner awareness of God is, in fact, an aspect of God dwelling within us all. It is the part of us called the self and in this book it is distinguished as the "SELF." According to the Hindu writings, we solve God's mysteries through the heart. The **Upanishad** says, "Truly, this SELF is in the heart. And the etymology of *hrdayam*, 'heart,' is this: *hrdyayam*, He is in the heart. Hence it is [called] *hrdayam*, 'Heart.' Whoever understands it in this way, day in and day out, goes to the heavenly world" (Chandogya Upanishad 8,3:3).

This book is a quest to understand spiritual wisdom through the sayings in the **Gospel of Thomas** with the assistance of the holy scriptures found in other major religious traditions of the world. This book is a search for inner eternal spiritual wisdom. In our own way, each person becomes a seeker of inner wisdom. Spiritual wisdom teaches that God provides us opportunities to learn, but each of us must be motivated and be able to recognize them. Of our own free will, we must choose to seek. Those who do will find great joy. As Jesus said, "If man keeps my saying, he shall never taste of death" (John 8:52).

SEEK UNTIL WE FIND

Question:
How long is the search?

Brief Answer:
We must search until we completely discover.

from the *Gospel of Thomas*

2. Jesus said, "Let one who seeks not stop seeking until one finds; and upon finding, the person will be disturbed; and being disturbed, will be astounded, will reign and will reign over the entirety."
(Based on the Layton translation from Greek fragments, p. 380.)

Longer Answer:

Spiritual wisdom is eternally optimistic. The **Gospel of Matthew** says, "Ask, and it shall be given you; seek, and ye shall find; knock, and it shall be opened unto you: For every one that asketh receiveth; and he that seeketh findeth; and to him that knocketh it shall be opened" (Matthew 7:7-8). According to the spiritual wisdom, anyone who truly seeks will find the answers; but we must continue to seek until we are successful. The **Koran** says, "Do not be quick to recite the **Koran** before its revelation is completed, but rather say: 'Lord, increase my knowledge'" (Koran 20:114). Success means understanding the truth, but it is more complex than one might think initially. The **Upanishad** says, "Understanding is greater than meditation. For it is with the understanding that one understands the Rig-Veda, the Vajur-Veda and the Sama-Veda, the Atharva-Veda and the ancient collections of stories ..." (Chandogya Upanishad 7, 7:1). We gain understanding by seeking the ancient wisdom in the holy scriptures and revering our new understanding of God.

Once an individual discovers the truth, that person has a special covenant with God. The **Hebrew Bible** says, "Incline your ear, and come unto me: hear, and your soul shall live; and I will make an everlasting covenant with you (Isaiah 55.3). God's pledge to all of us is: If you seek Him, He will ensure that you find Him. The **Gospel of Thomas** adds that upon finding, you will be disturbed and astounded. The search for spiritual wisdom often places the intense light of truth on the illusions of the physical and impermanent world. The magnitude of the difference between the illumined truth and the illusion is often shocking. That insight becomes the new and absolute reality. The significance of that reality is explained by the **Diamond Sutra**:

> "Subhuti, what do you think? If anyone filled three thousand galaxies of worlds with the seven treasures and gave all away in gifts of alms, would he gain great merit?"
>
> "Yes, indeed, World-Honored One, he would gain great merit!"
>
> "Subhuti, if such merit was real, the Tathagata would not have declared it to be great, but because it is without a foundation **the Tathagata characterized it as great.**" [emphasis added] (The Diamond Sutra 19)

The above is an example of the limited and illusionary nature of language. The term "great" is meaningless because the whole concept of gaining merit from wealth is without foundation. No amount of material wealth and honor is significant in our inner lives, whereas spiritual wisdom is significant in and of itself.

Once a mind is stretched by a new idea, it cannot be returned to its original dimension. Once seekers find spiritual wisdom, they are forever a changed person. The **Gospel of Thomas** says, "...upon finding, the person will be disturbed; and being disturbed, will be astounded, will reign, and will reign over the entirety." Once the seeker gains spiritual wisdom, they understand that they possess the greatest wealth possible. What person would not be *disturbed*? They *reign* because they become part of the Kingdom of God. They gain entirety because they have left the tumultuous illusionary Kingdom of Man and have entered the permanent and eternal Kingdom of God.

INSIDE AND OUTSIDE US

Question:

Where is the Kingdom of God?

Brief Answer:

It is both inside and outside us.

from the *Gospel of Thomas*

3. Jesus said, "If those who attract you, say to you, 'See, the kingdom is in the heaven,' then the birds of heaven will precede you. If they say to you, 'It is in the sea,' then the fish will precede you. But, the kingdom of god is inside you. And it is outside you. When you become acquainted with yourselves, then you will be recognized. And you will understand that it is you who are children of the living father. But if you do not become acquainted yourselves, then you are in poverty, and it is you who are the poverty."
(See Layton, p. 380.)

Longer Answer:

Spiritual wisdom tells us the Kingdom of God is a state of consciousness and being. It is not a particular place, but it is in part a process of inter-action between the individual and their environment. According to the **Koran**, the Angel of the Lord says, "We have ordained a law and assigned a path for each of you. Had God pleased, He could have made of you one community: but it is His wish to prove you by that which He was bestowed upon you. Vie with each other in good works, for to God you shall all return and he will resolve for you your differences" (Koran 5:49). God has selected an individual path for each of us and that path is made manifest in each of our lives. We are all free to choose to move down that path walking in either the Kingdom of God or in the Kingdom of Man.

The **New Testament** says, "And when he was demanded of the Pharisees, when the kingdom of God should come, he answered them and said, The kingdom of God cometh not with observation: Neither shall they say, Lo here! or, lo there! for, behold, the kingdom of God is within you" (Luke 17: 20-21). We must search within ourselves and come to comprehend exactly what are good works; and exactly what good works we must do in our individual lives. The Kingdom of God is a process that must originate within each person but be manifested outside each person.   The **Dhammapada** says, "If one practices equanimity even if adorned, if one is peaceful, restrained, disciplined, and chaste, that is the one who is priestly, the one who is religious, the one who is a mendicant" (Dhammapada 10:14).   In other words, anyone can walk their path of life in the Kingdom of God if that is their choice.

The "within you" aspect of the Kingdom of God is explained in the following poetry of the **Veda**, the **Upanishad**, and the **Hebrew Bible**:

Free from desire,
immortal,
wise and self-existent,
With [its own] savior satisfied,
and nothing lacking,—
Whoso knows him,
the SELF,
—wise, ageless, [ever] young,—
Of death will have no fear.
(Atharva-Veda 10,8:44)

Descry It in its Oneness,
Immeasurable,
firm,
Transcending space,
immaculate,
Unborn,
abiding,
great,—
[This is] SELF!
(Brihadaranyaka Upanishad 4,4:20)

Neither *is* it beyond the sea,
that thou shouldest say,
Who shall go over the sea for us,
and bring it unto us,
that we may hear it,
and do it?
But the word *is* very nigh unto thee,
in thy mouth,
and in thy heart,
that thou mayest do it.
(Deuteronomy 30:13-14)

Spiritual wisdom of all traditions tells us that by knowing the SELF we know the Kingdom of God and we are among the children of God. However, if we do not know the SELF, we remain in the illusionary Kingdom of Man with all its desires and spiritual poverty. Thus, we become that poverty ourselves.

CHILDLIKE INNOCENCE AND PURITY

Question:
Is spiritual wisdom a function of age?

Brief Answer:
Spiritual wisdom is a function of innocence and purity.

from the *Gospel of Thomas*

4. Jesus said, "The person advanced in days will not hesitate to ask a little child seven days old about the place of life. And that person will live. For many of the first will be last, and they will become one."
(See Layton, p. 380.)

Longer Answer:

Spiritual wisdom stresses the special quality of *childlike innocence and purity*. The **Gospel of Matthew** says, "At that time Jesus answered and said, I thank thee, O Father, Lord of heaven and earth, because thou hast hid these things from the wise and prudent and hast revealed them unto babes" (Matthew 11:25). Spiritual wisdom can be greater in children than in the so-called wise and prudent. The **Gospel of Luke** repeats the thought, "In that hour Jesus rejoiced in spirit, and said, I thank thee, O Father, Lord of heaven and earth, that thou hast hid these things from the wise and prudent, and hast revealed them unto babes: even so, Father; for so it seemed good in thy sight" (Luke 10:21). Spiritual wisdom is hidden from us by the complexities of our own minds.

Why do children often possess a superior ability to understand the spiritual wisdom of the Kingdom of God? Children live more in the heart than in the mind. They can easily grasp spiritual wisdom including spontaneous and unconditional love and trust because their minds have not yet developed doubt, cynicism, and suspicion. As children mature, especially in the teenage years, they often turn away from God's guidance as they focus on developing their individuality. As this is done, they begin to blunder around in the Kingdom of Man flitting from one desire to another. If the early experience with innocence and purity took firm root, their worldly experiences may eventually give them a greater awareness of the importance of spiritual wisdom.

God decides who and then when and how to guide us individually. "Exalted and throned on high, He lets the Spirit descend at His behest on those of His servants whom He chooses, that He may warn them of the day when they shall meet Him; the day when they shall rise up from their graves with nothing hidden from God" (Koran 40:16). Another answer comes from the second realization of Buddha. It says, "THE SECOND REALIZA-TION is the awareness that more desire brings more suffering. All hardships in daily life arise from greed and desire. Those with little desire and ambition are able to relax, their bodies and minds free from entanglement" (The Sutra on the Eight Realizations of the Great Being 2). Children are more likely to meet this condition than so-called wise and prudent adults because they are not yet caught in the web of responsibility to others, stress, expectations, and physical desires.

In reaching the Kingdom of God, the **Hebrew Bible** says, "Children's children *are* the crown of old men; and the glory of children *are* their fathers" (Proverbs 17:6). Innocence and purity are essential qualities for a seeker of spiritual wisdom. That advantage is explained best by the **Upanishad**:

> Just as [in a game of dice] all the lower throws go to the highest, to the winner, so do all the good deeds performed by [living] creatures go to him; and I say the same about whoever knows what he knows. (Chandogya Upanishad 4,1:6)

The seeker is the winner. As seekers, we learn more as we gain more spiritual wisdom, we perform more good deeds, and we increase in our spiritual capacity.

NOTHING HIDDEN FROM US

Question:
Where should we seek?

Brief Answer:
We should start seeking right where we are.

from the *Gospel of Thomas*

5. Jesus said, "Recognize what is before your face and what is hidden to you will become disclosed unto you. For there is nothing hidden unto you. For there is nothing obscure that will not become shown forth and nothing buried that [will not be raised]."
(See Layton, p. 361, using the Greek fragments.)

Longer Answer:

Spiritual wisdom is always right in front of us to grasp. The **Hebrew Bible** says, "I have set the Lord always before me; because he is at my right hand, I shall not be moved" (Psalms 16:8). The **New Testament** adds to that thought: "For nothing is secret, that shall not be made manifest; neither *any thing* hid, that shall not be known and come abroad" (Luke 8:17 and similar wording in Matthew 10:26). "For there is nothing covered, that shall not be revealed; neither hid, that shall not be known. Therefore whatsoever ye have spoken in darkness shall be heard in the light; and that which ye have spoken in the ear of closet shall be proclaimed upon the house tops" (Luke 12:2). Spiritual wisdom is available to all of us daily. It comes in many forms including our everyday life experiences.

In other words, God constantly makes His wisdom known to us. However, we can choose to slow down or even stop the process of gaining spiritual knowledge. Whenever we try to hide in darkness, doubt, and denial, we lose our ability to make spiritual progress. Sometimes we lose a great deal. God knows each and everyone of us intimately, and He knows and monitors our progress closely. The **Koran** says, "Then say: 'Praise be to God! He will show you His signs and you will recognize them. Your Lord is never heedless of what you do'" (Koran 27:93). Spiritual wisdom can be found in the little occurrences and lessons of daily life. The **Koran** says, "We have made known to you the **Koran** by gradual revelation; therefore await with patience the judgment of your Lord, and do not yield to the wicked and the unbelieving. Remember the name of your Lord morning and evening; in the night-time worship Him: praise Him all night long" (Koran 76:23). God is saying: Have patience. We may not recognize the experience as a spiritual lesson yet, but eventually we will. He is also creative in how He chooses to reveal Himself to us. As God is infinite, so is His use of time.

If spiritual wisdom is so common, why is it so hard to see? The **Diamond Sutra** answers as follows:

> "Subhuti, what do you think? Can the Buddha be perceived by his perfectly formed body?"
>
> "No, World-Honored One, the Tathagata cannot be perceived by his perfectly formed body, because the Tathagata teaches that a perfectly formed body is not really such; it is merely called a perfectly formed body."
>
> "Subhuti, what do you think? Can the Tathagata be perceived by means of any phenomenal characteristic?"
>
> "No, World-Honored One, the Tathagata may not be perceived by any phenomenal characteristic, because the Tathagata teaches that phenomenal characteristics are not really such; they are merely called phenomenal characteristics." (The Diamond Sutra 20)

We see bodies, faces, personalities, and other phenomenal or human characteristics in our daily experiences, but the mind has difficulty looking past those characteristics to the absolute permanent truths of spiritual wisdom.

The **Upanishad** illustrates the difficulty as follows:

> Then he said to them [all]:
>
> "You know,
> you eat food,
> although you [only] know this universal SELF
> as if it were something separate.

"But whoever reveres this universal SELF,
as having the measure of a span and [yet] as having limitless dimension,
eats food in all worlds,
all creatures,
all selves.

"The head of this universal SELF is indeed the brilliant [sky],
its eye is [the sun] which possesses every form,
its breath is [the wind] whose nature is to follow various paths,
its body is broad [space],
its bladder is the wealth [of water],
its feet are the earth,
its breast is the sacrificial altar,
its hair is the sacrificial strew [sic],
its heart is the householder's fire,
its mind is the southern sacrificial fire
and its mouth is the eastern sacrificial fire."
(Chandogya Upanishad 5, 18:1-2)

Although nothing is kept from us, our minds act as a veil, screen, or filter that prevents us from fully understanding God's messages. We create our own illusions, limitations, and diversions. Living in the Kingdom of Man clouds the mind from comprehending God's words and mysteries. Spiritual wisdom says if we can look past the so-called reality of human characteristics to see the subtle, God will reveal all that is hidden to us in time.

SINCERITY

Question:
What is required by spiritual wisdom?

Brief Answer:
All that is necessary is complete and sincere truthfulness.

from the *Gospel of Thomas*

6. His followers asked him and said to him, "Do you want us to fast? How should
we pray? Should we give to charity? What diet should we observe?"
Jesus said, "Do not lie, and do not do what you hate, because all things are
disclosed before heaven. For there is nothing hidden that will not be revealed, and
there is nothing covered that will remain undisclosed."

Longer Answer:

Spiritual wisdom tells us not to be hypocritical. The **Hebrew Bible**
says, "For what is the hope of the hypocrite, though he hath gained,
when God taketh away his soul?" (Job 27:8). If we wish to be a part of
the Kingdom of God, duplicity is just not the way. The **Dhammapada** says,
"Even if one speaks little of what is beneficial, one who acts on truth is
truthful; having abandoned lust, hatred, and folly, endowed with accurate
insight, liberated in mind, unattached to this world or the next one has a share
in spirituality" (Dhammapada 1:20). Even a small share of spirituality is
worth more than the whole Kingdom of Man. The **Koran** says, "God
forgives those who commit evil in ignorance and then quickly turn to Him in
repentance. God will pardon them. God is all-knowing and wise. But He will
not forgive those who do evil and, when death comes to them, say: 'Now we
repent!' Nor those who die unbelievers: for them We have prepared a woeful
scourge" (Koran 4:18). God forgives evil committed unknowingly through
ignorance but not the evil actions chosen repeatedly out of intentional malice
or perpetual ignorance.

The **Upanishad** says:

> Truth conquers,
> not untruthfulness:

> By truth is the path laid out that leads up to the gods:
> this [is the path] the sages tread,
> [all] their desires fulfilled,
> Leading to that place wherein
> Truth's highest treasure lies.
> (Mundaka Upanishad 3,1:6)

Without truth, we cannot reach the SELF; and without the full knowledge of SELF, we cannot reach the Kingdom of God. Furthermore, the ultimate ignorance is self-deception. The following quote clarifies the central role of heartfelt sincerity in spiritual wisdom:

> Take heed that ye do not (sic) your alms before men,
> to be seen of them:
> otherwise ye have no reward of your Father which is in heaven.

> Therefore when thou doest *thine* alms,
> do not sound a trumpet before thee,
> as the hypocrites do in the synagogues and in the streets,
> that they may have glory of men.
> Verily I say unto you.
> They have their reward.

> But when thou doest alms,
> let not thy left hand know what that thy right hand doeth:
> That thine alms may be in secret:
> and thy Father which seeth in secret himself shall reward thee openly.

> And when thou prayest,
> thou shalt not be as the hypocrites *are:*
> for they love to pray standing
> in the synagogues and in the corners of the streets,
> that they may be seen of men.
> Verily I say unto you,
> They have their reward.

> But thou,
> when thou prayest,
> enter into thy closet,

and when thou hast shut thy door,
pray to thy Father which is in secret;
and thy Father which seeth in secret shall reward thee openly.

But when ye pray,
use not vain repetitions,
as the heathen *do*:
for they think that they shall be heard for their much speaking.

Be not ye therefore like unto them:
for your Father knoweth what things ye have need of,
before ye ask him.

After this manner therefore pray ye:

Our father which art in heaven,
Hallowed be thy name.

Thy Kingdom come.
Thy will be done in earth,
as *it is* in heaven.

Give us this day our daily bread.

And forgive us our debts,
as we forgive our debtors.

And lead us not into temptation,
but deliver us from evil:
For thine is the kingdom,
and the power,
and the glory,
for ever.
Amen.

For if ye forgive men their trespasses,
your heavenly Father will also forgive you:
But if ye forgive not men their trespasses,
neither will your Father forgive your trespasses.

Moreover,
when ye fast,
be not,
as the hypocrites,
of a sad countenance:
for they disfigure their faces,
that they may appear unto men to fast.
Verily I say unto you.
They have their reward.

But thou, when thou fastest,
anoint thine head, and wash thy face;
That thou appear not unto men to fast,
but unto thy Father which is in secret:
and thy Father,
which seeth in secret,
shall reward thee openly.
(Matthew 6:1-18)

Our approach and attitude toward our own life and toward all of God's creation are of the utmost importance. We must sincerely hunger to be a good and righteous person. The goal must be to always grow as an individual and as a child of God. Simply performing rituals out of fear, obligation, or with the intent to gain or profit in some way from them will in fact gain us nothing in the sight of God.

THE IMPORTANCE OF
THE HUMAN EXPERIENCE

Question:
Can we reach the Kingdom of God
only through the human experience?

Brief Answer:
Yes, we need the experience of
physically being in the world
in order to understand and grow.

from the *Gospel of Thomas*

7. Jesus said, "Fortunate is the lion that the human will eat, so that the lion becomes
   human. And foul is the human that the lion will eat, and the lion will become
   human."

Longer Answer:

The human rather than the animal experience is central to spiritual
wisdom because it is only in the human experience that progress can
be made in reaching the Kingdom of God. The **Hebrew Bible** says,
"So foolish *was* I, and ignorant: I was *as* a beast before thee" (Psalms 73:22).
We must not behave like beasts. "Man *that is* in honour, and understandeth
not, is like the beasts *that* perish" (Psalms 49:20). When we have honor
without spiritual wisdom, then we are still acting like a beast. Honor must be
defined in the context of righteousness in order to be grounded in spiritual
wisdom. Righteousness in turn must be defined as the fundamental conduct
of spiritual wisdom in order to have spiritual substance. For example, people
claiming that they should kill someone who has insulted their honor are not
basing their assertion of the meaning of honor from the context of spiritual
wisdom. Rather, they are avenging their hurt egos. Thus, they would be
acting without spiritual substance, in spite of their claim that their honor justified their act of aggression.

What distinguishes humans from beasts? Humans can reason from spiritual wisdom and beasts cannot. The **Dhammapada** says, "Everything has

mind in the lead, has mind in the forefront, is made by mind. If one speaks or acts with a corrupt mind, misery will follow, as the wheel of a cart follows the foot of the ox. Everything has mind in the lead, has mind in the forefront, is made by mind. If one speaks or acts with a pure mind, happiness will follow, like a shadow that never leaves" (Dhammapada 1:1-2).

What allows us to transcend being a beast is the mind and its ability to comprehend. However, the mind must be firmly grounded in spiritual wisdom or we will remain in the consciousness of a beast concerned only with satisfying our desires. With the ability to reason, the human mind permits, though often with some difficulty, the understanding of spiritual wisdom, how to make good choices, and how to live on a higher plane of consciousness.

This does not mean that animals do not have hearts and souls, as demonstrated by the fact that they are often loving and faithful companions. However, the human condition alone has the ability to reason and make choices based on understanding spiritual wisdom through the heart. The **Koran** says, "All the beasts that roam the earth and all the birds that wing their flight are but communities like your own. We have left out nothing in the Book. They shall all be gathered before their Lord. Deaf and dumb are those that deny Our revelations: they blunder about in darkness. God confounds whom He will, and guides to the right path whom He pleases" (Koran 6:38).

Humans are different from beasts because humans have the *potential* to think and make choices with spiritual wisdom and therefore make conscious progress on their path. In spite of this fact, however, they often choose not to do so. The **Upanishad** describes the Brahman (the Kingdom of God) as follows:

> Some say that Brahman is food.
> But this is not so,
> for food goes bad without the breath of life.

> Others say that Brahman is the breath of life.
> But this is not so,
> for without food the breath of life dries up.

> Only when these two natural phenomena become one single substance,
> do they reach the highest state.
> (Brihadaranyaka Upanishad 5,12)

The combination of food and breath of life provide humans with the *potential* to think and act in the Kingdom of God. Both breath and food are provided by the Grace of God. Food gives daily nourishment but breath gives life itself. Together they sustain us and our *potential* for transcending the animal qualities within us to live in the Kingdom of God. Life's breath and food become the single substance called "you." We can reach the highest state of consciousness, the Kingdom of God. Spiritual wisdom indicates that both breath and food are necessary but they are not enough; in the same manner, life is necessary but not enough to reach the Kingdom of God. Man is able to transcend the beast within because of the heavenly food called spiritual wisdom. The **New Testament** tells us:

> Awake to righteousness,
> and sin not;
> for some have not the knowledge of God:
> I speak *this* to your shame.

> But some *man* will say,
> How are the dead raised up?
> and with what body do they come?

> Thou fool,
> that which thou sowest is not quickened,
> except it die:
> And that which thou sowest,
> thou sowest not that body that shall be,
> but bare grain,
> it may chance of wheat,
> or of some other *grain*:
> But God giveth it a body as it hath pleased him,
> and to every seed his own body.

> All flesh *is* not the same flesh:
> but *there is* one *kind of* flesh of men,
> another flesh of beasts, another of fishes,
> and another of birds.

> *There are* also celestial bodies,
> and bodies terrestrial:
> but the glory of the celestial is one,
> and the *glory* of the terrestrial is another.

There is one glory of the sun,
and another glory of the moon,
and another glory of the stars:
for *one* star differeth from *another* star in glory.

So also is the resurrection of the dead.
It is sown in corruption:
it is raised in incorruption:
It is sown in dishonour;
it is raised in glory:
it is sown in weakness;
it is raised in power:
It is sown a natural body;
it is raised a spiritual body.

There is a natural body,
and there is a spiritual body.

And so it is written,
The first man Adam was made a living soul;
the last Adam *was made* a quickening spirit.
(Corinthians 1, 15:34-45)

The key to understanding this spiritual wisdom is the word "potential." Although God gives us the potential to transcend our animal desires, we are also given the mind to reason and the right to choose. We must choose to use our potential to transcend our "natural body" and develop our individual "spiritual body."

FOCUS ON WHAT IS IMPORTANT

Question:
How should we seek spiritual wisdom?

Brief Answer:
We should not seek all that can be learned, but only focus on the truly important.

from the *Gospel of Thomas*

8. And He said, "Humankind is like a wise fisherman who cast his net into the sea and drew it up from the sea full of little fish. Among them the wise fisherman discovered a fine large fish. He threw all the little fish back into the sea and with no difficulty chose the large fish. Whoever has ears to hear should hear!"

Longer Answer:

Like a fisherman, we cast out and pull spiritual wisdom to us from the environment around us. The **New Testament** says, "Again, the kingdom of heaven is like unto a net, that was cast into the sea, and gathered of every kind: Which, when it was full, they drew to shore, and sat down, and gathered the good into vessels, but cast the bad away" (Matthew 13:47-48). We need to cast our nets far and wide, and when they are pulled in, examine the catch. If we are wise, we will keep the significant knowledge and throw away the insignificant. The **Hebrew Bible** helps us understand that there is a great deal of wisdom available to us. It says:

> And it shall come to pass,
> *that* every thing that liveth,
> which moveth,
> whithersoever the rivers shall come,
> shall live:
> and there shall be a very great multitude of fish,
> because these waters shall come thither:
> for they shall be healed;
> and every thing shall live whither the river cometh.
>
> And it shall come to pass,
> *that* the fishers shall stand upon it from En-gedi even unto En-eglaim;
> they shall be a *place* to spread forth nets;
> their fish shall be according to their kinds,
> as the fish of the great sea,
> exceeding many.
> (Ezekiel 47:9-10)

Although there is much wisdom always available, we must discriminate and appreciate the remarkable value of true spiritual wisdom.

The **Diamond Sutra** also stresses the importance of spiritual wisdom. It says:

> "Subhuti, what do you think? If anyone filled three thousand galaxies of worlds with the seven treasurers and gave always in gifts of alms, would he gain great merit?"
>
> Subhuti said: "Great indeed, World-Honored One! Wherefore? Because merit partakes of the character of no-merit, the Tathagata characterized the merit as great."
>
> Then Buddha said: "On the other hand, if anyone received and retained even only four lines of this discourse and taught and explained them to others, his merit would be the greater. Wherefore? Because, Subhuti, from this discourse issue forth all the buddhas and the consummation of incomparable enlightenment teachings of all the buddhas.
>
> "Subhuti, what is called 'the religion given by Buddha' is not, in fact, buddha-religion." (The Diamond Sutra 8)

A single piece of received and understood spiritual wisdom can result in a person moving forward on their path and possibly in turn being able to share their knowledge with others whom they meet along their path. Spiritual learning is by no means limited to only what is taught in a formal religion. We can draw spiritual wisdom into our "net" daily as we pass through life. Every experience, challenge, or conflict presents an opportunity to glean spiritual wisdom. Regardless of its source, any aspect of spiritual wisdom is more valuable than all the treasures of the galaxies because with it we can transcend our limitations and move closer to God. Because spiritual wisdom is more precious than the greatest treasures, it gives us great joy and happiness when we discover it. The **Upanishad** says, "Happiness is nothing less than the Infinite: there is no happiness in what is small (finite). Only the Infinite is happiness. So [you] should really want to understand the Infinite" (Chandogya Upanishad 7,23). Happiness in this sense should not be defined as pleasure but as a deep and abiding inner joy.

The **Upanishad** echoes the significance of the joys of spiritual wisdom as follows:

> Take a man who is rich and prosperous,
> master over others,
> possessing everything possible that could minister to human enjoyment:
> that is the highest [measure of] bliss on the human scale.

Now,
a hundred [measures of] bliss on the human scale make
one [measure of] bliss on the scale of the world-conquering ancestors.

A hundred [measurers of] bliss on the scale of the world-conquering ancestors
makes
one [measure of] bliss of the world of Gandharvas.

A hundred [measures of] bliss on the world of the Gandharvas make
one [measure of] bliss of the gods who have won divinity by their works.

A hundred [measures of] bliss of the gods who have won divinity by their works
make
one [measure of] bliss of the gods
who are destined to be gods by birth and
of the man well-versed in scripture
who is not crooked nor smitten with desire.

A hundred [measures of] bliss of the gods destined
to be gods by birth make
one [measure of] bliss of the world of Prajapati
and of the man versed in scripture
who is not crooked nor smitten with desire.

A hundred [measures of] bliss of the world of Prajapati make
one [measure of] bliss of the Brahman-world and
of the man well versed in scripture
who is not crooked nor smitten with desire.

This,
sire,
is indeed the highest bliss
— the Brahman world (that state of being which is Brahman).
(Brihadaranyaka Upanishad 4,3:33)

Spiritual wisdom tells us the highest bliss can only be reached in the
Kingdom of God. Bliss must not be confused with pleasure or enjoyment as

these are physical states of being and are always fleeting. The treasures of the Kingdom of Man can give us passing pleasure but never eternal bliss.

The best place to cast our nets in search of spiritual wisdom is among the people who are also seeking the bliss of the Kingdom of God and not the pleasures of the Kingdom of Man. We look for wise teachers and others of like mind and spirit. This is not a guarantee that we will find what we seek but only that it is the most likely place to find a good catch. We "fish" spiritually by being humble, living in peace, loving God, asking God's help only for spiritual progress, living a virtuous life and repenting our mistakes. If we consciously choose to not seek spiritual wisdom, we will never find eternal bliss of the Kingdom of God. According to the **Koran**, the Angel of the Lord says, "We will turn away their hearts and eyes from the Truth since they refused to believe in it at first. We will let them blunder about in their wrongdoing" (Koran 6:110).

GOD'S GIFT TO US

Question:
What is God's gift to us?

Brief Answer:
God's gift to us is giving us the opportunity to grow spiritually so that we can be in the Kingdom of God.

from the *Gospel of Thomas*

9. Jesus said, "Look, the sower went out, took a handful [of seeds], and scattered [them]. Some fell on the road, and the birds came and pecked them up. Others fell on rock, and they did not take root in the soil and did not produce heads of grain. Others fell on thorns, and they choked the seeds and worms devoured them. And others fell on good soil, and it brought forth a good crop: It yielded sixty per measure and one hundred twenty per measure."

Longer Answer:

Each life experience is a message of spiritual wisdom and an opportunity for us to grow. As agents of free choice, we can seize the opportunity or not. The **Koran** says, "They recognize God's favors, yet they deny them. Most of them are ungrateful" (Koran 16:83). Spiritual wisdom tells us that even though the opportunities are recognized, we are often most ungrateful to God. In the following parable, the ungrateful are represented by the poor soil and the grateful are represented by the good soil.

And he spake many things unto them in parables,
saying,

Behold,
a sower went forth to sow;
And when he sowed,
some *seeds* fell by the way side,
and the fowls came and devoured them up:
Some fell upon stony places,
where they had not much earth:
and forthwith they sprung up,
because they had no deepness of earth:
And when the sun was up,
they were scorched;
and because they had no root,
they withered away.

And some fell among thorns;
and the thorns sprung up,
and choked them:
But other (sic) fell into good ground,
and brought forth fruit,
some an hundredfold,
some sixtyfold,
some thirtyfold.

What hath ears to hear,
let him hear.
(Matthew 13:3-9; similar passages are Mark 4:2-9 and Luke 8:4-8)

By actively seeking spiritual wisdom, we consciously decide to be like the good soil. We choose to seize the opportunities. Through the Grace of God, we are given everything as noted by the **Upanishad**:

> As a spider emits and reabsorbs [its threads],
> As plants grow up upon the earth,
> As hair [grows] on the body and head of a living man,
> So does everything on earth arise from [this] Imperishable.
> (Mundaka Upanishad 1,1:7)

God created everything on this earth including us.

To continue the metaphor, mankind's ungrateful nature makes it possible for the weeds of the Kingdom of Man to overwhelm us as we seek God. The **Dhammapada** says:

> Weeds are the bane of the fields,
> passion is the bane of humankind;
> so a gift to the dispassionate bears great fruit.
>
> Weeds are the bane of the fields,
> hatred is the bane of humankind;
> so a gift to those free of hate bears great fruit.
>
> Weeds are the bane of the fields,
> folly is the bane of humankind;
> so a gift to those free of folly bears great fruit.
>
> Weeds are the bane of the fields,
> desire is the bane of humankind;
> so a gift to those free of desire bears great fruit.
> (Dhammapada 24:23-26)

The constant challenge is to be like the good soil and not permit the weeds to overtake us.

Although we ignore God, spiritual wisdom tells us that He does not ignore us. God is aware of all our actions. The **Koran** says, "Good soil yields fruit by God's will. But poor and scant are the fruits which spring from barren soil.

Thus do We make plain Our revelations to those who render thanks" (Koran 7:58). God reveals His spiritual wisdom to us in such a way as to reflect His awareness of our capacity and disposition. He reveals it to us in such a way that we can receive and understand it. The **Hebrew Bible** says:

> For my thoughts *are* not your thoughts,
> neither *are* your ways my ways,
> saith the Lord.
>
> For *as* the heavens are higher than the earth,
> so are my ways higher than your ways,
> and my thoughts than your thoughts.
>
> For as the rain cometh down,
> and the snow from heaven,
> and returneth not thither,
> but watereth the earth,
> and maketh it bring forth and bud,
> that it may give seed to the sower,
> and bread to the eater:
> So shall my word be that goeth forth out of my mouth:
> it shall not return unto me void,
> but it shall accomplish that which I please,
> and it shall prosper *in the thing* whereto I sent it.
>
> For ye shall go out with joy,
> and be led forth with peace:
> the mountains and the hills shall break forth before you into singing,
> and all the trees of the field shall clap *their* hands.
>
> Instead of the thorn shall come up the fir tree,
> and instead of the brier shall come up the myrtle tree:
> and it shall be to the Lord for a name,
> for an everlasting sign *that* shall not be cut off.
> (Isaiah 55:8-13)

When we choose to seize the opportunities of spiritual wisdom and become the good soil, doors open, barriers fall, and He reveals His higher ways to us.

OUR OPPORTUNITY AND CHALLENGE

Question:
What is life?

Brief Answer:
Life is both our opportunity and our challenge.

from the *Gospel of Thomas*
10. Jesus said, "I have thrown fire upon the world, and look, I am watching it until it blazes."

Longer Answer:

Spiritual wisdom transforms everything. Our individual paths in life are not easy; they are our challenge. The **New Testament** quotes Jesus, "I am come to send fire on the earth; and what will I, if it be already kindled?... Suppose ye that I am come to give peace on earth? I tell you, Nay; but rather division: For from henceforth there shall be five in one house divided, three against two, and two against three. The father shall be divided against the son, and the son against the father; the mother against the daughter and the daughter against the mother; the mother-in-law against her daughter-in-law, and the daughter-in-law against her mother-in-law" (Luke 12:49, 51-53). Life not only presents us with opportunities to learn but also with periodic tests. The **Koran** says, "Thus have We made some among them a mean for testing others, so that they should say: 'Are these the men whom God favors among us?' But does not God best know the thankful" (Koran 6:53). God maximizes our opportunities to accept and gain spiritual wisdom because He wants us to succeed in our search.

We are refined spiritually through our life challenges. The **Hebrew Bible** says, "But who may abide the day of his coming? and who shall stand when he appeareth? for he *is* like a refiner's fire, and like fullers' soap. And he shall sit *as* a refiner and purifier of silver: and he shall purify the sons of Levi, and purge them as gold and silver, that they may offer unto the Lord an offering in righteousness" (Malachi 3:2-3). God uses our lives as a crucible to purify us. The **Hebrew Bible** also says, "And the light of Israel shall be for a fire, and his Holy One for a flame: and it shall burn and devour his thorns and his briers in one day; and shall consume, the glory of his forest, and of his fruitful field, both soul and body; and they shall be as when a standard bearer fainteth. And the rest of the trees of his forest shall be few, that a child may write them" (Isaiah 10:17-19). No matter how bad, the negative experiences of our lives are part of His plan for us. They are not intended as punishments. They represent opportunities for us to grow, expand our understanding, and transcend our limitations.

Spiritual wisdom stresses that few will successfully meet the challenge, but the challenge itself is necessary to give everyone the opportunity and to reveal the true seekers. The **Hebrew Bible** says, "And the angel of the Lord appeared unto him in a flame of fire out of the midst of a bush: and he looked, and behold, the bush burned with fire, and the bush *was* not consumed" (Exodus 3:2). The metaphors of fire and burning in spiritual wisdom communicate not only purification but also represent our hazards. They are part of the test. The **Samyutta-nikaya** says as follows:

The body is burning,
tangible things are burning,
tactile consciousness is burning,
tactile impression is burning,
also whatever sensation,
pleasant or painful or neither-painful-nor-pleasant,
arises on account of the tactile sensation,
that too is burning.
Burning with what?
Burning with the fire of lust...

The mind is burning,
mental objects (ideas, etc.) are burning,
mental consciousness is burning,
mental impression is burning,
also whatever sensation,
pleasant or painful or neither-painful-nor-pleasant,
arises on account of the mental impression,
that too is burning.
Burning with what:
Burning with the fires of lust,

> with the fire of hate,
> with the fire of delusion;
> I say it is burning with birth,
> aging and death,
> with sorrows,
> with lamentations,
> with pains,
> with griefs,
> with despairs.
> (Samyutta-nikaya 35,28)

Life cannot be simply carefree and easy. It is an endless succession of learning experiences. Among those experiences there will be triumphs, disappointments, disasters, and challenges. All of these are opportunities for learning. When we are too comfortable in our lives, we forget to cry for God's love. We stop questioning and seeking. In spiritual wisdom, the metaphor "river" represents life's endless opportunities and sources of wisdom. The **Upanishad** explains the challenges as follows:

> We understand Him as a river of five streams
> From five sources,
> — crooked,
> cruel, —
> Its waves the five vital breaths,
> Its primal fount fivefold perception;
> Its five whirlpools swirl wildly
> With fivefold misery:
> Fifty tributaries it has,
> five branches.
> (Svetasvatara Upanishad 1:5)

God supplies His spiritual wisdom through the five religious traditions cited in this book and the many tributaries of those traditions. The sources of spiritual wisdom are not necessarily easy to read or comprehend. They can be "crooked, cruel." Learning spiritual wisdom can be a wild whirlpool that requires all our senses to be alert and our lifelong commitment.

WE MUST GROW SPIRITUALLY

Question:

How can we gain spirituality?

Brief Answer:

We can grow within ourselves.

from the *Gospel of Thomas*

11. Jesus said, "This heaven will pass away, and the one above it will pass away.
"The dead are not alive, and the living will not die.
"During the days when you ate what is dead, you made it alive. When you are in the light, what will you do?
"On the day when you were one, you became two. But when you become two, what will you do?"

Longer Answer:

When opportunities are provided, they are provided through God's Grace. The **Koran** says, "God brought you out of your mothers' wombs devoid of all knowledge, and gave you ears and eyes and hearts, so that you may give thanks" (Koran 16:78). Through life, we learn to appreciate the opportunities given to us by God. The **Hebrew Bible** says, "Thou hast granted me life and favour, and thy visitation hath preserved my spirit" (Job 10:12). God gives us hope to begin, continue, and even intensify our search. The **Koran** also says, "Your Lord is forgiving and merciful. Had it been His will to scourge them for their sins, He would have hurried on their punishment; but He has set for them a predestined time they cannot evade" (Koran 18:58). God is forgiving, merciful, and patient; however, there is an appointed time for everything. The **Hebrew Bible** says, "Is *there* not an appointed time to man upon earth? *Are not* his days also like the days of an hireling?" (Job 7:1). We must understand that time and opportunities are gifts that we must value and not waste.

God's spiritual wisdom says He will guide us and spiritually helps us grow. All the directions, signposts, and lessons are provided; however, we must train our eyes and ears to recognize them. The **Hebrew Bible** says, "For thou,

O God, hast proved us: thou hast tried us, as silver is tried. Thou broughtest up into the net; thou laidst affliction upon our loins. Thou hast caused men to ride over our heads; we went through fire and though water: but thou broughtest us out into a wealthy *place*" (Psalms 66:10-12). God knows we need His guidance through our life's experiences. The **Upanishad** states:

> "No one but a Brahman could put the matter so clearly," said [Gautama]. "Bring fuel, my dear boy; I will accept you as a pupil. You have not deviated from the truth."
>
> After he had accepted him as a pupil, he selected four hundred lean and feeble cows and told him to keep an eye on them. As he drove them on, he said: "I shall not come back with less than a thousand." So he lived away for many years, and when the number [of cows] had reached a thousand, — (Chandogya Upanishad 4,4:5b)

God happily takes us as His pupils, but we must be willing to be good students. The growth process more than likely will take great effort for the rest of our lives.

We can always gain from spiritual wisdom because it is eternal. It transcends the fads and fashions of time and culture. The **Gospel of Luke** says:

> Heaven and earth shall pass away:
> but my words shall not pass away.
>
> And take heed to yourselves,
> lest at any time your hearts be overcharged with surfeiting,
> and drunkenness,
> and cares of this life,
> and *so* that day come upon you unawares.

For as a snare shall it come on all them that dwell on the face of the whole earth.

> Watch ye therefore,
> and pray always,
> that ye may be accounted worthy to escape all these things that shall come to pass,
> and to stand before the Son of man.
> (Luke 21:33-36)

We can also gain from detaching ourselves from the ego and cultivating all kinds of goodness.

The spiritual wisdom sayings often use the terms *being one and two*. This is another way of saying that you have a choice. There are actually three possibilities. We can choose to live (a) only in the Kingdom of God, (b) only in the Kingdom of Man , or (c) both in the Kingdom of God and Kingdom of Man. Most of us select the last option. We try desperately to have a good heart and consciousness — while we surround ourselves with all the comfort and pleasures of the world. Yet even if we selected option (a), we still must exist in the Kingdom of Man while apprenticing in the Kingdom of God, because the human condition is the only form in which we can grow inwardly. Therefore, option (a) is really the same as option (c), except for one important difference. In the first option, one has consciously selected to *try* to not live in the Kingdom of Man. As discussed in the first Thomas quote, *trying* is the key to success. Therefore, we must be in the world but not of it to make the necessary progress. That is the supreme challenge. For example, even when we think we are acting in goodness, we need to use extreme caution. The **Diamond Sutra** explains the challenge as follows:

> "Furthermore, Subhuti, This is altogether everywhere, without differentiation or degree; wherefore it is called 'consummation of incomparable enlightenment.' It is straightly attained by freedom from separate personal selfhood and by cultivating all kinds of goodness.
>
> "Subhuti, though we speak of 'goodness,' the Tathagata declares that there is no goodness; such is merely a name." (The Diamond Sutra 23)

Because we conduct our lives in the Kingdom on Man with all its relativity, limitations, and illusions, what is goodness to one person is not necessarily goodness to another. Spiritual wisdom tells us that our goal should be the quest for the permanence of spirituality while appreciating the relative and contextual nature of "goodness" in the Kingdom of Man. Furthermore, the moment we characterize our actions as "good" or "righteous," we have allowed the ego to dominate and have pronounced judgment. Our actions must simply be natural and spontaneous reflexes, without any conscious judging.

GOD'S SPECIAL CHILDREN

Question:

Why should God love us?

Brief Answer:

God loves each and every one of us
because we have the potential of reaching
Oneness with Him and because He wants
each of us to succeed.

from the *Gospel of Thomas*

12. The followers said to Jesus, "We know that you are going to leave us. Who will
be our leader?"

Jesus said to them, "No matter where you are, you are to go to James the Just,
for whose sake heaven and earth came into being."

Longer Answer:

B ecause they were concerned who would lead them after Christ, the
followers of Jesus asked Him directly, "When you are no longer with
us, who should be the leader?" Jesus answered them: "You are to go to
James the Just." In our quest to understand spiritual wisdom, the rest of this
saying is important. For what reason did God create Heaven and Earth?
Christ told His disciples that God created Heaven and Earth for a particular
person, James the Just, and by inference, *for all people like him*. What qualities
made this man so special?

James the Just did succeed to the leadership of Christ's movement after His
death, but who was he? We have a good idea from the "Memoirs of
Hepesippus" that were preserved in Eusebius's *Ecclesiastical History* (2,23:4-7)
(Meyer, p. 73). James was called the brother of Christ not because of his
kinship, but because of his similarity in personality and character to Jesus.
According to Hepesippus, James was "holy from his mother's womb." He was
not concerned with temporal physical matters. He tried to observe the
religious traditions and rituals, not because they were traditions of man but
because he loved and honored God through them. He prayed with devotion

and cared deeply for the salvation of others. All considered him extraordinarily righteous in character. He died in 62 AD. The Jewish idiom at the time, "for whose sake heaven and earth came into being," is an expression of extreme praise and is used to reflect Jesus' high regard for this special disciple. In the context of this saying, Jesus is also presenting a role model that we would be wise to follow. The **Gospel of Luke** says:

> But ye *shall* not be so:
> but he that is greatest among you,
> let him be as the younger:
> and he that is chief,
> as he that doth serve.

> For whether *is* greater,
> he that sitteth at meat,
> or he that serveth?
> *is* not he that sitteth at meat?
> but I am among you as he that serveth.

> Ye are they which have continued with me in my temptations.

> And I appoint unto you a kingdom,
> as my Father hath appointed unto me;

> That ye may eat and drink at my table in my kingdom,
> and sit on thrones judging the twelve tribes of Israel.
> (Luke 22:26-30)

If we wish to be a part of the Kingdom of God, here is a clear message telling us how to conduct ourselves.

The **Dhammapada** captures that type of character as follows: "Who is capable of praising one like a coin of finest gold, one whom the knowing praise after finding him impeccable, controlled, intelligent, insightful, ethical, and composed day in and day out? Even the gods praise such a one, even the Creator" (Dhammapada 17:9-10). We must be wise and emulate this model. In addition to character, attitude toward life is extremely important. An attitude like that of James the Just is perhaps best captured by the following:

> The Lord *is* my shepherd;
> I shall not want.

> He maketh me to lie down in green pastures:
> he leadeth me beside the still waters.

He restoreth my soul:
he leadeth me in the paths of righteousness for his name's sake.

Yea,
though I walk through the valley of the shadow of death,
I will fear no evil: for thou *art* with me;
thy rod and thy staff they comfort me.

Thou preparest a table before me in the presence of mine enemies:
thou annointest my head with oil;
my cup runneth over.

Surely goodness and mercy shall follow me all the days of my life:
and I will dwell in the house of the Lord for ever.
(Psalms 23:1-6)

The Psalms tell us to let God be our guide as we move down our path of life. We should listen carefully to God's messages and directions. We should have no fear because God will take care of us every step of the way.

According to the spiritual wisdom, certain kinds of qualities are important to God. The **Bhagavad-Gita** says, "For the protection of the good, For the destruction of evildoers, For the setting up of righteousness, I come into being, age after age" (Bhagavad-Gita 4:8). God is always there for us. The **Gospel of Mark** says,

But they held their peace:
for by the way they had disputed among themselves,
who *should be* the greatest.

And he sat down,
and called the twelve,
and saith unto them,
If any man desire to be first,
the same shall be last of all,
and servant of all.

And he took a child,
and set him in the midst of them:
and when he had taken him in his arms,
he said unto them.

Whosoever shall receive one of such children in my name,
receiveth me:

and whosoever shall receive me,
receiveth not me,
but him that sent me.
(Mark 9:34-37)

God tells us to avoid power struggles because they are only battles between egos. There is a similar statement found in Luke:

Then there arose a reasoning among them,
which of them should be greatest.

And Jesus,
perceiving the thought of their heart,
took a child,
and set him by him,

And said unto them,
Whosoever shall receive this child in my name receiveth me:
and whosoever shall receive me receiveth him that sent me:
for he that is least among you all,
the same shall be great.
(Luke 9:46-48)

When selecting a spiritual leader, we should select the person whose consciousness is most like Jesus Himself, or like James the Just.

That God loves every one of us and He will act accordingly is perhaps the best understanding of spiritual wisdom. The **Koran** quotes the angel of God, "Then We raised a new generation, and sent forth to them an apostle of their own. 'Serve God,' he said, 'for you have no god but Him. Will you not take heed?'" (Koran 23:30). God has always tried to help us succeed and He keeps trying to help us to succeed. From the beginning, He has provided spiritual wisdom in many forms for us to have better access to it. According to the spiritual wisdom, there is no question of God's love for us, but there remains the question of our love for God.

Understanding God

◆————————

GOD CANNOT BE EXPLAINED

Question:

Can God be explained more specifically?

Brief Answer:

No. How can the unexplainable be explained?

from the *Gospel of Thomas*

13. Jesus said to his followers, "Compare me to something and tell me what I am like."

    Simon Peter said to him, "You are like a just messenger."

    Matthew said to him, "You are like a wise philosopher."

    Thomas said to him, "Teacher, my mouth is utterly unable to say what you are like."

Jesus said, "I am not your teacher. Because you have drunk, you have become intoxicated from the bubbling spring that I have tended."

And he took him, and withdrew, and spoke three sayings to him.

When Thomas came back to his friends, they asked him, "What did Jesus say to you?"

Thomas said to them, "If I tell you one of the sayings he spoke to me, you will pick up rocks and stone me, and fire will come from the rocks and consume you."

Longer Answer:

Spiritual wisdom tells us that God does not reveal all His complexities to us all at once. Inner knowledge is revealed to each seeker only as they are ready to receive it. The **New Testament** says, "When Jesus came into the coasts of Caesarea Philippi, he asked his disciples, saying, 'Whom do men say that I the Son of man am?' And they said, 'Some *say that thou art John* the Baptist: some, Elias; and others Jeremias, or one of the prophets.' He saith unto them, 'But whom say ye that I am?' And Simon Peter answered and said, 'Thou art the Christ, the son of the living God'" (Matthew 16:13-16; similar in Mark 8:27-33 and Luke 9:18-22). Who really was Jesus? The **Gospel of Thomas** says Peter and Matthew answered directly, in finite terms, but only Thomas, who was also called the twin because he was the most similar to Jesus, said that he could not compare Jesus to anyone or anything.

By a long incremental process of enlightenment, spiritual wisdom is granted us through the Grace of God. To Thomas, Christ was unexplainable and unfathomable. To us also, God is unexplainable and unfathomable. In a Diamond Sutra-like twist, Jesus told Thomas that he was ready to learn more as he had drunk from the spring Jesus was tending. In this metaphor, God is the spring of eternal truth and awareness, and the role of Jesus is to look after the spring. God bestows spiritual wisdom on whom He wishes, when He believes they are ready. God is the only one who gives us inner knowledge. We must all learn spiritual wisdom for ourselves directly from God.

How can the unexplainable, such as God, be explained? As good teachers know, a child learns a little at a time. Intellectually, students often grow slowly because they are able to digest only small pieces of knowledge until their capacity to comprehend grows. In time, a good student will understand the infinite. As seekers, we cannot know the infinite all at once, just as Adam and

Eve could not know the infinite when they ate of the tree of knowledge of good and evil. They were, as we today are, restricted by finite minds and limited hearts. The following is a helpful illustration:

> Who looked upon the water,
> [looked on them] with power,
> As they conceived insight,
> brought forth the sacrifice;
> Who,
> among the gods,
> was the One God above . . . .
> What god shall we revere with the oblation?
> (Rig-Veda 10,121:8)

God is not easy for anyone to comprehend. Understanding requires the efforts of an active and willing seeker of inner knowledge.

> This is the God in fire and in the waters;
> The whole world has He entered;
> In healing plants is He,
> He it is in the trees:
> To this God all hail,
> all hail!
> (Svetasvatara Upanishad 2:17)

God is everywhere and everything. That is hard for the human mind to grasp. If we can comprehend what appears to be a logical impossibility, then we can transcend the finite and understand God. If we can comprehend that God is in fire, water, healing plants, trees, and in fact in the whole world, then we can transcend and understand the infinite that is God.

Why is it so difficult to understand God? Spiritual wisdom gives three reasons. First, the **Hebrew Bible** says, "As thou knowest not what *is* the way of the spirit, *nor* how the bones *do grow* in the womb of her that is with child; even so thou knowest not the works of God who maketh all" (Ecclesiastes 11:5). There are many aspects of life that remain a mystery but that does not mean that they do not happen and that they do not affect us. Second, the **Diamond Sutra** says:

"Subhuti, if a good man or a good woman ground an infinite number of galaxies of worlds to dust, would the resulting minute particles be many?"

Subhuti replied: "Many indeed, World-Honored One! Wherefore? Because if such were really minute particles Buddha would not have spoken of them as minute particles. For as to this, Buddha has declared that they are not really such. 'Minute particles' is just the name given to them. Also, World-Honored One, when the Tathagata speaks of galaxies of worlds these are not worlds; for if reality could be predicated of a world it would be a self-existent cosmos, and the Tathagata teaches that there is really no such thing. 'Cosmos' is merely a figure of speech."

[Then Buddha said:] "Subhuti, words cannot explain the real nature of a cosmos. Only common people fettered with desire make use of this arbitrary method." (The Diamond Sutra 30)

We must use language as it is our everyday tool to communicate. But like any tool, it has limitations and it can sometimes create more misunderstandings than clarity. For example, language creates categories called definitions that limit our ability to perceive larger truths. Given our imprecise limited language, we find comprehending the infinite and the eternal very difficult. The third difficulty can be expressed through the **Koran**:

But the unbelieving elders of his people, who denied the life to come and on whom We had bestowed the good things of this life, said: "This man is but a mortal like yourselves nourished by the same food and drink. If you obey a mortal like yourselves, you shall indeed be lost. Does he threaten you that when you are dead and turned to dust and bones, you will be raised to life? A foolish threat, indeed. There is no other life but this, our earthly life: we die and live, never to be restored to life. This man is but an impostor who tells of God what is untrue. Never will We believe him." (Koran 23:37)

In a world full of people arguing about the truth and who are skillful at creating division and disharmony, anyone can easily become confused.

GESTURES, NO — COMMITMENT, YES

Question:

What does God want from us?

Brief Answer:

God wants our total commitment, not mere gestures.

from the *Gospel of Thomas*

14. Jesus said to them, "If you fast, you will bring sin upon yourselves, and if you pray, you will be condemned, and if you give to charity, you will harm your spirits.

"When you go into any region and walk through the countryside, when people receive you, eat what they serve you and heal the sick among them. For what goes into your mouth will not defile you; rather, it is what comes out of your mouth that will defile you."

Longer Answer:

Spiritual wisdom notes that once we begin to believe in God, there is a strong tendency to focus on physical manifestations or gestures of devotion and rituals such as fasting, praying, and giving charity. The problem is not that we perform these gestures and rituals but rather that we think our commitment and faith are defined in terms of them. They are not and cannot be. Commitment requires our total attention. Faith requires reflection and examination. This is illustrated in the following long **Upanishad** spiritual lesson:

> The threefold offspring of Prajapati, — **gods, men and demons** [emphasis added], — dwelt with their father, Prajapati, as chaste students of sacred knowledge. After they had stayed [with him for some time] as students, the **gods** said: "Speak to us, sir."
>
> To them he uttered this [one] syllable: "Da. Did you understand?"
>
> "We did understand," they said. "What you said to us was 'damyata, restrain yourselves,'"
>
> "Yes (om)," he said, "you did understand."

Then the **men** said to him: "Speak to us, sir."
To them he uttered this [one] syllable: "Da. Did you understand?"
"We did understand," they said. "What you said to us was 'datta, give.'"
"Yes," he said, "you did understand."

The **demons** said to him: "Speak to us, sir."
To them he uttered this [one] syllable: "Da. Did you understand?"
"We did understand," they said. "What you said to us was 'dayadhvam, be compassionate.'"
"Yes," he said, "you did understand."
This is indeed what the divine voice, the thunder, echoes: "Da-da-da: restrain yourselves, give, be compassionate." This threefold lesson must be learnt: restraint, giving and compassion.
(Brihadaranyaka Upanishad 5,2)

Without commitment, we hear only the "da" and do not learn the three-tiered lesson of restraint, giving, and compassion. Without faith, we believe that physically performing rituals that are empty of feeling will some how give us salvation.

Spiritual wisdom tells us time after time that God wants us to live in His Kingdom. The Kingdom of God is a mind-set or attitude that we can adopt with discipline and self-control. The **Dhammapada** says, "For one who is self-controlled and always disciplined in action, victory over the self is better than victory over others. The victory of someone like this cannot be made into defeat, even by a god, an angel, or a devil" (Dhammapada 8:5-6). The following quotes describe in part that mind-set:

> He that soweth iniquity shall reap vanity:
> and the rod of his anger shall fail.

> He that hath a bountiful eye shall be blessed;
> for he giveth of his bread to the poor.

> Cast out the scorner,
> and contention shall go out;
> yea,
> strife and reproach shall cease.

He that loveth pureness of heart,
for the grace of his lips the king *shall be* his friend.
(Proverbs 22:8-11)

Commitment means always acting with the pureness of heart. Faith means loving unconditionally.

And as ye go,
preach,
saying,
The kingdom of heaven is at hand.

Heal the sick,
cleanse the lepers,
raise the dead,
cast out devils:
freely ye have received,
freely give.
(Matthew 10:7-8)

Commitment means you must always perform the good deed. Faith means never looking for reward or recognition.

And in the same house remain,
eating and drinking such things as they give:
for the labourer is worthy of his hire.
Go not from house to house.

And into whatsoever city ye enter,
and they receive you,
eat such things as are set before you:
And heal the sick that are therein,
and say unto them,
The kingdom of God is come nigh unto you.
(Luke 10:7-9)

Commitment does not mean proselytizing, but does mean accepting the hospitality of those that offer it. Faith means demonstrating our belief throughout our lives.

If any of them that believe not bid you *to a feast*,
and ye be disposed to go;
whatsoever is set before you,
eat,
asking no question for conscience sake.
(Corinthians 1,10:27)

Commitment means accepting generosity from the heart without question.
Faith means that no outside occurrence can disturb our inner peace.

And he called the multitude,
and said unto them.

Hear,
and understand:
Not that which goeth into the mouth defileth a man;
but that which cometh out of the mouth,
this defileth a man.
(Matthew 15:10-11)

Commitment means always being sensitive about what we say and do. It
does not mean that our spirituality is defined by what we eat. Faith is confi-
dently living our spirituality by God's standards, not waiting for others to
define it by their standards.

As for those that have faith and do good works,
God will bestow on them their rewards and enrich them from His own
abundance.

But those who are scornful and proud He will sternly punish,
and they will find none besides God to protect or help them.
(Koran 4:173)

Commitment means not scorning others and being proud. Faith is knowing inwardly that our actions are correctly motivated by God and not by our
human desires.

Wealth and children are the ornaments of this life.

But deeds of lasting merit are better rewarded by your Lord and
hold for you a greater hope of salvation.
(Koran 18:46)

Commitment means knowing that having wealth and children in our lives really means nothing. Faith is finding our personal fulfillment in our relationship with God — not in other mortal beings.

Believers,
let no man mock another man,
who may perhaps be better than himself.

Let no woman mock another woman,
who may perhaps be better than herself.

Do not defame one another,
nor call one another my nicknames.

It is an evil thing to be called by a bad name after embracing the true Faith.

Those that do not repent are wrongdoers.
(Koran 49:11).

Commitment means refraining from using hurtful names. Faith is demonstrating a universal and unconditional love for all God's creation.

DO NOT REDEFINE GOD IN OUR IMAGE

Question:
Can God be explained in human terms?

Brief Answer:
We must not limit God by our inability to understand Him.

from the *Gospel of Thomas*

15. Jesus said, "When you see one who was not born of woman, fall on your faces and worship. That is your father."

Longer Answer:
Using poetry, the **Upanishad** compares man to God:

> Then Vidagdha Sakalya questioned him, saying:
> "How many gods are there,
> Yajnavalkya?"
> He answered by [reciting] this invocatory formula:
> "As many as are mentioned in the invocatory formula in the hymn to the All-gods,
> — three hundred and three and three thousand and three (= 3306)."
> "Yes (om),"
> said he,
> "but how many gods are there really,
> Yajnavalkya?"
> "Thirty-three."
> "Yes,"
> he said,
> "but how many gods are there really,
> Yajnavalkya?"
> "Six."
> "Yes,"
> he said,
> "but how many gods are there really,
> Yajnavalkya?"
> "Three."
> "Yes,"

he said,
"but how many gods are there really,
Yajnavalkya?"
"Two."
"Yes,"
he said,
"but how many gods are there really,
Yajnavalkya?"
"One and a half."
"Yes,"
he said,
"but how many gods are there really,
Yajnavalkya?"
"One."
"Yes,"
he said,
"but which are those three hundred and three and those three thousand and
three?"
(Brihadaranyaka Upanishad 3,4:1)

Spiritual wisdom is really saying there is only one God, but any number such as 3,306 can also represent the one God as long as we are using it to express His infinite and limitless quality. On first impression, the **Upanishad** says there are 3,306 gods but the concluding realization is that God cannot be described by any finite number except one.

Man is finite and God is infinite. For example, the **Hebrew Bible** says, "Man *that is* born of a woman *is* of few days, and full of trouble" (Job 14:1). As soon as children enter the world, desires shape their existence. The finite is filled with the troubles caused by the desires of the Kingdom of Man. In contrast, the **Upanishad** says:

Endless and beginningless is God:
In the midst of chaos He
All things doth emanate,
— how manifold his forms! —
The One Encompasser of all:
By knowing Him a man is from every fetter freed.
(Svetasvatara Upanishad 5:13)

God has no beginning and no end. He is everything; and in everything, He is omniscient and omnipresent. The **Koran** declares, "Say: 'God is One, the Eternal God, He begot none, nor was He begotten. None is equal to Him'" (Koran 112:1). Humans, who are prolific and exist on earth for only for a short time, are dependent for their physical existence and are motivated by their corporeal desires. We live in the finite and God in the infinite. There can be no comparison.

Spiritual wisdom tells us to try not to put limits on our understanding of God based on our worldly experiences. Too often we fail. We allow our human mind to limit our ability to grasp God's vastness, especially when we think of Him in physical terms. In the **Gospel of Thomas**, Jesus tells us to free ourselves from such worldly limitations if we really want to see God, because He is beyond material existence. He has no beginning or end. As we start to spiritually grow, we begin to understand how confining our temporal finite world is. As we continue to grow, we transcend its limitations and begin to recognize the Kingdom of God in ourselves and in the world around us.

How can mankind with such limitations comprehend our limitless God? According to the **Gospel of John**, Jesus answered, "Verily, verily, I say unto thee, Except a man be born of water and *of* the Spirit, he cannot enter into the kingdom of God. That which is born of the flesh is flesh; and that which is born of the Spirit is spirit. Marvel not that I said unto thee, Ye must be born again" (John 3:5-7). We are born of water at birth, but what we must realize is that we are also born of the Spirit. With the Spirit, we can transcend the limits of the physical world and move toward the Kingdom of God. Spiritual wisdom tells us that we *are born again* when our inner perspective changes from being centered in the material and ego-driven world (also called the Kingdom of Man mind-set) to being altruistic and God-centered (or the Kingdom of God mind-set).

Changing our inner perspective can be very difficult, as the following notes: "Even the gods wish to be as the wise ones devoted to meditation, delighting in the calm of detachment, perfectly awakened, imbued with mindfulness. It is hard to get to be human; the life of mortals is hard. Teaching of truth is hardly ever heard; Buddhas hardly ever appear" (Dhammapada 14:3-4). Difficult though it may be, we can change our inner perspective.

The Path Called Life

GOD'S CHALLENGE

Question:
What will a seeker find in life?

Brief Answer:
A seeker will not necessarily find outer peace but may in fact find a life of conflict.

from the *Gospel of Thomas*

16. Jesus said, "Perhaps people think that I have come to impose peace upon the world. They do not know that I have come to impose conflicts upon the earth: fire, sword, war. For there will be five in a house: There will be three against two and two against three, father against son and son against father, and they will stand alone."

Longer Answer:

The Hindu **Bhagavad-Gita** story of Arjuna is spiritual wisdom. Arjuna was about to begin a remarkable battle that would require him to kill almost all his cousins and many of his former friends. Krishna, who is an incarnation of God, is Arjuna's charioteer and thus is Arjuna's guide along his path of life. The **Bhagavad-Gita** says:

> Then (Arjuna,) whose banner is an ape,
> Gazed upon the serried ranks
> Of Dhritarashtra's sons.
> The clash of arms
> Began.
> He lifted up his bow.
>
> To Krishna then
> These words he spake:
> "Halt thou my chariot [here]
> Between the armies twain,
>
> That I may see these men drawn up,
> Spoiling for the fight,
> [That I may see] with whom I must do battle
> In this enterprise of war."
> (Bhagavad-Gita 1:20-22)

Arjuna is told that he must fight this difficult and distasteful battle for the sake of righteousness. His only responsibilities were to righteousness and the fulfillment of his own soul's path. That is every seeker's responsibility also.

Spiritual wisdom stresses the personal difficulty and the challenge of being faithful to one's path. The **Hebrew Bible** says, "For the son dishonoureth the father, the daughter riseth up against her mother, and daughter-in-law against her mother-in-law; a man's enemies *are* the men of his own house" (Micah 7:6). When we follow God's guidance, we may discover our closest loved ones become our strongest enemies. The very people who claim to love us the most may try to keep us from realizing our spiritual goals. They are fearful of the changes they see in us and are afraid that these changes will alter their relationship with us. The **New Testament** says, "And ye shall be betrayed both by parents, and brethren, and kinsfolks, and friends; and *some* of you shall then cause to be put to death. And ye shall be hated of all *men* for my name's sake" (Luke 21:16-17).

Spiritual wisdom does not tell us that as seekers we will have easy lives, but rather that we must anticipate hardship and conflict from directions where we least expect them. The **Hebrew Bible** also says, "For wickedness burneth as the fire: it shall devour the briers and thorns, and shall kindle in the thickets of the forest, and they shall mount up *like* the lifting up of smoke. Through the wrath of the Lord of hosts is the land darkened, and the people shall be as the fuel of the fire; no man shall spare his brother" (Isaiah 9:18-19). Spiritual wisdom assures us that though challenges may be significant, we can win on the battlefield of life with God's Grace. The **New Testament** goes on to say, "But there shall be not a hair of your head perish. In your patience possess ye your souls" (Luke 21: 18-19). If we are patient in our beliefs and diligent in our actions, spiritual wisdom tells us that ultimately we will be all right.

God's special messengers are not immune from these challenges. The **Koran** says, "We sent forth apostles before you to other nations, and afflicted them with calamities and misfortunes so that they might humble themselves. If only they humbled themselves when Our scourge overtook them! But their hearts were hardened, and Satan made their deeds seem fair to them" (Koran 6:42). Even the apostles did not escape the challenges of life. We must accept and embrace all our experiences as opportunities for spiritual growth and not let ourselves be drawn into feeling anger or sorrow about our predicament. The **Dhammapada** says, "Cut off five, abandon five, rise above five; a mendicant who has surmounted the five fetters is said to have crossed over the torrent" (Dhammapada 25:11). The mendicant is a beggar. Regardless of status or position, every person must face and overcome life's challenges.

Often the way we learn best — and sometimes the only way we learn — is through difficult experiences. The ultimate gift of inner peace from God is most commonly learned from a challenging life, rarely from a tranquil one. God's daily gifts are lessons that allow us to move along our individual path. Major lessons or "gifts from God" can include aggression, violence, war, and all other adversities that change our lives, test our priorities, challenge our values and beliefs, and raise doubts in our minds. Even small and seemingly trivial irritations can be gifts or opportunities, like quarrels with friends, traffic tickets, and uncooperative coworkers. Thinking of such negative events as *gifts* may seem odd, but growth and change for most people rarely come without some turmoil or trauma.

If left to our own devices, we would rarely choose a life of adversity. Yet we learn the most and the fastest through adversity. If we are wise and use our hearts, such events bring reflection and introspection. They can enhance our appreciation and commitment to understanding life and our search for God. The fire and conflict noted by Jesus can bring pain, but hopefully the experience awakens us to spiritual growth. Sometimes these gifts are not understood or appreciated at the moment because we are too busy living the episode. Often, we need time to digest and assimilate the experiences before we can comprehend the lesson. We should not consider an unavoidable conflict as negative, but only as an experience. Although a crisis can destroy the strongest will, it can also move us forward along our paths in positive ways if we help our minds transcend the crisis.

We need to shift our view from seeing the crisis as a disaster or potential disaster to seeing it as an opportunity to fulfill our true goal in life. Our tactical approach should be to neutralize or turn the conflict into something positive for all parties involved, including the attackers. Conflict should not be viewed as a win or lose situation, but rather as an experience in which significant learning can take place.

<hr />

THE GIFT OF GOD'S LOVE

Question:
What should we expect from God?

Brief Answer:
Expect the greatest gift imaginable.

from the *Gospel of Thomas*

17. Jesus said, "I shall give you what no eye has seen, what no ear has heard, what no hand has touched, what has not arisen in the human heart."

Longer Answer:

According to spiritual wisdom, God has given and continues to give us the perfect gift. For Christians, the metaphor is Jesus Christ. The **New Testament** says, "Who gave himself for our sins, that he might deliver us from this present evil world, according to the will of God and our Father" (Galatians 1:4). The **Hebrew Bible** describes the gift a little differently: "And *if* thou draw out thy soul to the hungry, and satisfy the afflicted soul: then shall thy light rise in obscurity, and thy darkness *be* as the noon day: And the Lord shall guide thee continually, and satisfy thy soul in drought, and make fat thy bones; and thou shalt be like a watered garden, and like a spring of water, whose waters fail not" (Isaiah 58:10-11). The gift is not in or through another but given directly to each of us individually and privately. If we are in the Kingdom of God mind-set, God's gift is His continual guidance as we travel our paths of life. He satisfies our real needs by providing for us spiritually. He is our perpetual comforter and provider.

How significant is this gift? The following quote from the **Diamond Sutra** sheds some light on its greatness:

> "Subhuti, if there were as many Ganges rivers as the sand grains of the Ganges, would the sand grains of them all be many?"
>
> Subhuti said: "Many indeed, World-Honored One! Even the Ganges rivers would be innumerable; how much more so would be their sand grains!"
>
> "Subhuti, I will declare a truth to you. If a good man or good woman filled three thousand galaxies of worlds with the seven treasures for each sand grain in all those Ganges rivers, and gave all away in gifts of alms, would he gain great merit?"
>
> Subhuti answered: "Great indeed, World-Honored One!"
>
> Then Buddha declared: "Nevertheless, Subhuti, if a good man or good woman studies this discourse only so far as to receive and retain four lines, and teaches and explains them to others, the consequent merit would be far greater." (The Diamond Sutra 11)

According to the Buddha, the gift of inner knowledge and understanding of spiritual wisdom, even in a limited amount, is far more valuable and precious a gift than all the treasures of the galaxy.

The **New Testament** is very specific about God's special gifts to us. It says, "Every good gift and every perfect gift is from above, and cometh down from the Father of lights, with whom is no variableness, neither shadow of turning" (James 1:17). It also says, "For the wages of sin *is* death; but the gift of God *is* eternal life through Jesus Christ our Lord" (Roman 6:23). To Christians, Jesus is the living symbol and the deliverer of God's gift, as the following notes: "Then saith the woman of Samaria unto him, How is it that thou, being a Jew, askest a drink of me, which am a woman of Samaria? for the Jews have no dealings with the Samaritans. Jesus answered and said unto her, If thou knewest the gift of God, and who it is that saith to thee, Give me to drink; thou wouldest have asked of him, and he would have given thee living water" (John 4:9-10).

God's gift is the spiritual wisdom that allows us to see and live the Kingdom of God. The gift of spiritual wisdom is perhaps best described as follows:

But as it is written,
Eye hath not seen,
nor ear heard,
neither have entered into the heart of man,
the things which God hath prepared for them that love him.

But God hath revealed *them* unto us by his Spirit:
for the Spirit searcheth all things,
yea,
the deep things of God.

For what man knoweth the things of a man,
save the spirit of man which is in him?
even so the things of God knoweth no man,
but the Spirit of God.

Now we have received,
not the spirit of the world,
but the spirit which is of God;
that we might know the things that are freely given to us of God.
(Corinthians 1,2:9-12)

Another way to describe the gift of spiritual wisdom is, "God is the light of the heavens and the earth. His light may be compared to a niche that enshrines a lamp, the lamp within a crystal of star-like brilliance. It is lit from a blessed olive tree neither eastern nor western. Its very oil would almost shine forth, though no fire touched it. Light upon light; God guides to His light whom He will" (Koran 24:35). God guides whom He wills to His light but each of us must choose to accept the gift. Each of us must choose to see it or ignore it.

Yet another way to describe the same gift is as follows:

> The self-existent [Lord] bored holes facing the outside world;
> Therefore a man looks outward,
> not into [him]self.
>
> A certain sage,
> in search of immortality,
> Turned his eyes inward and saw the SELF within.
> (Katha Upanishad 4:1)

With our two eyes, we view the world; but the Eastern cultures believe we have a third eye. With it, we have inner vision and the ability to look inward. We can always choose to look inward for God's gift of light rather than to the outer world. When we choose to look inward for His light, He will guide us toward a greater and deeper understanding.

TO REACH THE END, START AT THE BEGINNING

Question:
What is salvation?

Brief Answer:
Salvation begins with spiritual wisdom. Salvation can not be understood until spiritual wisdom is understood.

from the Gospel of Thomas

18. The followers said to Jesus, "Tell us how our end will be."
Jesus said, "Have you discovered the beginning, then, so that you are seeking the end? For where the beginning is, the end will be. Fortunate is one who stands at the beginning: That one will know the end and will not taste death."

Longer Answer:

The end for seekers is Oneness, but that can only be found through the truth of spiritual wisdom. The Buddha said, "This is the Noble Truth of Suffering: such was the vision, the knowledge, the wisdom, the science, the light, that arose in me with regard to things not heard before. This suffering, as a noble truth, should be fully understood: such as the vision, the knowledge, the wisdom, the science, the light, that arose in me with regard to things not heard before. This suffering, as a noble truth, has been fully understood: such was the vision, the knowledge, the wisdom, the science, the light, that arose in me with regard to things not heard before" (The First Sermon of the Buddha). Our path begins in seeking inwardly and realizing that God guides and teaches us privately as we proceed through life. The Noble Truth of Suffering is one of those private and silent lessons.

Only with the spiritual wisdom that God gives us can we reach our goal. The **Koran** says, "Or like darkness on a bottomless ocean spread with clashing billows and overcast with clouds: darkness upon darkness. If he stretches out his hand he can scarcely see it. Indeed the man from whom God withholds His light shall find no light at all" (Koran 24:40). Commonly in the holy scriptures, light is used as a metaphor meaning spiritual wisdom or inner knowledge. God's Grace gives us opportunities to discover spiritual wisdom, but unless we seize the opportunity we remain metaphorically in the dark. We cannot begin to understand the vastness of the Kingdom of God without first discovering spiritual wisdom. Only by recognizing and seizing the opportunities as they are presented to us can we begin to move toward the light more effectively

As discussed in Thomas 15, God has neither beginning nor end. God is everything, since there is none before and none after God. The **Hebrew Bible** says, "Ye *are* my witness, saith the Lord, and my servant whom I have chosen: that ye may know and believe me, and understand that I *am* he: before me there was no God formed, neither shall there be after me" (Isaiah 43:10). The **Hebrew Bible** also says, "Thus saith the Lord the King of Israel, and his redeemer the Lord of host; I *am* the first, and I am the last; and beside me *there is* no God" (Isaiah 44:6). God is our only guide, our only redeemer, our strength, and our inspiration. The **Upanishad** says,

> In the beginning this [universe] was Not-Being only,
> Therefrom was Being born:
> [And Being] itself made [for itself] a SELF;
> Hence is it called "well-done."
> What that "well-done" really is,
> is the [essential] saviour [in all things].
> Once a man has tasted this savior,
> he tastes bliss.
> For who could breathe,
> who could live,
> were this bliss not [diffused] throughout space?
> For this [saviour] alone brings bliss.
> (Taittiriya Upanishad 2:7)

God is the beginning. He is everything and exists everywhere, omnipotent and omnipresent. God is the saviour that offers us bliss — a state of happiness that surpasses physical or intellectual understanding.

God is central to discovering spiritual wisdom. As we begin our path, God must be there and He is there at the end of it. The **New Testament** says, "And when I saw him, I fell at his feet as dead. And he laid his right hand upon me, saying unto me, Fear not; I am the first and the last: I *am* he that liveth, and was dead; and, behold, I am alive for evermore, Amen . . ." (Revelations 1: 17-18). For Christians, Jesus is the model for living spiritual wisdom and for being One with God.

When we achieve Oneness with God, we have reached both the beginning and the end. When we reach Oneness, the individual's consciousness is merged with God. There is no separation between the creator and His creation. The journey of a single drop of water starts in the heavens as falling rain and travels down the mountain in small streams to an ever-growing river until it merges finally with the great ocean. The journey of light also starts as a small drop of Grace and grows until it finally merges with the vastness called Oneness with God. The single individual drop then exists inside the vastness with God. Once we have experienced the bliss of Oneness, how can we exist without it? There was no one before or after God — He is the alpha and the omega, omnipotent and omniscient. With Oneness, we become a part of His infinite.

SOURCES OF SPIRITUAL NOURISHMENT

Question:
Are there constant sources of nourishment to help us reach greater spirituality?

Brief Answer:
Yes, there are five constant sources of spiritual nourishment.

from the *Gospel of Thomas*

19. Jesus said, "Blessed is the person who existed before coming into being." If you exist as my disciples and listen to my sayings, these stones will minister unto you. "Indeed you have five trees in paradise which do not move in summer or winter, and whose leaves do not fall. Whoever is acquainted with them will not taste death."
(See Layton, p. 383.)

Longer Answer:

Seekers of spiritual wisdom must always listen and learn in order to understand even more and act with wisdom. Buddha says, "THE FIFTH REALIZATION is the awareness that ignorance is the cause of the endless round of birth and death. Therefore, bodhisattvas always remember to listen and learn in order to develop their understanding and eloquence. This enables them to educate living beings and bring them to the realm of great joy" (The Sutra on the Eight Realizations of the Great Beings 5). Bodhisattvas are seekers. In their training, they begin to appreciate that the lack of spiritual wisdom (that is, ignorance) is the reason salvation is not reached. Buddhists and Hindus believe in reincarnation. For them, there will be continual reincarnation or rebirths until salvation or enlightenment is reached through spiritual wisdom. Although we do not remember the details of our past lives, we gain spiritual wisdom from them. The wisdom we bring to this life is likely to have a positive impact made on the kinds of experiences and the amount of inner knowledge we can achieve. In other words, we begin each life with a better vantage point for learning and understanding more. We are blessed indeed if we are able to build on our past life experiences to make spiritual progress in this life.

How do we make progress in a given lifetime? The **Upanishad** says:

> When the five senses stand,
> [their action stilled,]
> Likewise the mind;
> and when the soul
> No longer moves or acts, —
> Such,
> have men said,
> is the all-highest Way.
> (Katha Upanishad 6,10)

Spiritual wisdom tells us that we must still the five human senses, the mind, and the soul. The human senses fill our minds with the everyday desires of the world. If we can calm the mind so that it does not focus on matters of the Kingdom of Man, then we can instead focus all our attention and energy on learning and living the spiritual wisdom of the Kingdom of God.

Saying 19 presents a mystery. What are the five trees in paradise? The **Upanishad** says, "This sacrifice is fivefold; cattle are fivefold; man is fivefold; this whole universe is fivefold, — everything that exists. Whoso thus knows wins this whole universe" (Brihadaranyaka Upanishad 1,4:17). The **Hebrew Bible** says, "And out of the ground made the Lord God to grow every tree that is pleasant to the sight, and good for food; the tree of life also in the midst of the garden, and the tree of knowledge of good and evil" (Genesis 2:9). Two of the trees are the well-known tree of life and the tree of knowledge of good and evil. The **Hebrew Bible** also says, "The fruit of the righteous *is* a tree of life; and he that winneth souls *is* wise" (Proverbs 11:30). Therefore, righteousness is an aspect of the tree of life and we should not consider it as a separate tree.

What are the other three trees? We know that they are eternal and of a similar nature to the other two trees. One possible clue is that there are five major religious traditions. The oldest stresses the importance of life. The next oldest stresses knowledge of good and evil. The next three, in order, stress enlightenment, love, and Oneness. Perhaps the answer to the mystery of Saying 19 is (1) life, (2) knowledge of good and evil, (3) enlightenment, (4) love, and (5) Oneness. Maybe the answer to the mystery is in the collective holy scriptures of the five religious traditions. Maybe the answer to the mystery is really what we have referred to in this book as "spiritual wisdom."

The spiritual wisdom tells us that the sources of nourishment are everlasting. The **Hebrew Bible** says, "And by the river upon the bank thereof, on this side and on that side, shall grow all trees for meat, whose leaf shall not fade, neither shall the fruit thereof be consumed: it shall bring forth new fruit according to his mouths, because their waters they issued out of the sanctuary: and the fruit thereof shall be for meat, and the leaf thereof for medicine" (Ezekiel 47:12). The trees are also for our spiritual nourishment. The **New Testament** is also clear about this:

> And he shewed me a pure river of water of life,
> clear as crystal,
> proceeding out of the throne of God and of the Lamb.

In the midst of the street of it,
and on either side of the river *was there* the tree of life,
which bare twelve *manner of* fruits,
and yielded her fruit every month:
and the leaves to the tree *were* for the healing of the nations.

And there shall be no more curse;
but the throne of God and of the Lamb shall be in it;
and his servants shall serve him:

And they shall see his face;
and his name *shall be* in their foreheads.

And there shall be no night there;
and they need no candle,
neither light of the sun;
for the Lord God giveth them light:
and they shall reign for ever and ever.

And he said unto me,
These sayings *are* faithful and true;
and the Lord God of the holy prophets sent his angel to shew unto his servants the
things which must shortly be done.

Behold,
I come quickly:
blessed *is* he that keepeth the sayings of the prophecy of this book.
(Revelations 22:1-7)

The **Koran** says, "Do you not see how God compares a good word to a good tree? Its root is firm and its branches are in the sky; it yields its fruit in every season by God's leave. God speaks in parables to men so that they may take heed. But an evil word is like an evil tree torn out of the earth and shorn of all its roots. God will strengthen the faithful with His steadfast Word, both in this life and the hereafter. He leads the wrongdoers astray. God accomplishes what He pleases" (Koran 14:27). The use of the tree as a metaphor for sustenance and nourishment is consistent with all religious traditions. The **New Testament** says, "He that hath an ear, let him hear what the Spirit saith unto the churches; To him that overcometh will I give to eat of the tree of life, which is in the midst of the paradise of God" (Revelations 2:7). The **Upanishad** also uses the same metaphor:

> "[Look at] this great tree, my dear. If you were to strike at its root, it would bleed but live on; if you were to strike it in the middle, it would bleed but live on; if you were to strike it at the top, it would bleed but live on. Strengthened by the living SELF, it still stands, drinking in the moisture and exulting.
>
> "If life leaves one of its branches, it dries up; if it leaves a second, that too dries up; if it leaves a third, that too dries up. If it leaves the whole [tree], the whole [tree] dries up. This, my dear boy, is how you ought to understand it," said he.
>
> "When the life has gone out of it, this [body] dies; [but] the life does not die.
>
> "This finest essence, — the whole universe has it as its SELF: That is the Real: That is the SELF: That you are, Svetaketu!" (Chandogya Upanishad 6,11)

Another mystery in Saying 19 is "Blessed is the person who existed before coming into being." One possible answer to this conundrum is simply the concept of being reborn or reincarnation. The **Koran** says, "It is He who has given you life, and He who will cause you to die and make you live again. Surely man is ungrateful" (Koran 22:66). This statement clearly says that God can make us be reborn after we die and that we really do not appreciate the magnitude and importance of this gift. The **Koran** also says, "He created you only as one soul, and only as one soul will He bring you back to life. God hears all and observes all" (Koran 31:29). Although we might have many lives, we have only one soul. The soul is the continuum and the vessel or receptacle for the lessons we learn and the spiritual wisdom we gain from life to life.

Hindu and Buddhist traditions tell us that reincarnation is our challenge to escape the circle of "endless" life. In contrast, the Jewish, Christian, and Islam traditions are not overtly associated with reincarnation. Although some religious leaders in the Islam, Jewish, and Christian traditions tell us that reincarnation exists, most say it does not exist. However, the **Koran** says, "They say: 'There is this life and no other. We die and live; nothing but Time destroys us.' Surely of this they have not knowledge. They are merely guessing" (Koran 45:24). The **Koran** also says, "They shall say: 'Lord, twice have You made us die, and twice have You given us life. We now confess our sins. Is there no way out?'" (Koran 40:11). Is there a circle of life and death? The **Koran** says, "Behold then the tokens of God's Mercy; how He resurrects the earth after its death. It is He who will resurrect the dead. He has power over all things" (Koran 30:50).

Can reincarnation be possible according to the other wisdom messages? The **New Testament** says, "Verily, verily, I say unto you, If a man keep my saying, he shall never see death" (John 8:51). If we are seekers and lead righteous lives, will we truly never see death? Does that mean we will be reborn? The **Upanishad** says:

> Some to the womb return, —
> Embodied souls,
> to receive another body;
> Others pass into a lifeless stone
> In accordance with their works,
> In accordance with [the tradition] they had heard.
> (Katha Upanishad 5:6)

Spiritual wisdom tells us the circle of life-death-rebirth is extended to those who demonstrate their faith, as defined by their tradition, with their actions. Those who care nothing for the inner life and who act inappropriately in their lives are passed by and left behind. The **New Testament** says, "Marvel not that I said unto thee, Ye must be born again" (John 3:7). Being reborn is a significant part of spiritual wisdom. Compare the following two quotes from the **New Testament** to the previous **Upanishad** writings:

> Verily,
> verily,
> I say unto you,
> He that heareth my word,
> and believeth on him that sent me,
> hath everlasting life,
> and shall not come into condemnation;
> but is passed from death unto life.

Verily,
verily,
I say unto you,
The hour is coming,
and now is,
when the dead shall hear the voice of the Son of God;
and they that hear shall live.
(John 5:24-25)

Now if we be dead with Christ,
we believe that we shall also live with him:
Knowing that Christ being raised from the dead dieth no more;
death hath no more dominion over him."
(Romans 6:8-9)

God provides us with all we need to transcend ignorance and reach Oneness with Him. This is true regardless of time or place. As we have discussed earlier, certainly language is a major barrier to our understanding, especially of the concept of the infinite. Nevertheless, the five sources of spiritual nourishment are constantly available to us in spiritual wisdom. They are described in this book as life, knowledge of good and evil, enlightenment, love, and Oneness. Only our own ignorance blinds us to these sources of God's nourishment. In our search, the five sources permit us to gain greater spiritual wisdom because they live on in spite of our all-too-common abuse of them. For example, let us say the Hindu and Buddhist belief that life continues on in an endless cycle of being born, dying, and being reborn is correct. Then each time our soul is born into a new body, the Supreme is giving us a new opportunity to make spiritual progress. Each time we are reborn, we can use all five trees of paradise as nourishment as we seek further inner growth.

The treatment of reincarnation differs in the **Hebrew Bible**, the **New Testament** and the **Koran** from what is found in the Hindu and Buddhist scriptures. The **Hebrew Bible** discusses two trees in paradise and Ezekiel discusses various nurturing trees. Although some aspects of the Jewish tradition believe in reincarnation, direct references to it or to being reborn were not found in the **Hebrew Bible** by these authors. However, the **Hebrew Bible** does say, "Behold, I will send my messenger, and he shall prepare the way before me: and the Lord, whom ye seek, shall suddenly come to his temple, even the messenger of the covenant, whom ye delight in: behold, he shall come, saith the Lord of hosts. But who may abide the day of his coming? and who shall stand when he appearth? for he *is* like a refiner's fire, and like a fullers' soap. And he shall sit *as* a refiner and purifer of silver: and he shall purify the sons of Levi, and purge them as gold and silver, that they may offer unto the Lord an offering in righteousness" (Malachi 3:1-3).

Possibly, the process of refining and purifying refers to reincarnation, but that can be easily contested. In contrast, the **New Testament** and the **Koran** have many references that could easily be interpreted to mean that reincarnation exists. Many early Christians, including the Gnostics, believed that a major gift or accomplishment of Jesus Christ was the "defeat of death" or establishment of reincarnation, much in the **Hebrew Bible** tradition of Malachi. A good ancient source on this subject found in the **Nag Hammadi Library** is **The Secret Book According to John** ("Apocryphon of John") written before 180 A.D. and attributed to John, the son of Zebedee, one of Jesus' twelve original disciples.

A reincarnation interpretation of the words of the **New Testament** and **Koran** is possible. Given the infinite compassion of God, such a gift is logically consistent with viewing life as a continuing opportunity given us by God. Certainly, if the Kingdom of God is now present and obtainable for each of us, then reincarnation is merely an added gift to us from God to allow us to achieve the final goal called Oneness. As optimists and believers in the remarkable love of God for humankind, the authors find it comforting to believe in reincarnation. Each of us has far too much learning and growing to do in order to reach Oneness in only one lifetime. We do not believe God would place us in such a nearly impossible position, and we believe with our hearts that reincarnation is a reflection of God's infinite and unconditional love for us.

THE KINGDOM OF GOD GROWS WITHIN

Question:
How does the Kingdom of God grow within us?

Brief Answer:
It grows through our individual relationship with Him.

from the *Gospel of Thomas*

20. The followers said to Jesus, "Tell us what heaven's kingdom is like."
    He said to them, "It is like a mustard seed. <It> is the smallest of all seeds, but
    when it falls on prepared soil, it produces a large plant and becomes a shelter for
    birds of heaven."

Longer Answer:
Our spiritual growth starts with God. The **Upanishad** says:

> He who consists of mind, whose body is the breath of life, whose form
> is light, whose idea is the real, whose self is space, through whom are all
> works, all desires, all scents, all tastes, who encompasses all this universe,
> who does not speak and has no care, — he is my SELF within the heart,
> smaller than a grain of rice or barley-corn, or a mustard-seed, or a grain
> of millet, or the kernel of a grain of millet; this is my SELF within my
> heart, greater than the earth, greater than the atmosphere, greater than
> the sky, greater than all these worlds.
>
> All works, all desires, all scents, all tastes belong to it: it encompasses
> all this universe, does not speak and has no care. This my SELF within
> the heart is that Brahman. When I depart from hence I shall merge into
> it. He who believes this will never doubt.
>
> So did Sandilya say, — so did he say. (Chandogya Upanishad 3,14:3-5).

Knowing the self begins in the heart, as SELF is God. The **Hebrew
Bible** says, "Blessed *is* the man that trusteth in the Lord, and whose hope the
Lord is. For he shall be as a tree planted by the waters, and *that* spreadeth out
her roots by the river, and shall not see when heat cometh, but her leaf shall
be green; and shall not be careful in the year of drought, neither shall cease

from yielding fruit" (Jeremiah 17:7-8). Spiritual wisdom tells us to trust and have hope in God. He will provide us with ample opportunity to grow. He will nourish us with spiritual wisdom.

However, that does not absolve us from taking responsibility for our own growth. We must be good students also. We must complete our assignments and do the right work. The **Diamond Sutra** says:

> Buddha said: "Subhuti, what do you think? In the remote past when the Tathagata was with Dipamkara Buddha, did he have any degree of attainment in the good law?"
>
> "No, World-Honored One. When the Tathagata was with Dipamkara Buddha he had no degree of attainment in the good law."
>
> "Subhuti, what do you think? Does a bodhisattva set forth any majestic buddha-lands?"
>
> "No, World-Honored One. Wherefore? Because 'setting forth majestic buddha-lands' is not a majestic setting forth; this is merely a name."
>
> [Then Buddha continued:] "Therefore, Subhuti, all bodhisattvas, lesser and great, should develop a pure, lucid mind, not depending upon sound, flavor, touch, odor, or any quality. A bodhisattva should develop a mind that alights upon nothing whatsoever; and so should he establish it.
>
> "Subhuti, this may be likened to a human frame as large as the mighty Mount Sumeru. What do you think? Would such a body be great?"
>
> Subhuti replied: "Great indeed, World-Honored One. This is because Buddha has explained that no body is called a great body." (The Diamond Sutra 10)

We must develop a pure and clear mind that is not influenced by the filters that cloud our perceptions of the world. In other words, we must remove the layers of ignorance that taint our perception of, and in some cases blind us from, the truth. The **New Testament** says:

> Another parable put he forth unto them,
> saying,
> The kingdom of heaven is like to a grain of mustard seed,
> which a man took,
> and sowed in his field:

Which indeed is the least of all seeds:
but when it is grown,
it is the greatest among herbs,
and becometh a tree,
so that the birds of the air come and lodge in the branches thereof.

Another parable spake he unto them;
The kingdom of heaven is like unto leaven,
which a woman took,
and hid in three measures of meal,
till the whole was leavened.
(Matthew 13:31-32; similar Luke 13:18-19 and Mark 4:30-32)

Note the **Gospel of Thomas** saying and the New Testament quote from three gospels are almost identical except that the **Gospel of Thomas** says "but when it falls on prepared soil." This expression makes the same implication as the **Diamond Sutra**. We must prepare ourselves as seekers just as a farmer prepares the soil to plant his crop.

In this way we can ensure a good harvest. The **Koran** says:

Muhammad is God's apostle. Those who follow him are ruthless to the unbelievers but merciful to one another. You see them adoring on their knees, seeking the grace of God and His good will. Their marks are on their faces, the traces of their prostrations. Thus are they described in the Torah and in the Gospel: they are like the seed which puts forth its shoot and strengthens it, so that it rises stout and firm upon its stalk, delighting the sowers. Through them He seeks to enrage the unbelievers. Yet to those of them who will embrace the Faith and do good works God has promised forgiveness and a rich reward. (Koran 48:29)

Interestingly, the **Koran** cites the **Hebrew Bible** and the **New Testament** on this very subject. We must prepare the soil by praying, seeking God's Grace, and doing good works just as a farmer uses fertilizer, removes weeds, and otherwise prepares the ground to receive the seed.

There is the smallest spark within each of us as we start life. Like dough and a mustard seed, it can grow with our proper care, love, stimulation, and diligence. We always have the guidance of the Holy Spirit. God provides us with His word through Holy Scriptures and continuing lessons throughout our lives. His light reveals more and more to us until we reach our goal of Oneness with Him. That Oneness is a shelter for all of God's creation. We participate with God in the proper preparation of our heart and soul through our discipline and devotion. With that preparation and God's love and guidance, the vastness of the universe grows from the tiniest of seeds within us. God has clearly told us that He starts with the smallest and creates the most magnificent. He wishes to see the seed grow within each of us. He wants it to blossom into something magnificent, and finally, He wants us to merge with Him. Everything is concentrated in this tiny space within the heart.

The seed is given to all those who seek it, regardless of religious tradition, because He wants His seeds to grow. This can be done when we repattern our lives by first seeing the SELF inside ourselves. Next, we need to revisit our experiences with a new awareness so that we grow our inner light and knowledge. We need to seek enlightenment with newly found awareness and enthusiasm. As all seeds, time is needed from the first planting to finally reaping a bumper crop. Therefore, we also need patience as we let our aspirations grow our "plants" tall and strong.

BE WATCHFUL

Question:
Is there an important warning to those who are seeking spiritual wisdom?

Brief Answer:
Yes, always be on guard.

from the *Gospel of Thomas*

21. Mary said to Jesus, "What do your disciples resemble?"
    He said, "What they resemble is children living in a plot of land that is not theirs.

When the owners of the land come they will say, 'Surrender our land to us.' They, for their part, strip naked in their presence in order to give it back to them, and they give them their land.

"Thus I say that the owner of an estate, knowing that a bandit is coming, will keep watch before the bandit comes and not let the bandit break into the house of his kingdom and steal the possessions. You, then, be on your guard against the world. Arm yourself with great power lest the brigands find a way to get to you; for the trouble that you expect will come. Let an experienced person dwell in your midst!

"When the crop had matured, that person came in haste, sickle in hand, and harvested it. Whoever has ears to hear should listen!"

(See Layton, p. 384.)

Longer Answer:

Spiritual wisdom must include watchfulness. As previously discussed, childlike innocence is an essential quality in our spiritual lives but we must temper it with caution. Possibly, the **Hebrew Bible** provides the best warning about the pitfalls of that childlike innocence and purity that is so central to spiritual wisdom. It says, "The rod and reproof give wisdom: but a child left *to himself* bringeth his mother to shame" (Proverbs 29:15). Mothers need to be watchful of their children. So too do seekers need to be watchful of their precious gifts. The **Dhammapada** warns, "One who lives as though the things of the world were pure, with senses unguarded and appetite immoderate, lazy and weak, will be overpowered by bedevilment, like a weak tree blown over by the wind" (Dhammapada 1:7). Without watchfulness, our senses can be overcome by the unending array of desires of the Kingdom of Man, and we may lose our awareness and desire for seeking the Kingdom of God.

We need to also be watchful of others. The **Koran** says, "Some there are who would indulge in frivolous talk, so that they may without knowledge lead men away from the path of God and hold it up to ridicule. For these there shall be shameful punishment" (Koran 31:2). Without watchfulness, we can easily become diverted by others who are misguided and who are very willing to misguide whomever they can. The **Koran** also says:

We send Our apostles only to proclaim good news and to give warning. But with false arguments the unbelievers seek to confute the truth,
scoffing at My revelations and My warnings.

Who is more wicked than the man who, when reminded of his Lord's
revelations, turns away from them and forgets what his own hands have
done? We have cast veils over their hearts lest they understand Our
words, and made them hard of hearing. Call them as you may to the
right path, they shall never be guided.

Your Lord is forgiving and merciful. Had it been His will to scourge
them for their sins, He would have hurried on their punishment; but He
has set for them a predestined time they cannot evade. (Koran 18:56)

God is well aware that there are those who attempt to turn us away from
our spiritual path. God has a plan for everyone and we must trust that He will
attend to their needs. We do not have to be concerned about them because
we must only be concerned with protecting and preserving our own spiritual
aspirations. This does not mean we should be selfish, however. We must
instead be prudent and careful with our newly found treasure. The **New
Testament** explains:

Be watchful,
and strengthen the things which remain,
that are ready to die:
for I have not found thy works perfect before God.

Remember therefore how thou hast received and heard,
and hold fast,
and repent.
If therefore thou shalt not watch,
I will come on thee as a thief,
and thou shalt not know what hour I will come upon thee.
(Revelations 3:2-3)

We must always be mindful of the spiritual wisdom we have learned or we
may fail in God's opportunity called life. The **Upanishad** says, "Now, [this]
too has been said elsewhere: There can be no reversal of any deed once it has
been performed any more than the [direction of] the waves [can be reversed]

in a great river. The approach of death cannot be warded off any more than the ocean tide" (Matri Upanishad 4:2). Our deeds and actions in life are how we are known. Jesus tells us that we have a most difficult challenge as we must try to maintain our innocence and childlike qualities. However, because of these very qualities, we may act inappropriately, especially when confronted by a hostile authority. We must recognize this limitation of ours and be on guard in order to marshal the strength to resist the inappropriate demands of others. We must not be derailed from our path of seeking Oneness with God because, being human, we can grow faint of heart and lack the vision to realize that courage is required to resist evil. Vigilance is always necessary, or all our spiritual accomplishments may be swept away in a moment of weakness, hesitation, or doubt. The outer world always has apparent pleasures and hazards. Thus, the true seeker must recognize the traps and remain on guard at all times.

GROW INTO THE KINGDOM OF GOD

Question:
What is the secret to reaching the Kingdom of God?

Brief Answer:
We must try to be One with God.

from the Gospel of Thomas

22. Jesus saw some babies nursing. He said to his followers, "These nursing babies are like those who enter the kingdom."
They said to him, "Then shall we enter the kingdom as babies?"
Jesus said to them, "When you make the two into one, and when you make the inner like the outer and the outer like the inner, and the upper like the lower, and when you make male and female into a single one, so that the male will not be male nor the female

be female, when you make eyes in place of an eye, a hand in place of a hand, a foot in place of a foot, an image in place of an image, then you will enter [the kingdom]."

Longer Answer:

Achieving Oneness with God is the central goal of spiritual wisdom. Although they can be "good" people, nonseekers live for the Kingdom of Man. There is often a temptation for new seekers to try to walk with one foot in the Kingdom of Man and the other in Kingdom of God. For example, they may enthusiastically participate in church services on Sunday and be completely consumed by the desires of the world on the other days of the week. Spiritual wisdom tells us that there is nothing gained from this dualistic life. The physical pleasures of the Kingdom of Man and the altruistic Kingdom of God are not harmonious but discordant.

As spiritual progress can only be made while in the body, we must live in the Kingdom of Man, but spiritual wisdom tells us that our overwhelming *desire* must be to live only in the Kingdom of God. Although we live in a world in which physical distinctions exist, we must try to transcend such differences if we are to raise our consciousness. We need to live only in the soul and to look past such fundamentally unimportant characteristics as sex, nationality, religion, and race. We need to let petty egos disappear from our minds. The infant perceives no such differences as it feeds from the mother. The baby and mother are one and the same. We also need to perceive no such differences, as we must see everything as being merely a part of the same Oneness of God. The **New Testament** tells us, "There is neither Jew nor Greek, there is neither bond nor free, there is neither male nor female: for ye are all one in Christ Jesus" (Galatians 3:28; similar Corinthians 1,12:13).

Living in the Kingdom of God means identifying with God's consciousness. The **Koran** says, "There they shall hear no idle talk, but only the voice of peace. And their sustenance shall be given them morning and evening. Such is the Paradise which We shall give the righteous to inherit" (Koran 19:62). Identification with God's consciousness is not idle talk to those concerned with spiritual wisdom. For seekers, only the voice of peace has real meaning. We are challenged to appreciate that although God allowed division, He wants unity. But He also wants us to freely choose unity for ourselves. The **Hebrew Bible** says, "So God created man in his *own* image, in the image of God created he him; male and female created he them" (Genesis

1:27). To be truly in the image of God, we must be One with God regardless of our sex, size, color, or anything else.

How can we live in the Kingdom of Man and transcend our physical being to become the consciousness of the Kingdom of God? Buddha tells us the answer lies in the Middle Path. Buddha says, "Avoiding both these extremes, the Tathagata has realized the Middle Path: it gives vision, it gives knowledge, and it leads to calm, to insight, to enlightenment, to Nirvana. And what is that Middle Path. . . ? It is simply the Noble Eightfold Path, namely right view, right thought, right speech, right action, right livelihood, right effort, right mindfulness, right concentration. This is the Middle Path realized by the Tathagata, which gives vision, which gives knowledge, and which leads to calm, to insight, to enlightenment, to Nirvana" (The First Sermon of the Buddha). Spiritual wisdom is not easily lived while existing in the Kingdom of Man. The life of desire confronts us at every turn and the mind is difficult to tame. The **Upanishad** clarifies the challenge as follows:

> Who knows not how to discriminate
> With mind undisciplined the while, —
> Like vicious steeds untamed,
>   his senses
> He cannot master,
> — he their charioteer.

> But he who does know how to discriminate
> With mind [controlled and] disciplined, —
> Like well-trained steeds,
>   his senses
> He masters [fully],
> — he their charioteer.

> But he who knows not how to discriminate,
> Mindless,
>   never pure,
> He reaches not that [highest] state,
>   returns
> To this round of never-ending birth and death.

But he who does know how discriminate,
Mindful,
always pure,
He gains [indeed] that [highest] state
From which he's never born again.

The man whose charioteer is wisdom,
Whose reins a mind [controlled],
Reaches the journey's end [indeed],
Vishnu's final state.

Higher than the senses are the [senses'] objects,
Higher than these the mind,
Higher than mind is soul,
Higher than soul the SELF,
the "great."

Higher than the "great" the Unmanifest,
Higher than that the "Person:"
Than "Person" there's nothing higher;
He is the goal,
He the All-Highest Way.

This is the SELF,
deep-hidden in all beings,
[The SELF that] shines not forth, —
Yet it *can* be seen by men who see things subtle,
By the subtle soul,
[man's] noblest [part].
(Katha Upanishad 3:5-12)

Saying 22 explains the condition of Oneness. We need to replace our dualistic personality with abiding Oneness. Today, we live in the body and the soul because we let our vital desires and our spiritual learning both serve as goals. We need to completely replace who and what we are with an entirely new person. When we achieve living in the soul, the small ego, that is, the personality identification, disappears, and we become one with the Supreme. When we receive nourishment from spiritual wisdom, we are One with God's consciousness. As we move from childhood to adulthood, our minds create a separate identity and personality defined as "I, me, and mine." This separation is folly and can never lead us to enlightenment. We do not always know how to discriminate correctly. We need to discipline our minds so that we can choose correctly between (a) right and wrong, (b) good and evil, and (c) desire and transcendence. In all these examples of spiritual wisdom, the common theme is to stop thinking of ourselves as being separate from God. He is ready and anxious to be One with us. As long as we cling to the physical world, we need an identity, personality, and individuality that perpetuates our separation. God is in us all. We are in Him. Only our awareness, or more properly the lack of our awareness, keeps us from seeing this clearly.

FEW ARE CHOSEN

Question:
Is heaven easily attainable for all?

Brief Answer:
God anxiously waits for all of us but expects only a few to reach the the goal of Oneness.

from the *Gospel of Thomas*

23. Jesus said, "I shall choose you, one from a thousand and two from ten thousand, and they will stand as a single one."

Longer Answer:

Spiritual wisdom clearly says that few will attain the highest goal. Few will even be interested enough to pursue it. The **Dhammapada** says, "Few are the people who reach the Beyond; the others run along this shore" (Dhammapada 6:10). The **New Testament** says, "For many are called, but few *are* chosen" (Matthew 22:14). It also says, "So the last shall be first, and the first last: for many be called, but few chosen" (Matthew 20:16). The **Hebrew Bible** says, "*Thou* whom I have taken from the ends of the earth, and called thee from the chief men thereof, and said unto thee, Thou *art* my servant: I have chosen thee, and not cast thee away" (Isaiah 41:9). Why will so few reach the ultimate goal? The **Upanishad** explains,

> Many there are who never come to hear of Him,
> Many,
> though hearing of Him,
> know Him not:
> Blessed the man who,
> skilled therein,
> proclaims Him,
> grasps Him;
> Blessed the man who learns from one so skilled and knows Him!
> (Katha Upanishad 2:7)

There are several reasons why everyone does not reach the goal of Oneness. Some never hear about spiritual wisdom. Some hear about it but really do not understand it. Some hear and understand but do not want to apply themselves to the discipline required, while some deliberately choose to stay in the world of physical desire. The **Koran** says, "Say: 'Show us your proof. Here are the Scriptures of today and those of long ago.' But most of them do not know the Truth, and this is why they give no heed" (Koran 21:24). A few gain mastery of spiritual wisdom and thus understand the Kingdom of God. The **Hebrew Bible** says,

> For they *are* a nation void of counsel,
> neither *is there any* understanding in them.
>
> O that they were wise,
> *that* they understood this,
> *that* they would consider their latter end!
> (Deuteronomy 32:28-29)

Another reason why only a few reach the goal of Oneness is the Grace of God. The **New Testament** says, "Ye have not chosen me, but I have chosen you, and ordained you, that ye should go and bring forth fruit, and *that* your fruit should remain: that whatsoever ye shall ask of the Father in my name. He may give it you" (John 15:16). God chooses us first for reasons that are only known to Him. The **New Testament** also says, "But the Lord said unto him, Go thy way: for he is a chosen vessel unto me, to bear my name before the Gentiles, and kings, and the children of Israel: For I will shew him how great things he must suffer for my name's sake" (The Acts 9:15-16). If we are lucky enough to be chosen, do not think that the hardships of walking the righteous path can somehow be avoided, because this will not be the case. There are no shortcuts in the process of learning, but some are more receptive than others and therefore can learn faster.

Although God makes the decisions, spiritual wisdom tells us that our actions largely determine His decision. The **New Testament** says, "And he said, The God of our fathers hath chosen thee, that thou shouldest know his will, and see that Just One, and shouldest hear the voice of his mouth. For thou shalt be his witness unto all men of what thou hast seen and heard" (The Acts 22:14-15). God selects whom He chooses to know His wisdom through His messengers and Grace. As individuals, we must still choose to accept the invitation and become His willing students or not. Once His wisdom is made known to us, then all our future actions bear witness to Him and the nature of His spiritual wisdom. The following parable explains this in more depth:

> Then shall the kingdom of heaven be likened unto ten virgins,
> which took their lamps,
> and went forth to meet the bridegroom.
>
> And five of them were wise,
> and five *were* foolish.
>
> They that *were* foolish took their lamps,
> and took no oil with them:
> But the wise took oil in their vessels with their lamps.
>
> While the bridegroom tarried,
> they all slumbered and slept.
>
> And at midnight there was a cry made,
> Behold,
> the bridegroom cometh;
> go ye out to meet him.

Then all those virgins arose,
and trimmed their lamps.

And the foolish said unto the wise,
Give us of your oil;
for our lamps are gone out.

But the wise answered, saying,
Not so;
lest there be not enough for us and you:
but go ye rather to them that sell,
and buy for yourselves.

And while they went to buy,
the bridegroom came;
and they that were ready went in with him to the marriage:
and the door was shut.

Afterward came also the other virgins,
saying,
Lord,
Lord,
open to us.

But he answered and said,
Verily I say unto you,
I know you not.

Watch,
therefore,
for ye know neither the day nor the hour wherein the Son of man cometh.
(Matthew 25:1-13)

We must be wise and prudent in our actions. We do not know the moment or moments in which God will reveal Himself to us. Therefore, we must always be prepared or we may miss our opportunities. Certainly, God will choose but His preference is to select those of us who have willingly accepted His earlier gifts through our own choice and have tried sincerely to live in His ways. Thus, few will be selected. Again, as always, the starting point in the selection process rests with each individual's response to Grace. Very few even recognize the presence of the SELF within themselves. Fewer still recognize that God gives them a continuing treasure of gifts and opportunities on a daily basis. Fewer yet are willing to truly work for their own enlightenment. God will eagerly receive the receptive. He challenges each person to increase their capacity. Each person will receive light according to his or her own strength and depth. As we grow and are able to receive more, we are given more.

THE LIGHT WITHIN

Question:
Where should we search for spiritual wisdom?

Brief Answer:
The best place is to look inside ourselves.

from the Gospel of Thomas

24. His disciples said, "Show us the place where you are, for we must seek it."
    He said to them, "Whoever has ears should listen! There is light existing within a person of light. And it enlightens the whole world: And it does not enlighten, if it is darkness."
    (See Layton, p. 385.)

Longer Answer:

Spiritual wisdom is first and foremost found within ourselves. If we have found it, our actions radiate its presence. The **Upanishad** says, "[Abiding] among the senses there is a 'person' who consists of understanding, a light within the heart: this is he. Remaining ever the same, he skirts both worlds, seemingly thinking, seemingly moving. For, having fallen asleep, he transcends this world, — the forms of death" (Brihadaranyaka Upanishad 4,3:7). We must cultivate that light within our hearts. Buddha says, "This is the Noble Truth of the Path leading to the Cessation of suffering. . . such was the vision, . . . This Path leading to the Cessation of suffering, as a noble truth, should be followed (cultivated): such was the vision, . . . This Path leading to the (cultivated): such was the vision, the knowledge, the wisdom, the science, the light, that arose in me with regard to things not heard before" (The First Sermon of the Buddha). We must cultivate and grow that spark into a flame as we would build a fire. We can use the metaphor of the spark and flame to describe the growing aspiration within us. Spiritual wisdom says the good news is that we have the spark, we can understand spiritual wisdom, and we can grow with God as our guide and teacher, and with His help we can transcend our limitations into the Oneness of God.

Spiritual wisdom must grow within us. The **Koran** says, "Prophet, say to those you have taken captive: 'If God finds goodness in your hearts, He will give you that which is better than what has been taken from you, and He will forgive you, God is forgiving and merciful.' But if they seek to betray you, know they have already betrayed God. Therefore He has made you triumph over them. God is forgiving and merciful'" (Koran 8:70). If the spark of goodness is within us, God will help us cultivate it into a soaring flame though His spiritual wisdom. The **New Testament** says, "The light of the body is the eye: if therefore thine eye be single, thy whole body shall be full of light. But if thine eye be evil, thy whole body shall be full of darkness. If therefore the light that is in thee be darkness, how great is that darkness!" (Matthew 6:22-23; similar Luke 11: 34-35). The converse is also true because ignorance and malice will extinguish our flame and lead us into complete darkness. Spiritual wisdom is positive and asserts that God is on our side. He loves each of us unconditionally and He wants all of us to succeed. The **Hebrew Bible** says:

He will deliver his soul from going into the pit,
and his life shall see the light.

Lo,
all these *things* worketh God oftentimes with man,

To bring back his soul from the pit,
to be enlightened with the light of the living.
(Job 33:28-30)

Spiritual wisdom does not exist within us because we simply declare it exists. It must be carefully nurtured. The **Koran** says, "The Arabs of the desert declare: 'We are true believers.' Say: 'Believers you are not.' Rather say: 'We profess Islam, for faith has not yet found its way into your hearts. If you obey God and His apostle, He will not deny you the reward of your labours. God is forgiving and merciful'" (Koran 49:14). Saying we are true seekers may impress our friends and colleagues but our mere words are meaningless to God; instead, real seekers bear witness to His wisdom through their sincere daily actions and not with their claims and assertions to others. By the very nature of our own enlightenment, we enlighten the whole world. As the soul grows and strengthens with the light from our aspiration, it radiates through our very being into the world. The disciples of Jesus asked to see where Jesus was. They were seekers. Jesus answered that He was within all those with light; and as each adds their light, the whole world has more light. If one loses light, then that person is lost in darkness and the whole world is darker.

LOVE AND PROTECT OUR BROTHERS

Question:
How do we cultivate spiritual wisdom?

Brief Answer:
We cultivate it by loving one another.

from the *Gospel of Thomas*

25. Jesus said, "Love your brother like your soul, protect that person like the pupil of your eye."

Longer Answer:

Spiritual wisdom is much more than words in a lesson. It is also a process and a mind-set. We begin to develop spiritual wisdom by living it. One good place to start is by loving our brothers and sisters or fellow seekers as much as we love our own soul. In loving our spiritual family, we naturally try to protect them just as we would ourselves. In other words, just like the reflex action of our hands covering our eyes to protect them is instinctive, so too is our reflex to protect our spiritual family. The **Hebrew Bible** says, "Thou shalt not hate thy brother in thine heart: thou shalt in any wise rebuke thy neighbour, and not suffer sin upon him. Thou shalt not avenge, nor bear any grudge against the children of thy people, but thou shalt love thy neighbour as thyself: I *am* the Lord" (Leviticus 19:17-18). Notwithstanding the human cry for revenge throughout history in the Kingdom of Man, spiritual wisdom clearly says NO! The **Koran** says, "The believers are a band of brothers. Make peace among your brothers and fear God, so that you may be shown mercy" (Koran 49:10).

Spiritual wisdom calls for peace. Unfortunately the limitations of our language is revealed once more. Religious writers sometimes use the terms "believers" and "seekers" interchangeably. Thus one word is often confused for the other. In many cases these terms have come to mean a self-selected set of people who exclude others rather than the broader inclusive meaning. The **Koran** says clearly, "Be courteous when you argue with the People of the Book, except with those among them who do evil. Say: 'We believe in that which is revealed to us and which was revealed to you. Our God and your God is one. To Him we surrender ourselves'" (Koran 29:46).

Loving our spiritual brothers and sisters is the beginning. Many people can accomplish this first step. However, the challenge becomes larger when we meet someone whose intent in life is to do harm. To meet this larger challenge, we must be able to distinguish among ignorance, lethargy, and true evil. If our challenge is to conquer true evil, we must realize that anger and hatred will conquer nothing and our only solution is to try to find even greater light from within. Starting with our fellow seekers is appropriate but we need to learn not to hate anyone. Instead, we must be friendly and compassionate to all. We must replace the "I, me, mine" pronouns in our lives with "we, us, ours." In this way, we begin to expand ourselves into God's entire creation.

The **Bhagavad-Gita** says,

> Let a man feel hatred for no contingent being,
> Let him be friendly,
> compassionate,
> Let him be done with thoughts of "I" and "mine,"
> The same in pleasure as in pain,
> long-suffering.
> (Bhagavad-Gita 12:13)

The **Metta-sutra** tells us:

> He who is skilled in good and who wishes to attain the state of Calm should act
> (thus):
> He should be able,
> upright,
> perfectly upright,
> compliant,
> gentle,
> and humble.
>
> Contented,
> easily supported,
> with few duties,
> of simple livelihood,
> controlled in senses,
> discreet,
> not impudent,
> he should not be greedily attached to families.
> (Metta-sutra 1-3)

When we adopt a more detached but loving approach to life, everything looks different because our appreciation for all things and all people changes dramatically. People of all traditions have ignored this elemental lesson of spiritual wisdom. For example, many have allowed their actions to bear witness not to their love of humanity but to their hatred and distrust of all those with different beliefs. Some of the most bloody wars in history were fought in the name of God. The following **New Testament** quotes require reflection and need to be contrasted to the daily experiences of Christian nations:

If ye fulfil the royal law according to the scripture,
Thou shalt love thy neighbour as thyself,
ye do well:
(James 2:8)

And the second *is* like unto it,
Thou shalt love thy neighbour as thyself.
(Matthew 22:39)

And the second *is* like,
namely,
this,
Thou shalt love thy neighbour as thyself.
There is none other commandment greater than these.
(Mark 12:31)

For this,
Thou shalt not commit adultery,
Thou shalt not kill.
Thou shalt not steal,
Thou shalt not bear false witness,
Thou shalt not covet;
and if *there be* any other commandment,
it is briefly comprehended in this saying,
namely,
Thou shalt love thy neighbour as thyself.
(Romans 13:9)

For all the law is fulfilled in one word,
even in this:
Thou shalt love thy neighbour as thyself.
(Galatians 5:14)

A new commandment I give you:
That you love one another;
as I have loved you,
that you have love one to another.
By this shall all *men* know that you are my disciples,
if you have love one to another.
(John 13:34-35)

Spiritual wisdom tells us to love our spiritual brothers and sisters more than our own bodies. We must love them like our own soul, because, as God exists in everyone, we are merely loving the divine in others. If we look carefully and deep into the hearts of others, we will be amazed to find higher spiritual qualities in everyone. We must love all humanity as we love our own soul, because humanity is God's creation. We need to perceive with sadness those who are lost in darkness, but we must realize that our love can raise the collective awareness of the world's darkness because we can lead by following God's example of unconditional love. However, we must grant others the same free choice that God gives us by not imposing our will on them.

Divine love is the absence of all hate and discord toward fellow beings; it is being friendly and compassionate; it is thinking and acting without the ego; and it is viewing equally the experiences of pleasure and pain. We must love all people like ourselves. This absolute standard of God's unconditional love is difficult for us to maintain, but it is His love for us.

FOCUS ON OUR OWN LIMITATIONS FIRST

Question:

Are there any particular pitfalls to avoid in seeking spiritual wisdom?

Brief Answer:

Yes, we must focus on correcting our own limitations before having any thought of being concerned about the faults of others.

from the *Gospel of Thomas*

26. Jesus said, "You see the speck that is in your brother's eye, but you do not see the beam that is in your own eye. When you take the beam out of your own eye, then you will see clearly to take the speck out of your brother's eye."

Longer Answer:

Most of us are quick to see even the smallest faults in someone else's behavior while never even noticing our own. Spiritual wisdom tells us to rethink our priorities and focus on our own faults first. The **Dhammapada** says, "It is easy to see the faults of others, hard to see one's own. One sifts the faults of others like chaff, but covers up one's own, as a crafty cheater covers up a losing throw" (Dhammapada 18:18). It also says, "Do not look at the faults of others, or what others have done or not done; observe what you yourself have done and have not done" (Dhammapada 4:7). The **Bhagavad-Gita** adds:

> Better one's own duty [to perform],
> though void of merit,
> Than to do another's well:
> Better to die within [the sphere of] one's own duty:
> Perilous is the duty of other men.
> (Bhagavad-Gita 3:35)

Why should we focus on our own faults first? The **Dhammapada** answers, "Do not neglect your own need for another's, no matter how great; having discerned your own need, do what is really useful" (Dhammapada 12:10). If we look toward others, we tend to neglect our own spiritual growth problems. The **Hebrew Bible** says, "Woe unto them that seek deep to hide their counsel from the Lord, and their works are in the dark, and they say, Who seeth us? and who knoweth us? Surely your turning of things upside down shall be esteemed as the potter's clay: for shall the work say of him that made it, He made me not? or shall the thing framed say of him that framed it, He had no understanding?" (Isaiah 29:15-16).

If we do not focus on our own problems, we not only continue the problem but we do not allow ourselves to increase our inner light and gain in spirituality. The **Koran** says, "Let not the rich and honorable among you swear to withhold their gifts from their kindred, the destitute, and those who have fled their homes for the cause of God. Rather let them pardon and forgive. Do you not wish God to forgive you? God is forgiving and merciful" (Koran 24:22). The rich, honorable, and powerful have a special responsibility because they above all must pardon and forgive the problems and shortcomings of others, especially subordinates and those entrusted to their care. The **New Testament** says:

> For with what judgment ye judge,
> ye shall be judged:
> and with what measure ye mete,
> it shall be measured to you again.

> And why beholdest thou the mote that is in thy brother's eye,
> but considerest not the beam that is in thine own eye?

> Or how wilt thou say to thy brother,
> Let me pull out the mote out of thine eye;
> and,
> behold,
> a beam *is* in thine own eye?

> Thou hypocrite,
> first cast out the beam out of thine own eye:
> and then shall you see clearly to cast out the mote out
> of thy brother's eye.
> (Matthew 7:2-5; similar Luke 6:41-42)

We must take care not to be hypocrites. Our first responsibility is to correct our own problems, faults, and failings. Only when we have done that should we worry others about their problems. Often, if we feel close enough to those around us, we are quick to not only point out faults but to go the next step and freely condemn them for their faults. Spiritual wisdom tells us to take responsibility for our own life and first correct our own faults. Certainly, we should help others and share what spiritual wisdom we have acquired. However, we must do so only after we have addressed our own inner problems and shortcomings, because our primary responsibility is to proceed down our individual spiritual path. Often, we are inclined to focus on the shortcomings of others and decide to address those problems, because they are less painful to us than confronting our own. Unless we have taken the beam out of our eye, we cannot clearly see the needs of others, since our vision is distorted. God explains that our full enlightenment is necessary before we can stand in judgment of others.

OUR TOTAL COMMITMENT

Question:
In seeking spiritual wisdom, must the commitment be total?

Brief Answer:
Yes, total.

from the *Gospel of Thomas*
27. Jesus said, "If you do not fast unto the world you will not find the kingdom of God. If you do not make the sabbath a sabbath, you will not behold the father." (See Layton, p. 385, using Greek fragments.)

Longer Answer:
Spiritual wisdom requires the total commitment of the seeker in always making an effort to grow and to live a spiritual life. The **Dhammapada** says, "It is easy to do what is bad and harmful to one-self; what is beneficial and good is supremely hard to do" (Dhammapada 12:7). The **Bhagavad-Gita** says:

> Works of sacrifice,
> the gift of alms and works of penance
> Are not to be surrendered;
> these must most certainly be done;
> It is sacrifice,
> alms-giving and ascetic practice
> That purify the wise.
> (Bhagavad-Gita 18:5)

Although difficult, trying to live spiritual wisdom is essential. However, total commitment does not mean blind or mindless ritualism. The **Koran** says, "The Sabbath was ordained only for those who differed about it. On the Day of Resurrection your Lord will judge their disputes" (Koran 16:124). Religious ritual has its purpose but it is not the definition of commitment. The **New Testament** says:

> *And* having spoiled principalities and powers,
> he made a shew of them openly,
> triumphing over them in it.
> Let no man therefore judge you in meat,
> or in drink,
> or in respect of an holyday,
> or of the new moon,
> or of the sabbath *days*:
> (Colossians 2:15-16)

Observing the holy days is not a critical factor in a person's commitment. Every day should be treated as though it is a holy day. We should not judge or label others in terms of their religious practices. Spiritual nourishment is not found in rote ritual but rather in sincere acts of devotion inspired by our discoveries of spiritual wisdom. Total commitment is a matter of the mind and the heart. The **Hebrew Bible** says, "Blessed *is* the man *that* doeth this, and the son of man *that* layeth hold on it; *that* keepeth the sabbath from polluting it, and keepeth his hand from doing any evil" (Isaiah 56:2). Performing rituals is merely a tool to inspire us and keep us focused on the goal of Oneness with God. The **New Testament** says,

> Then was Jesus led up of the spirit into the wilderness to be tempted of the devil.

> And when he had fasted forty days and forty nights,
> he was afterward an hungred.

> And when the tempter came to him,
> he said,
> If thou be the Son of God,
> command that these stones be made bread.

> But he answered and said,
> It is written,

man shall not live by bread alone,
but every word that proceedeth out of the mouth of God.
(Matthew 4:1-4)

Our focus and energy should not be on the daily coming and goings of the world but rather on God's messages to us. The **Koran** says, "Children of Adam, dress well when you attend your mosques. Eat and drink, but avoid excess. He does not love the intemperate" (Koran 7:31). We observe the sabbath and dress appropriately for certain rituals because we choose to honor God. These are signs of deep love and respect; however, the true sign is how we conduct our lives each minute of every day. Our unconditional commitment to God is not found in ritual; it is found only in our personal intimate relationship with Him. The **New Testament** says:

Or have ye not read in the law,
how that on the sabbath days the priest in the temple profane the sabbath,
and are blameless?

But I say unto you,
That in this place is *one* greater than the temple.

But if ye had known what *this* meaneth,
I will have mercy,
and not sacrifice,
ye would not have condemned the guiltless.

For the Son of man is Lord even of the sabbath day.
(Matthew 12:5-8)

Perhaps the **New Testament** explains the difference best with the following words:

Two men went up into the temple to pray;
the one a Pharisee,
and the other a publican.

The Pharisee stood and prayed thus with himself,
God,

I thank thee,
that I am not as other men *are*,
extortioners, unjust adulterers, or even as this publican.

I fast twice in the week,
I give tithes of all that I possess.

And the publican,
standing afar off,
would not lift up so much as *his* eyes unto heaven,
but smote upon his breast saying,
God be merciful to me a sinner.

I tell you,
this man went down to his house justified *rather* than the other:
for every one that exalteth himself shall be abased;
and he that humbleth himself shall be exalted.
(Luke 18:10-14)

Spiritual wisdom gives the performance of certain rituals like fasting and observing the sabbath much deeper meaning. With knowledge of God's spiritual wisdom, fasting is done as a offering of surrender to God. Observing the sabbath is the positive act of going to a place of worship with our prayers of thanks and requests for forgiveness. It is done as an offering of celebration and gratitude to God. With spiritual wisdom, we need to transcend the earthly bonds that bind us to our vital desires and emotional needs. Therefore, we must make every moment a sabbath and see our sacred offerings as our gifts to God. Our every thought and action should be a gift to the Supreme. Oneness is not something we do for a while in a particular way then stop and live a "normal life" because Oneness is a complete commitment. Oneness is our gift of love and devotion to God.

Acquiring Spiritual Wisdom

---◆---

OUR IGNORANCE

Question:

Are most people considered spiritual?

Brief Answer:

Most people are content to be satisfied with worldly pleasures but a few are seekers of spiritual wisdom.

from the *Gospel of Thomas*

28. Jesus said, "I stood at rest in the midst of the world. And unto them I shown forth incarnate; I found them all intoxicated. And I found none of them thirsty. And my soul was pained for the children of humankind, for they are blind in their hearts and cannot see. For, empty did they enter the world, and again

empty they seek to leave the world. But now they are intoxicated. When they
shake off their wine, then they will repent."
(See Layton, p. 385, using Greek fragments.)

Longer Answer:

Saying 28 tells us that when Jesus began His ministry He looked like a common villager, and therefore people treated him accordingly. From that vantage point, Jesus found humanity ignorant of spiritual wisdom. A common metaphor in spiritual wisdom meaning ignorace is "drunk," or sometimes, "intoxicated." Just as intoxication slows and even paralyzes our bodily functions, a lack of understanding slows and paralyses our souls from comprehending the essential knowledge around us, by halting our interest in seeking. Buddha described that "intoxication" as follows:

> THE FIRST REALIZATION is the awareness that the world is
> impermanent. All political regimes are subject to fall; all things com-
> posed of the four *elements* (that is earth, air, water, fire) are empty and con-
> tain the seeds of suffering. Human beings are composed of five skand-
> has (that is forms, feelings, perceptions, mental formations, conscious-
> ness), and are without a separate self. They are always in the process of
> change — constantly being born and constantly dying. They are empty
> of self, without sovereignty. The mind is the source of all confusion, and
> the body is the forest of all impure actions. If we meditate on these facts,
> we can gradually be released from *samsara*, the round of birth and death.
> (The Sutra on the Eight Realizations of the Great Beings 1)

If our only reality is that we live in the physical world, spiritual wisdom tells us our world is both impermanent and transient. In other words, we are empty of SELF and thus unaware of the divine spark within us, we have a confused mind, and the only desires driving our actions are those of the physical body. For many, life is defined by a long succession of unmet and unsatisfied desires that we call "needs." The **Hebrew Bible** says, "For the drunkard and the glutton shall come to poverty: and drowsiness shall clothe *a man* with rags" (Proverbs 23:21). Such individuals are not thirsty for spiritual wisdom. The **Hebrew Bible** also says, "Woe to the crown of pride, to the drunkards of Ephraim, whose glorious beauty *is* a fading flower, which *are* on the head of the fat valleys of them that are overcome with wine!" (Isaiah 28:1).

No matter how pleasing to the eye, all worldly beauty fades and is lost in time. If this is our highest value, then we are also lost. The **Hebrew Bible** goes on to say, "Awake, ye drunkards, and weep; and howl, all ye drinkers of wine, because of the new wine; for it is cut off from your mouth" (Joel 1:5). If one is ignorant of spiritual wisdom, one cannot place any value on seeking it. The **New Testament** directly references Joel and says:

For these are not drunken,
as ye suppose,
seeing it is *but* the third hour of the day.

But this is that which was spoken by the prophet Joel;

And it shall come to pass in the last days,
saith God,
I will pour out of my Spirit upon all flesh:
and your sons and your daughters shall prophesy,
and your young men shall see visions,
and your old men shall dream dreams:

And on my servants and on my handmaidens I will pour out in those days of my
Spirit;
and they shall prophesy:

And I will shew wonders in heaven above,
and signs in the earth beneath;
blood,
and fire,
and vapour of smoke:

The sun shall be turned into darkness,
and the moon into blood,
before that great and notable day of the Lord come:

And it shall come to pass,
that whosoever shall call on the name of the Lord shall be saved.
(The Acts 2:15-21)

Like any good teacher, God wishes us to be motivated to learn but He realizes that some students willingly choose ignorance. Each of us comes into this world ignorant; however, many even strive to depart it ignorant. The **Dhammapada** says, "Just as a fragrant, delightful lotus grows from a heap of suet thrown off the road, so also in the midst of blind mortals, who are like so much dust, do disciples of the truly enlightened shine" (Dhammapada 4:15-16). In spite of our appalling ignorance, spiritual wisdom tells us that some will emerge to seek Oneness with God. However, we can emerge only if we listen to God's messengers and are grateful for God's unconditional Grace. The **Koran** says, "We have sent you forth to all mankind, so that you may give them good news and forewarn them. But most men have no knowledge. They ask: 'When will this promise be fulfilled, if what you say be true?'" (Koran 34:27).

We must not be impertinent or impatient with God. The **Koran** says, "Perish Man! How ungrateful he is! From what did God create him? From a little germ He created him and proportioned him. He makes his path smooth for him, then causes him to die and stows him in a grave. He will surely bring him back to life when He pleases. Yet he declines to do His bidding" (Koran 80:17-27). God created us, shaped us, established a path called life for us, and He will surely bring us back when we stray from Him. Yet, many remain ungrateful, refusing to follow His guidance. Instead, the **Upanishad** says:

> [The individual self] is like a lame man [weighed down] by fetters made up of the fruits of good and evil deeds; like a prisoner, not his own master, bound; like one in the realm of death, beset by all manner of fear; like a man drunk with wine, intoxicated with the wine of delusion; like one possessed by an evil [spirit], driven haplessly this way and that; like one bitten by a great snake, bitten by the attractions of sense; like [one groping his way] in thick darkness, blinded by passion; [like the victim] of a jugglers's tricks, subject to deception; like [a man in] a dream, seeing a false appearance; like the inside of a reed, empty of pith; like an actor, wearing the same costume for only a moment, like painted scenery, falsely attractive. (Maitri Upanishad 4:2b)

For many, life is fraught with perceived problems defined in terms of our unmet desires. Our egos drive us to seek instant gratification or, failing that, temporary fulfillment. We avoid change because it is unsettling, unpleasant, and requires too much effort. We seek gratification, fantasize about fulfillment, and are concerned primarily with pain avoidance. Jesus found humanity blind in its heart because people were ignorant of their souls and the important inner knowledge associated with spiritual growth. Humanity was not only ignorant of inner knowledge, it was also unable to seek such knowledge or recognize its importance. This condition caused Him to ache and God's wisdom messages were sent to address that anguish.

IS THERE HOPE FOR US?

Question:
Is there spiritual hope for us?

Brief Answer:
Of course, there is always hope.

from the *Gospel of Thomas*

29. Jesus said, "It is amazing if it was for the spirit that flesh came into existence. And it is amazing indeed if spirit (came into existence) for the sake of the body. But as for me, I am amazed at how this great wealth has come to dwell in this poverty."
(See Layton, p. 385.)

Longer Answer:

The Spirit is very special in spiritual wisdom. The **Upanishad** says, "This earth is the honey of all beings, and all beings are honey for this earth. That radiant, immortal Person who indwells this earth and, in the case of the [human] self, that radiant, immortal Person who consists of the body, is indeed that very SELF; this is the Immortal, this Brahman, this the All" (Brihadaranyaka Upanishad 2,5:1). The Spirit is called SELF in the Hindu tradition. For example, the **Hebrew Bible** repeats the same message as follows: "But *there is* a spirit in man: and the inspiration of the Almighty giveth them understanding" (Job 32:8). The Spirit is a very important concept. For example, the **Hebrew Bible** says, "And it came to pass, when they were gone over, that Elijah said unto Elisha, Ask what I shall do for thee, before I be taken away from thee. And Elisha said, I pray thee, let a double portion of thy spirit be upon me" (Kings 2,2:9).

The Spirit is our direct link to God. The **Hebrew Bible** also says, "And I shall come down and talk with thee there: and I will take of the spirit which *is* upon thee, and will put *it* upon them; and they shall bear the burden of the people with thee, that thou bear *it* not thyself alone" (Numbers 11:17). What else do we know about the Spirit? The **Koran** says, "They put questions to you about the Spirit. Say: 'The Spirit is at my Lord's command. Little indeed is the knowledge vouchsafed to you'" (Koran 17:85). The Spirit is God's personal agent within us. The Spirit helps us to grow. Although it is lengthy, the **Diamond Sutra** explains the importance of spiritual growth as follows:

> Subhuti said to Buddha: "World-Honored One, will there always be men who will truly believe after coming to hear these teachings?"
>
> Buddha answered: "Subhuti, do not utter such words! At the end of the last five-hundred-year period following the passing of the Tathagata, there will be self-controlled men, rooted in merit, coming to hear these teachings, who will be inspired with belief. But you should realize that such men have not strengthened their root of merit under just one buddha, or two buddhas, or three, or four, or five buddhas, but under countless buddhas; and their merit is of every kind. Such men, coming to hear these teachings, will have an immediate uprising of pure faith, Subhuti; and the Tathagata will recognize them. Yes, he will clearly perceive all these of pure heart, and the magnitude of their moral excellences. Wherefore? It is because such men will not fall back to cherishing the idea of an ego entity, a personality, a being, or a separated individuality. They will neither fall back to cherishing the idea of

things as having intrinsic qualities, nor even of things as devoid of, intrinsic qualities.

Wherefore? Because if such men allowed their minds to grasp and hold to anything they would be cherishing the idea of an ego entity, a personality, a being, or a separated individuality; and if they grasped and held on to the notion of things as having intrinsic qualities they would be cherishing the idea of an ego entity, a personality, a being, or a separated individuality. Likewise, if they grasped and held on to the notion of things as devoid of intrinsic qualities they would be cherishing the idea of an ego entity, a personality, a being, or a separated individuality. So you should not be attached to things as being possessed of, or devoid, of intrinsic qualities.

This is the reason why the Tathagata always teaches this saying: My teaching of the good law is to be likened unto a raft. The buddha-teaching must be relinquished; how much more so misteaching!" (The Diamond Sutra 6)

God is amazing. We know that God created us. Yet, we identify ourselves as body and flesh. Is it not God's body? What is amazing is God's desire to take finite beings such as ourselves and help us to become infinite with Him. Maybe even more amazing is that in spite of the ignorance in the world and our indifference to God's word, great spiritual wealth has grown in this place of spiritual poverty. Possibly the following **New Testament** quote captures the Spirit and God's amazing accomplishment that we call "life":

There is therefore now no condemnation to them which are in Christ Jesus,
who walk not after the flesh,
but after the Spirit.

For the law of the Spirit of life in Christ Jesus hath made me free from the law of sin and death.

For what the law could not do,
in that it was weak through the flesh,
God sending his own Son in the likeness of sinful flesh,

and for sin,
condemned sin in the flesh:
That the *righteousness* of the law might be fulfilled in us,
who walk not after the flesh,
but after the Spirit.

For they that are after the flesh do mind the things of the flesh;
but they that are after the Spirit change the things of the Spirit.
(Romans 8:1-5)

Spiritual growth requires our effort and determination. Both the Buddhist Sutras and the **New Testament** scriptures stress the importance of spiritual growth and the challenge of achieving that growth. We must not allow ourselves to fall back on the ego. Instead, we must take great strength and direction from the Spirit or SELF within us. The SELF is God's greatest gift to us because it enables us to move forward down the path of life with spiritual wisdom in spite of having enormous limitations created by the body. The Spirit gives us hope and faith to approach the unknowable and unseeable. The Spirit gives us comfort and strength on our challenging journey to enlightenment and Oneness with God. The Spirit is the constant outpouring of God's love for us. The Spirit feeds, strengthens, and guides each of us.

DO NOT LIMIT OUR UNDERSTANDING OF GOD

Question:
Can God be explained in simpler terms?

Brief Answer:
God has no limits, so we must not let the mind create limits that do not exist.

from the *Gospel of Thomas*

30. Jesus said, "Where there are [three, they are] godless. And where there is [one] alone, I say that I myself am with that one. Lift a stone and you will find me there. Split a piece of wood, and I am there."
(See Layton, p. 386 using the Greek version from available fragments.)

The Meyer translation based on the Coptic is as follows:
Jesus said, "Where there are three deities, they are divine. Where there are two or one, I am with that one."

Longer Answer:

Spiritual wisdom clearly says God is one. The **Hebrew Bible** says, "Hear, O Israel: the Lord our God *is* one Lord" (Deuteronomy 6:4). God is one. The **Koran** says, "The apostles We sent before you were but men whom We inspired with revelations and with scriptures. Ask the People of the book, if you doubt this. To you We have revealed the Admonition, so that you may proclaim to men what was sent down for them, and that they may give thought" (Koran 16:42). God has sent many messengers but there is only one God. Ironically, religions are defined more by the messengers than by God. We should look past religions and their rites and rituals to focus only on God. The **Koran** also says, "Your God is one God. There is no God but Him. He is the Compassionate, the Merciful" (Koran 2:163). God is one meaning; God is everything. The **New Testament** says, "But to us *there is but* one God, the Father, of whom *are* all things, and we in him; and one Lord Jesus Christ, by whom *are* all things, and we by him" (Corinthians 1, 8:6). God is inside us and outside us. The **Veda** says:

> He is their father,
> he their son,
> He their eldest brother and their youngest:
> The One God,
> entering the mind,
> Is the first-born;
> [yet] he is in the womb.
> (Atharva-Veda 10,8:28)

Unfortunately, in trying to understand spiritual wisdom, we tend to think of God in human finite terms. Often we misunderstand not only the wisdom of other traditions but sometimes even our own traditions. The **Koran** says, "Unbelievers are those that say: 'God is one of three.' There is but one God. If they do not desist from so saying, those of them that disbelieve shall be sternly punished" (Koran 5:73). God is only one and not three. The **New Testament** says, "I and *my* Father are one" (John 10:30). The **New Testament** also says, "And Jesus answered him, The first of all command-ments *is* Hear, O Israel; the Lord our god is one Lord: And thou shalt love the Lord thy God with all thy heart, and with all thy soul, and with all thy mind, and with all thy strength: this *is* the first commandment" (Mark 12:29-30). Like much of spiritual wisdom, what God is and is not appears a mystery to us largely because our finite minds more easily see parts rather than the whole. The **Koran** says,

> People of the Book (Christians), do not transgress the bounds of your religion. Speak nothing but the truth about God. The Messiah, Jesus the son of Mary, was no more than God's apostle and His Word which He cast to Mary: a spirit from Him. So believe in God and His apostles and do not say: 'Three.' Forbear, and it shall be better for you. God is but one God. God forbid that He should have a son! His is all that the heavens and the earth contain. God is the all-sufficient protector. The Messiah does not disdain to be a servant of God, nor do the angels who are nearest to Him. Those who through arrogance disdain His service shall all be brought before Him. (Koran 4:171)

Are the **Koran** and the **New Testament** in conflict? No, but perhaps religious leaders are. The **New Testament** says, "But what went ye out for to see? A prophet? Yea, I say unto you, and much more than a prophet. This is *he*, of whom it is written, Behold, I send my messenger before thy face, which shall prepare thy way before thee" (Luke 7:26-27). Is that in conflict with the following?

> Praise be to God who has revealed the Book to His servant shorn of falsehood and unswerving from the truth, so that he may give warning of a dire scourge from Himself, proclaim to the faithful who do good works that a rich and everlasting reward awaits them and admonish those who

say that God has begotten a son. Surely of this they could have no knowledge, neither they nor their fathers: a monstrous blasphemy is that which they utter. They preach nothing but falsehood. (Koran 18:1)

Possibly a third tradition can help us see past the apparent contradictions within spiritual wisdom. The **Dhammapada** says, "The noble one, the excellent one, the valiant one, the great seer, the victorious one, the passionless one, the purified one, the awakened one, is one that I call priestly. One who knows former abodes, and sees paradise and hell, the sage established in higher knowledge who has reached the end of birth, the one who has accomplished all that is to be accomplished, is one that I call priestly" (Dhammapada 26:40-41).

What is important is that we take the high ground and not argue over the nature of God. All the religious traditions say God is limitlessness yet religious leaders engage in discussions and arguments that presume we can grasp the concept of limitlessness. We should focus instead on what is important. The **Koran** says, "We have given you (Muhammad) a glorious victory, so that God may forgive you your past and future sins, and perfect His goodness to you; that He may guide you to a straight path and bestow on you His mighty help" (Koran 48:1). The **New Testament** says, "As it is written in the prophets, Behold, I send my messenger before thy face, which shall prepare thy way before thee" (Mark 1:2). God has sent us prophets and messengers to help us understand and live His spiritual wisdom. All we have to do is listen and learn from them.

The **Bhagavad-Gita** makes the critical point as follows:

> [Yet] even those who worship other gods with love
> And sacrifice to them,
> full filled with faith,
> Do really worship Me,
> Though the rite differ from the norm.
> (Bhagavad-Gita 9:23)

The **Gospel of Thomas** adds to our knowledge by saying: "Where there are three, they are godless." If we limit our understanding of God to three or anything less than everything, we are not speaking of God as was pointed out in **Gospel of Thomas** Saying 15. One means everything, therefore to place another number associated with God is technically wrong because, ironically, higher numbers limit the vastness of God even more. This does not mean the **Bhagavad-Gita** is incorrect in saying there are many gods, because it clearly communicates the infinite nature of God. The identification of other gods is merely a localized understanding of the vastness of one God. However, if we say there is only the Trinity, then we are permanently limiting our understanding of an infinite God.

In the largest, most appropriate understanding of God, there can be no separate identity as elements merge into the Oneness of the Supreme. There is one whole and it is indivisible. We must not let our minds think in terms of ourselves as separate egos. Individuality is merely an illusion. We are simply a part of God's entire creation. No part appears to stand alone except for the Grace of God. As we learn and grow in our understanding of His Oneness, we can appreciate this uniqueness. He permits it out of His love for us. If we refuse to learn this truth, then we have limited our own vast potential. Jesus was born of flesh and began his earthly journey as an apparent separate entity. By example, though, He taught us that He was One with the Father's Oneness because that was His message and His purpose. We are all God's "sons" and "daughters" who are born with apparent separate identities and personalities; but if we fulfill God's plan for us, we can and indeed we must realize that we are One with our Eternal Father.

God knows that we are simply on the path to a realization of Oneness. If we truly love God, then we love everything and everyone because they are also part of the Oneness. God's messengers are sent to prepare the way for us to move along our path toward God. He tells us that we think we are going to see possibly a prophet, but what we really see is God, Himself. For example, Jesus and the Father are One. Messengers of God, the Father, are by definition One with Him. When we see His messenger, we see God. When we hear His messenger, we hear God. Spiritual wisdom is telling us not to limit our understanding of the Oneness of the Supreme.

APPROPRIATE REGARD IS NOT GIVEN TO THE MESSENGER

Question:

If God has continually given humankind spiritual wisdom, why do we not appreciate His messagers?

Brief Answer:

Because we hear them but fail to listen properly.

from the *Gospel of Thomas*

31. Jesus said, "A prophet is not acceptable in the prophet's own town; a doctor does not heal those who know the doctor."

Longer Answer:

God has many faces. The **Upanishad** says, "The best [of them], the breath of life, said to them: 'Make no mistake about it. It is I who divided [my]self into five parts and who prop this trunk up and support it.' They did not believe him" (Prasna Upanishad 2:3). Since God created us and gave us free choice, He knows we are diverse. Not surprisingly, He communicates to each of us in ways that can best be understood by the receiver of the message. The **Koran** says, "We have recounted to you the history of those nations. Their apostles came to them with veritable proofs, yet they persisted in their unbelief. Thus God seals up the hearts of the unbelievers" (Koran 7:101). History tells us that God has sent many messages and many messengers. He has even demonstrated His spiritual wisdom by living among us, but people persist in not listening. They have chosen to remain ignorant partly because we are at perfect liberty to seal up our hearts to Him.

How can we know the true messenger of God? The **Hebrew Bible** explains how as follows:

Also,

thou son of man,

the children of thy people still are talking against thee

by the walls and in the doors of the houses,

and speak one to another,

every one to his brother,

saying,

come,

I pray you,

and hear what is the word that cometh forth from the Lord.

And they come unto thee as the people cometh,

and they sit before thee,

as my people,

and they hear thy words,

but they will not do them:

for with their mouth they shew much love,

but their heart goeth after their covetousness.

And,

lo,

thou *art* unto them as a very lovely song of one that hath,

a pleasant voice,

and can play well on an instrument;

for they hear thy words,

but they do them not.

And when this cometh to pass,

(lo, it will come,)

then shall they know that a prophet hath been among them.

(Ezekiel 33:30-33)

Unfortunately, only a few comprehend or appreciate God's messengers. The **New Testament** says, "And they were offended in him, But Jesus said unto them, A prophet is not without honour, save in his own country, and in his own house" (Matthew 13:57). It also says, "But Jesus said unto them, A prophet is not without honour, but in his own country, and among his own kin, and in his own house" (Mark 6:4). Similarly, the **Gospel of John** says, "For Jesus himself testified, that a prophet hath no honour in his own country" (John 4:44).

Why do we have difficulty accepting God's messengers and their messages? The **Koran** says, "They marvel that a prophet of their own has risen amongst them. The unbelievers say: 'This is indeed a strange thing. When we are dead and turned to dust . . .? Such a return is most improbable!'" (Koran 50:1). Part of the answer is that we doubt God's prophets can be people that we know. The **New Testament** says, "And he said unto them, Ye will surely say unto me this proverb, Physician, heal thyself: whatsoever we have heard done in Capernaum, do also here in thy country. And he said, Verily I say unto you, No prophet is accepted in his own country" (Luke 4:23-24). Another part of the answer is that people simply fail to understand and believe. Most people operate primarily in the Kingdom of Man and they expect an important person such a messenger from God to act like an important person in the Kingdom of Man. Even if they see some dramatic divine quality in the messenger, their doubting minds dismiss it as a strange light, or the wind, or some other natural phenomena rather than accept it as a manifestation from God.

The **Dhammapada** says, "None can measure the virtue of one who is making offerings to one worthy of offering, whether a Buddha or a disciple, to one who has gone beyond false rationalizations and crossed over sorrow and grief; none can measure the virtue of one making offerings to such as have attained nirvana and are free from all fear" (Dhammapada 14:17-18). Part of the answer is that unless we realize the Kingdom of God is some small measure within ourselves, we cannot fully appreciate the accomplishment of someone who has fully realized Oneness.

The phrase "familiarity breeds contempt" is a recognition that an accomplished person is unappreciated by his or her associates. Because we all know accomplished people on the human level, our minds can only appreciate what is defined in terms of worldly success. Thus our minds filter out the divine and dismisses the greatness that may have grown in someone we know well over a long period of time. We recall only their earthly activities and manifestations; we turn our minds so that seeing their spiritual growth is impossible. Our minds act as a filter limiting our ability to see their greater knowledge, because it is beyond our own capacity to comprehend. Our pride blinds us even to the growing light that is present within ourselves. Strangers do not have the same filters. Therefore, they can more easily see the goodness, recognize it, and thus seek it out.

BE PREPARED

Question:

What can we do to gain from spiritual wisdom?

Brief Answer:

We can prepare by taking steps to fortify ourselves and realize
our preparation will not go unnoticed.

from the *Gospel of Thomas*

32. Jesus said, "A city built upon a high hill and fortified cannot fall, nor can it be
hidden."

Longer Answer:

Learning from spiritual wisdom in an optimal manner requires personal preparation. The **New Testament** says, "Therefore whosoever
heareth these sayings of mine, and doeth them, I will liken him unto a
wise man, which built his house upon a rock: And the rain descended, and the
floods came, and the winds blew, and beat upon that house; and it fell not: for
it was founded upon a rock" (Matthew 7:24-25; similar Luke 6:47-48).
Reading the messages such as those found in the holy scriptures of all religious
traditions is a good place to start. Familiarity with these scriptures will provide a firm foundation that will fortify us when our faith is challenged. The
Koran says, "When Our revelations are recited to them in all their clarity,
you will note denial in the faces of the unbelievers. Barely can they restrain
themselves from assaulting those who recite Our revelations" (Koran 22:72).
Many who do not share our beliefs will most assuredly try to assault us. The
New Testament says, "Ye are the light of the world. A city that is set on an
hill cannot be hid" (Matthew 5:14). We may become an obvious target. Why
is this negative reaction so typical to those who seek? The **Upanishad**
answers as follows:

For by the mind one sees, by the mind one hears. Desire, conception, doubt, faith, infidelity, tenacity and the lack of it, modesty, thought and fear, — all this indeed is mind.

Swept away by the currents of Nature's constituents, made turbid by them, unstable, fickle, mutilated, full of longing, restless, a man reaches [the stage of individual] self-consciousness. "This I am, this is mine," he thinks, and so of his own accord he binds [him]self as a bird [entangled] in a net. Hence the man who has the marks of will, conception and [individual] self-consciousness is bound: the man who is the opposite of this is free. Therefore let a man remain without will, without conceptions, without [individual] self-consciousness: this is the sign of [his spiritual] liberation. This is the path [that leads] to Brahman here; this is the hole in the door through which one will reach the farther shore beyond the darkness. For herein all desires are concentrated. On this point here is the following quotation:

> "When the five senses and the mind
> Are stilled,
> When intellect is motionless,
> That, they say, is the highest Way."
> (Maitri Upanishad 6:30d)

This **Upanishad** statement helps us realize what disturbs so many people as we begin our spiritual journey. They are not free, and they act without free will. They are continually reacting to and are trapped in the cross currents of life. They can escape the trap, but because they lack the will to do so, they do not see the way out. Individuals who have chosen to seek spiritual wisdom are in stark contrast. They are freed from the things that bind us to the physical world and they have no fear of striking out into the infinite vastness of God.

What is our foundation or rock? The **Dhammapada** says, "One who lives as though the things of the world are impure, with senses guarded and appetite moderate, faithful and diligent, will not be overpowered by bedevilment, like a rock mountain unshaken by the wind" (Dhammapada 1:8). Our rock is spiritual wisdom. The **Hebrew Bible** says, "And he said, The Lord *is* my rock, and my fortress, and my deliverer; The God of my rock; in him will I trust: *he is* my shield, and the horn of my salvation, my high tower, and my refuge, my saviour; thou savest me from violence" (Samuel 2,22:2-3). God is the rock for all of us. The **Hebrew Bible** also says, "Be thou my strong habitation, whereunto I may continually resort: thou hast given commandment to save me; for thou *art* my rock and my fortress" (Psalms 71:3). God's wisdom messages are our solid foundation. However, seeking God and reading the scriptures are never a final place; they are only the beginning point for achieving Oneness. The **Diamond Sutra** says:

> "Subhuti, if you should conceive the idea that the Tathagata attained the consummation of incomparable enlightenment by reason of his perfect form, do not countenance such thoughts. The Tathagata's attainment was not by reason of his perfect form. [On the other hand] Subhuti, if you should conceive the idea that anyone in whom dawns the consummation of incomparable enlightenment declares that all manifest standards are ended and extinguished, do not countenance such thoughts. Wherefore? Because the man in whom the consummation of incomparable enlightenment dawns does not affirm concerning any formula that it is finally extinguished." (The Diamond Sutra 27)

If we achieve inner knowledge in Oneness, the bedrock of His love will provide us safety and security regardless of our enemies' strength. Such a remarkable strength will be obvious to both friend and foe. How is such strength achieved? In stilling the five senses and the mind to motionlessness, meditation is an important tool to gain inner strength. Faith is important in developing our trust in God. We need to continually seek inner knowledge. God's revelations are so powerful that nothing can disturb the steadfastness of our rock. There is no formula to follow in achieving the bedrock of His love and Oneness with Him, because we gain strength only through God's love, His guidance, and our individual effort in following His charted path.

ONCE WE HAVE LEARNED SPIRITUAL WISDOM WE MUST RADIATE IT

Question:

Once spiritual wisdom is learned, what must we do with it?

Brief Answer:

We must live it with our words through our actions.

from the *Gospel of Thomas*

33. Jesus said, "What you hear in your ear, proclaim upon your rooftop into someone else's ear. Indeed, no one lights a lamp and puts it under a vessel, nor puts
it in a hidden place. Rather, it is put on a lampstand so that each who enters and
leaves might see its light."
(See Layton, p. 386, using Greek fragments.)

Longer Answer:

Knowing a spiritual lesson is not enough, it must be lived. Buddha tells us:

> THE EIGHTH REALIZATION is the awareness that the fire of
> birth and earth is raging, causing endless suffering everywhere. We
> should take the Great Vow to help everyone, to suffer with everyone, and
> to guide all beings to the realm of great joy. (The Sutra on the Eight
> Realizations of the Great Beings 8)

With spiritual wisdom, we become more aware of the Kingdom of Man
and its endless desires and suffering. Our challenge is to take the "Great Vow"
of the Kingdom of God to love all of God's creation unconditionally. The
New Testament says, "What I tell you in darkness, *that* speak ye in light: and
what ye hear in the ear, *that* preach ye upon the house tops" (Matthew 10:27;
similar Luke 12:3). It also says, "Neither do men light a candle, and put it
under a bushel, but on a candlestick; and it giveth light unto all that are in the
house" (Matthew 5:15). As a metaphor, darkness is commonly ignorance and
light is wisdom. The **Upanishad** says:

When by means of SELF as it really is as with a lamp
An integrated man sees Brahman as It really is,
[Then will he know] the unborn,
undying God,
the Pure,
Beyond all essences as they really are,
[And] knowing Him,
from all fetters he'll be freed.
(Svetasvatara Upanishad 2:15)

Once we know of God's presence and begin to seek His inner knowledge, we must try to live the lessons as we learn them. The **Hebrew Bible** says, "And he said, It is a light thing that thou shouldest be my servant to raise up the tribes of Jacob, and to restore the preserved of Israel: I will also give thee for a light to the Gentiles, that thou mayest be my salvation unto the end of the earth" (Isaiah 49:6). Repeating this thought the **New Testament** says, "For so hath the Lord commanded us, *saying*, I have set thee to be a light of the Gentiles, that thou shouldest be for salvation unto the ends of the earth" (The Acts 13:47). We cannot keep knowledge to ourselves, but we must understand that our actions speak louder than words. As we live the learned messages in our daily lives, we will serve as a beacon in the dark for others because they will know us by our actions.

The **New Testament** says, "No man, when he hath lighted a candle, putteth *it* in a secret place, neither under a bushel, but on a candlestick, that they which come in may see the light. The light of the body is the eye: therefore when thine eye is single, thy whole body also is full of light; but when *thine eye* is evil, thy body *is* full of darkness" (Luke 11:33-34). We cannot hide or deny our spirituality. Just as we can see light or darkness in the eye of another, others can see it in us. The **New Testament** explains, "For there is nothing hid, which shall not be manifested; neither was any thing kept secret, but that it should come abroad" (Mark 4:22; similar Luke 8:16). The light cannot be hidden if we manifest the lessons learned from the spiritual wisdom in our lives.

There is a need to openly claim God's wisdom messages as our own. The **Koran** says, "When God made a covenant with those to whom the Scriptures were given He said: 'Proclaim these to mankind and do not suppress them.' But they cast the Scriptures behind their backs and sold them for a paltry

price. Evil was their bargain" (Koran 3:187). Because God has shared His
spiritual wisdom with us, we have a covenant with Him that requires us to not
suppress our new knowledge. The **Koran** also says, "Fight for the cause of
God with the devotion due to Him. He has chosen you, and laid on you no
burdens in the observance of faith, the faith of Abraham your father. In this,
as in former scriptures, He has given you the name of Muslims, so that the
Apostle may testify against you, and that you yourselves may testify against
your fellow-men" (Koran 22:78). If needed, we must be ready to fight for His
cause. The **Upanishad** adds to our understanding by saying:

> Thought is greater than will.
> For when a man thinks,
> then he wills,
> then he has it in mind,
> then he utters speech and formulates it in a name.
> In name the sacred formulas become one
> as do [sacred] actions in the sacred formulas.
>
> [All] these meet in one place only,
> — in thought.
> Thought is their very self,
> and thought is their foundation.
> And so even if a man knows a great deal but is unthinking,
> people say of him:
> "He is nothing, whatever he may know.
> For if he were [really] wise,
> he would not be so very unthinking."
> On the other hand,
> even if a man knows only a little but knows how to think,
> people are anxious to listen to him.
> For thought is the one point
> at which [all] these [other faculties] meet:
> thought is [their] self,
> though [their] foundation.
> Revere thought.
>
> Whoso reveres thought
> as Brahman [attains to] states of being that have been properly thought out;
> being himself abiding,

firmly based and unperturbed,
he attains to abiding,
firmly based and unperturbed states of being.
He gains freedom of movement in the whole sphere of thought, — whoso reveres
thought as Brahman.
(Chandogya Upanishad 7,5)

Spiritual wisdom tells us our proclamation of faith is not so much about will power as it is about thought power. We proclaim our faith and beliefs by living them. With thoughtfulness, we manifest the SELF in our proclamation of faith through our deeds. Proselytizing or acting superior to others is not part of such a proclamation. Words can never change a person's heart — only the individual with God's guidance can do that. We can only live the lessons God has revealed to us.

◆

CHOOSING HELP

Question:
Is seeking help for finding and increasing spiritual wisdom helpful?

Brief Answer:
Yes, but be selective as only a true master of spiritual wisdom can help.

from the *Gospel of Thomas*
34. Jesus said, "If a blind person leads a blind person, both of them will fall into a hole."

Longer Answer:

The ignorant cannot teach wisdom. The **New Testament** says, "Let them alone: they be blind leaders of the blind. And if the blind lead the blind, both shall fall into the ditch" (Matthew 15:14). If we are just learning and have not yet mastered spiritual wisdom, we only compound our ignorance by selecting a poor teacher. The **Dhammapada** says, "Whoever rejects the teaching of the worthy and noble who live the truth, an imbecile fixated on wrong opinion, produces self-destructive results, like the cane that dies on fruiting" (Dhammapada 12:8). We are told to be careful and not select a limited teacher, but we are also cautioned not to reject a knowledgeable one. Thus, selecting the right teacher is a delicate decision.

If we ourselves are ignorant, how can we select the right teacher? The **Upanishad** answers:

> "'Better" and "agreeable" present themselves to men:
> Considering them carefully the wise man discriminates,
> Preferring the better to what only pleasure brings:
> Dull men prefer the "agreeable." —
> For the getting and keeping [of what they crave].
>
> Thou,
> Naciketas,
> has well considered [all objects of] desire,
> [All] that's agreeable in form,
> — thou has rejected them;
> Thou wouldst not accept this garland of wealth compacted
> In which how many a man has been [dragged down,]
> submerged!
>
> Different opposed,
> wise separated these, —
> Unwisdom and what men as wisdom know:
> Wisdom [it is that] Naciketas seeks,
> I see;
> Not thou to be distracted by manifold desire!

Self-wise,
puffed up with learning,
some
Turn round and round [imprisoned] in unwisdom['s realm];
Hither and thither rushing,
round they go,
the fools,
Like blind men guided by the blind!

No glimmering has such of man's destiny, —
Unheeding,
childish fools,
by wealth delude:
"This world alone exists,
there is no other,"
so think they;
Again and ever again they fall into my hands.
(Katha Upanishad 2:2-6)

If we live in the darkness of ignorance, how can we choose the correct teacher? The **Hebrew Bible** says, "Therefore is judgment far from us, neither doth justice overtake us: we wait for light, but behold obscurity; for brightness, *but* we walk in darkness. We grope for the wall like the blind, and we grope as if *we had* no eyes: we stumble at noon day as in the night; *we are* in desolate places as dead *men*" (Isaiah 59:9-10). We need a true master of spiritual wisdom. The **Upanishad** says, "So too does the man who has a teacher [to show him the way] know that he will remain [in this phenomenal world] only so long as he is not released: then he will arrive home. This finest essence, — the whole universe has it as its SELF: That is the Real: That is the SELF: That you are, Svetaketu" (Chandogya Upanishad 6,14)!

The true master provides a clear path or direction, but we must still walk down that path. The **Upanishad** also says, "My dear boy, you are radiant as is a man who knows Brahman. Now, who has been instructing you? 'Not human beings,' he confessed, 'but it is you alone whom I should like to teach me; for I have heard from men like you that wisdom learnt from a teacher produces the best results'" (Chandogya Upanishad 4,9:2). Even those that have made progress in spiritual wisdom are wise to seek the true master to achieve the best results. Who is the true master? The **Koran** tells you to say, "Can any of your idols guide you to the truth? God can guide you to the truth. Who is more worthy to be followed: He that can guide you to the truth, or he that cannot and is himself in need of guidance? What has come over you that you so judge?"(Koran 10:35). The real guide to spiritual wisdom is always God, but some illumined souls have appeared from time to time to help us find our path and direction. The **Upanishad** says, "The teacher is the first element, the pupil the last element, knowledge the connection [between the two], teaching the operative conjunction. So much for its application to knowledge" (Taittiriya Upanishad 1:3). We sometimes believe that learning is merely having a teacher tell us what we need to know. However, the teacher is only the first element. Between the student and the teacher is the "operative conjunction" called knowledge.

Learning is not an event but a process. The **Koran** tells us to say, "I do not tell you that I possess God's treasures or know what is hidden, nor do I claim to be an angel. I follow only that which is revealed to me." It tells you to say, "Are the blind the seeing equal? Can you not think?" (Koran 6:51). Only God reveals lessons that are appropriate to the individual being taught. The teacher guides, assists, and encourages. The responsibility of the student is to learn that which is revealed, as it is revealed.

Spiritual wisdom tells us to seek guidance and reach enlightenment, but we should not seek the help of someone who has not already seen the light, as is demonstrated by his or her actions. One can learn to play the piano by finding one note after another, until they together make up a desired tune. A better approach to learning is to seek an accomplished musician who can provide instruction on not only how to play many beautiful melodies but also how to create new melodies. In the spiritual life, we can also gain from a knowledgeable and enlightened teacher. Such teachers are often called rabbi, priest, minister, guru, master, or simply teacher. With such help, we avoid false paths and many mistakes. They help us discover richer rewards and more direct routes to our goal. We need to discriminate wisely and select the right teacher for us. How will we know the right teacher? We will know him by his actions and deeds. When we meditate with him, our hearts will recognize him.

SUBDUE OUR OWN DESIRES

Question:
What is the first step in learning spiritual wisdom?

Brief Answer:
First, we must control our own worldly desires.

from the *Gospel of Thomas*

35. Jesus said, "No one can enter the house of the strong and wreck it without first tying that person's hands. Thereafter, one can overturn the person's house." (See Layton translation, p. 386.)

Longer Answer:

The first step in learning spiritual wisdom is to develop self-control. The **Dhammapada** says, "One who has vomited out all filth and concentrates on moral practices has self-control and is genuine, thus is worthy of the saffron robe" (Dhammapada 1:10). We must first learn to reject the ignorance and desires of the Kingdom of Man through the discipline of self-control. The **New Testament** repeats the **Gospel of Thomas**. It says, "Or else how can one enter into a strong man's house, and spoil his goods, except he first bind the strong man? and then he will spoil his house" (Matthew 12:29).

This step is not easily accomplished and we may spend a long time trying to perfect it. The **Hebrew Bible** notes that even a person as strong as Samson can be overcome due to a lack of self-control. It says, "And it came to pass afterward, that he loved a woman in the valley of Sorek, whose name *was* Delilah. And the lords of the Philistines came up unto her, and said unto her, Entice him, and see wherein his great strength *lieth*, and by what *means* we may prevail against him, that we may bind him to afflict him: and we will give thee every one of us eleven hundred *pieces* of silver" (Judges 16:4-5). In more poetic language, the **New Testament** presents the same message using a parable. It says:

And he called them *unto him*,
and said unto them in parables,
How can Satan cast out Satan?

And if a kingdom be divided against itself,
that kingdom cannot stand.

And if a house be divided against,
itself,

that house cannot stand.

And if Satan rise up against himself,
and be divided,
he cannot stand,
but hath an end.

No man can enter into a strong man's house,
and spoil his goods,
except he will first bind the strong man;
and then he will spoil his house.
(Mark 3:23-27)

The two houses are the Kingdom of Man and the Kingdom of God. We cannot let the kingdoms become divided. If we exercise self-control over the Kingdom of Man, the two will not be divided.

We can achieve self-control by knowing our SELF, including the very breath of life. But how do we know our SELF? The **Upanishad** answers with the following poetry:

Then Kausalya Asvalayana asked him: "Master, whence is this breath of life born? Once it has divided [it]self, how does it settle down? What makes it go away? How does it correlate itself with the outside world? How with itself?"

To him [the Master] answered: "You ask a great may questions, so you must know a great deal about Brahman. Well, that is a [good] reason for my speaking up.

"[Your first question: Whence is this breath of life born?]

"This breath of life is born of SELF. As his shadow is to a man, so in this case there is an extension. It comes into the body with the mind as its artifact.

"[Your second question: How does it come into the body?]

"As a king commands his officials, saying, '[Go and] govern this group of villages or the group of villages,' so does this breath of life allot to each of the other breaths their appointed task.

"[Your third question: Once it has divided itself, how does it settle down?]

"The breath of life [allots] (sic) the out-breath to the organs of generation and excretion, and itself settles in the eye and ear, the mouth and nostrils. In the middle is the 'concentrated' (digestive) breath, for it is this ["breath"] that reduces the food offered up [in the body] to the same [consistency]. From this arise the seven flames.

"[Your fourth question: What makes it go away?]

"The SELF is in the heart. Here there are a hundred and one channels, each subdivided a hundred times, and these again are divided into seventy-two thousand branches. Within them moves the diffused breath.

"Then the upper breath, [rising] up through one [of these], leads [the transmigrating soul] to a good world by means of his good [deeds], or to an evil [world] by means of his evil [deeds], or to the world of men by means of both.

"[Your fifth question: How does it correlate itself with the outside world?]

"The sun assuredly is the breath of life in the outside world: it rises, and [in so doing] it shows favour to the life-breath in the eye. That power which [resides] in the earth supports the out-breath in man. What is between [the sun and the earth], that is, space, is the concentrated breath. The wind is the diffused breath.

"[Your sixth question: How does it correlate itself with itself?]

"Heat is the upper breath; and so when the heat [of the body] is extinguished, one is reborn from it with the sense concentrated in the mind.

"With whatever thoughts [he may have had in his previous life] he comes [back] to life. [And] this breath of life, combines with heat and accompanied by the SELF lead [him] on to whatever world he had [previously] conceived of.

"Whoever possesses this knowledge knows the breath of life; his off-spring will not fail, [while he himself] will become immortal. On this there is the following verse:

> 'How did it originate?
> How approach [the body]?
> How did it [there] remain?
> How extend itself fivefold?
> What its relation to the SELF?
> Whoso should know
> [All this] concerning the breath of life,
> Attains to immortality: to immortality attains!'
> (Prasna Upanishad 3)

Fighting and overcoming the vital temporal world cannot be done without discipline, concentration, and extensive preparation. We must first tie the hands of desire before we can succeed. The desire for sensuous pleasures are very strong and our will power is weak. In order to be triumphant over the lower elements of the physical world, we must cleverly defeat our desires. Even Samson, the strongest man, was defeated because the "attack" of desire is so very powerful. Although we are vulnerable, we can and we will succeed because God gives us guidance; but we need to transcend our desires rather than just suppress them. If they are only suppressed, they will return more powerfully in other forms to strike us again. Therefore, we should exercise our self-control by developing concentration techniques through meditation and increase our abilities to resist spiritual vulnerability through something as easy as breathing exercises.

Although the first step is essential, we must not forget the second step, which is to seek God's assistance through His messengers and then to act accordingly. The **Koran** says, "It is He who has sent His apostle with guidance and the Faith of Truth, so that He may exalt it above all religions, much as the pagans may dislike it. Believers! Shall I point out to you a profitable course that will save you from a woeful scourge? Have faith in God and His apostle, and fight for God's cause with your wealth and your persons. That would be best for you, if you but knew it" (Koran 61:9).

DO NOT FOCUS ON THE SUPERFICIAL

Question:

What clothing should be worn and what food should be eaten in order to be spiritual?

> *Brief Answer:*
>
> We should not be so concerned about superficial matters.

from the *Gospel of Thomas*

36. Jesus said, "Do not worry, from dawn to dusk and from dusk to dawn, about what [food] you [will eat], [or] what [clothing] you will wear. [You are much] better than the [lilies], which [neither] card nor spin. And for your part, what [will you wear] when you have no clothing? Who would add to your stature? It is he who will give you your clothing."
(See Layton, p. 386, using the Greek fragments.)

Longer Answer:

Vanity belongs to the Kingdom of Man and not to the Kingdom of God. The **Hebrew Bible** says, "Vanity of vanities, saith the Preacher, vanity of vanities; all *is* vanity. What profit hath a man of all his labour which he taketh under the sun?" (Ecclesiastes 1:2-3). The **Dhammapada** says, "Come, look at this world, like a painted royal chariot; fools sink in it, the knowing have no attachment to it" (Dhammapada 13:5). The **Koran** says, "The unbelievers, love this fleeting life too well, and thus prepare for themselves a heavy day of doom. *We* created them, and endowed their limbs and joints with strength; but if We please, We can replace them by other men. This is indeed an admonition. Let him that will, take the right path to his Lord. Yet you cannot will, except by the will of God. God is all-knowing and wise" (Koran 76:29-30). Spiritual wisdom tells us the right path to God is following the wisdom message of the Kingdom of God. Food, clothing, position, and status symbols are all fleeting aspects of the physical world. The **New Testament** says:

Therefore I say unto you,

Take no thought for your life,

what ye shall eat,

or what ye shall drink;

nor yet for your body,

what ye shall put on.

Is not the life more than meat,

and the body than raiment?

Behold the fowls of the air:

for they sow not,

neither do they reap,

nor gather into barns;

yet your heavenly Father feedeth them.

Are ye not much better than they?

Which of you by taking thought can add one cubit unto his stature?

And why take ye thought for raiment?

Consider the lilies of the field,

how they grow;

they toil not,

neither do they spin:

And yet I say unto you,

That even Solomon in all his glory was not arrayed

like one of these.

Wherefore,

if God so clothe the grass of the field,

which to day (sic) is,

and to morrow (sic) is cast into the oven,

shall he not much more *clothe* you,

O ye of little faith?

Therefore take no thought,
saying,
What shall we eat?
or,
What shall we drink?
or,
Wherewithal shall we be clothed?
(Matthew 6:25-31; similiar Luke 12:22-29)

We do not need to focus our attention on what to eat or what clothes to wear. Instead we should focus on our spiritual awakening and the search for our path to Oneness. The **Upanishad** explains what is really important in verse:

Where one sees nothing else,
hears nothing else,
knows nothing else,
that is the Infinite.

But where one sees something else,
hears something else,
knows something else,
that is something small [because finite].

The Infinite is the same as the immortal;
the small [and finite] is the same as what is mortal.

Sir, on what is this [Infinite] based?

On its own greatness, or else,
— not on any greatness at all.

Cows and horses men here on earth call "greatness,"
— so too elephants,
gold,

slaves,

wives,

fields and dwelling-places.

This is not the way I talk:

this is not the way I talk,

said he,

"for [in these cases] one is based on another."

(Chandogya Upanishad 7,24)

Too often apparel, habits, and food are used as statements of devotion to ourselves, our peers, and the outside world. Such behavior does not reflect a true awareness of the light or greatness of God. Only He can provide us with spiritual wisdom. We cannot gain an iota of spiritual wisdom from such outer manifestations of custom, desire, or insecurity. Vanity in any form is our enemy. We cannot use anything to measure spiritual wisdom such as cows, horses, gold, land, dwelling places. Any finite thing we possess that is considered valuable is vanity and not a real measure of greatness. Spiritual wisdom tells us that only fools see the "painted royal chariot" as a measure of greatness, because by definition it has a transient nature. We should not cherish the fleeting world of material objects nor should we try to demonstrate or measure our devotion to God with them.

Like other religious rituals, as discussed in Gospel of Thomas Saying 27, what we wear and what we eat when done in the right consciousness become expressions of our love and devotion to our spiritual lives. For instance, clothing chosen for modesty or dressing appropriately for worship can be expressions of respect for God and our fellow seekers. Likewise, a seeker may be inspired to fast for the purpose of purification or devotion. However, these things in and of themselves cannot move us an inch along our paths; but inspiration, aspiration, love, and devotion can. The sincerity and the mind-set are the critical factors in determining if these activities are a waste of time or a heartfelt offering.

ABANDON THE WAYS OF
THE KINGDOM OF MAN

Question:
What attitude is needed for spiritual wisdom?

Brief Answer:
We should have no concern for the conventions of man.

from the *Gospel of Thomas*

37. His followers said, "When will you appear to us and when shall we see you?" Jesus said, "When you strip without being ashamed and you take your clothes and put them under your feet like little children and trample them, then [you] will see the child of the living one and you will not be afraid."

Longer Answer:

Spiritual wisdom tells us to abandon the worldly concerns. The **New Testament** says, "Verily I say unto you, Whosoever shall not receive the kingdom of God as a little child, he shall not enter therein" (Mark 10:15 and Luke 18:17). Childlike innocence is critical. Buddha teaches, "This is the Noble Truth of the Origin of Suffering: such was the vision . . . This Origin of suffering, as a noble truth, should be abandoned" (The First Sermon of the Buddha). We must put the Kingdom of Man, with all its limitations and suffering, behind us. If we do, the **Koran** tells us, "The day will surely come when you shall see the true believers, men and women, with their light shining before them and on their right hands, and a voice saying to them: 'Rejoice this day. You shall enter gardens watered by running streams in which you shall abide for ever.' That is the supreme triumph" (Koran 57:12).

Concerns of man are very real to us as illustrated by the following story of Joseph and the Pharaoh: "And Pharaoh said unto Joseph, I have dreamed a dream, and *there is* none that can interpret it: and I have heard say of thee, *that* thou canst understand a dream to interpret it. And Joseph answered Pharaoh, saying, *It is* not in me: God shall give Pharaoh an answer of peace.

. . . And Joseph said unto Pharaoh, the dream of Pharaoh *is* one: God hath shewed Pharaoh what he *is* about to do" (Genesis 41:15-16, 25). Pharaoh's problem was that he existed in the Kingdom of Man and could not see past it. Joseph could see God's message in spite of all his unfortunate experiences of being sold into slavery and imprisoned. He lived in the Kingdom of God and He understood God's wisdom messages. The **Upanishad** tells us how to live in the Kingdom of God:

> So let a Brahman put away learning with disgust
> and lead a childlike life.
> Let him then put away both the childlike life
> and learning with disgust,
> and [become] a silent sage.
> Let him then put away both silence
> and its opposite with disgust,
> and [become a true] Brahman
> (a man who really knows Brahman).
>
> And what is it that makes him a Brahman?
>
> Whatever really makes him such.
> What is other than [the SELF] suffers?
> (Brihadaranyaka Upanishad 3,5)

We must try to liberate ourselves from the body's desires so that it is not the driving force within us, because freeing the mind liberates the bondage of the heart. If we can do that, we become as free and happy as little children. Children's joy is not rooted in the kind of mindfulness that values being clever. Instead, it comes from the depth of their own souls and radiates outward through their hearts which are larger than our adult minds. Look into a child's face and see the reflection of love in their eyes. The face is of one who is simple, uncomplicated, nonjudgmental, loving, surrendered, and completely abandoned in unconditional joy.

GOD'S SILENCE

Question:
How is God's guidance distinguished from His silence?

Brief Answer:
It takes time and practice to distinguish between the two.

from the *Gospel of Thomas*

38. Jesus said, "Often you have desired to hear these sayings that I am speaking to you, and you have no one else from whom to hear them. There will be days when you will seek me and you will not find me."

Longer Answer:

Spiritual wisdom tells us that there will be times that we will not hear God. For example, the **New Testament** says, "Then said Jesus again unto them, I go my way, and ye shall seek me, and shall die in your sins: whither I go, ye cannot come" (John 8:21). Given we live in the busy modern world, we often have trouble "hearing" God above the noise and chatter. We sometimes have difficulty even hearing our own thoughts. The **Hebrew Bible** says, "Why art thou cast down, O my soul? and *why* are thou disquieted in me? hope thou in God: for I shall yet praise him *for* the help of his countenance" (Psalms 42:5). Feeling disconnected from God is not unusual. The **Hebrew Bible** says, "Why are thou cast down, O my soul? and why art thou disquieted within me? hope in God: for I shall yet praise him, *who is* the health of my contenance, and my God" (Psalms 43:5). We must maintain our hope and faith in God. The **Bhagavad-Gita** says:

> By a rare privilege may someone behold him,
> And by a rare privilege indeed may another tell of him,
> And by a rare privilege may such another hear him,
> Yet even having heard there's none that knows him.
> (Bhagavad-Gita 2:29)

Seeing God is indeed a fine and rare privilege, but none can really know Him in our limited bodies and with our limited minds.

Spiritual wisdom requires our patience. The **Hebrew Bible** tells us, "Arise, O God, plead thine own cause: remember how the foolish man reproacheth thee daily" (Psalms 74:22). Sometimes we foolishly reproach God because of our expectations and impatience. The **Dhammapada** says, "Even one who is good may see ill as long as the good has not developed; but when the good has developed, the good one sees good" (Dhammapada 9:5). Frankly, the reason so few people "hear" God is because they are too involved in themselves and the desires and demands of the Kingdom of Man. The **Koran** says, "We have sent no apostles before you who did not eat or walk about the market-squares. We test you by means of one another. Will you not have patience? Your Lord observes all. Those who entertain no hope of meeting Us ask: 'Why have no angels been sent to us? Why can we not see our Lord? How arrogant they are, and how gross is their iniquity!" (Koran 25:20-21). We all need to practice greater patience. The **New Testament** says:

And I will pray the Father,
and he shall give you another Comforter,
that he may abide with you for ever;
Even the Spirit of truth;
whom the world cannot receive,
because it seeth him not,
neither knoweth him:
but ye know him;
for he dwelleth with you,
and shall be in you.

I will not leave you comfortless:
I will come to you.

Yet a little while,
and the world seeth me no more;
but ye see me:
because I live,
ye shall live also.

At that day ye shall know that I *am* in my Father,

and ye in me,

and I in you.
(John 14:16-20)

In this quote, Jesus tells us that God will send us another comforter. The quote tells us that Jesus is in God, we are in Jesus, and Jesus is in us. When we allow ourselves to mentally live in the Kingdom of God, all is One. Once we have come to the realization that the Word of the Light is important to us, and we decide to be true seekers of Oneness with God, there will be days when we cry for God but will not find Him. However, we can and will see Him in our everyday occurrences and actions. For example, a stranger will extend an unexpected kindness or the beauty of a child's smile will melt our hearts. There are always clear messages in life's daily events that address our growing enlightenment.

With the realization that the Word of the Light is important and that God is ever-present in our lives, we have a tendency to want to cling like a child to Him. Some distance is often necessary for our new spiritual development. God is our only source of true knowledge, but we need to take time to absorb His knowledge and lessons. His seeming lack of presence when we cry for Him tends to make us anxious, much like a child is anxious about a misplaced parent. Faith and surety of His presence in our lives take time to grow and strengthen in us. He will reveal Himself to us again when He is ready for us to move forward in our growth process.

Being One with God is indeed a rare privilege, given to us out of His love for us. To bring God's message to others is also a great honor and privilege. Even hearing His message is a gift that occurs only because of His love for us. However, God cannot be truly known from only reading the holy scriptures, because we must experience Him through the revelation of the spiritual wisdom lessons that grow within us individually. The mind is important in learning about God, but we can only **know** God with our heart. We should not become discouraged because we need to keep hope in our hearts and pray for His assistance. With inner growth, we appreciate that the mind filters what we hear but it also can grow to transcend our former limitations. Although God may not seem to be present when we cry, He is always with us, but He may be waiting to reveal Himself more until we can demonstrate our inner capacity. Our "filter" must evolve to allow us to grow even more, because God always provides a new comforter as we grow. We must be patient and not lose hope in Him.

HIDDEN THE TRUTH

Question:
Will religious leaders and scholars provide spiritual wisdom?

Brief Answer:
Often they will, but not always.

from the *Gospel of Thomas*

39. Jesus said, "The Pharisees and the scribes have taken the keys of knowledge and have hidden them. They have not entered, nor have they allowed those who want to enter to do so. As for you, be as shrewd as snakes and as innocent as doves."

Longer Answer:

Spiritual wisdom is not very positive about religious leaders and scholars. The **Dhammapada** says, "Many who wear the saffron robe are evil and unrestrained. Evildoers go to hell by their evil deeds" (Dhammapada 22:2). Although they may wear the uniforms of religious leaders, they can remain in darkness or simply be unwise. We will know them by their deeds and actions, not by their titles. The **Koran** says, "Those to whom We gave the Scriptures know Our apostle as they know their own sons. But some of them deliberately conceal the truth. This is the truth from your Lord: therefore never doubt it" (Koran 2:146). Although religious leaders may know some spiritual wisdom, some have a personal agenda and deliberately conceal or withhold it. The **New Testament** says:

> Woe unto you,
> lawyers!
> for ye have taken away the key of knowledge:
> ye entered not in yourselves,
> and them that were entering in ye hindered.

> And as he said these things unto them,
> the scribes and the Pharisees began to urge *him* vehemently,
> and to provoke him to speak of many things:

> Laying wait for him,
> and seeking to catch something out of his mouth,
> that they might accuse him.
> (Luke 11:52-54)

Jesus is very negative toward lawyers who in His time interpreted the scriptures. Even to Jesus, they attempted to confuse the truth in order to further their own purposes. The very people who should be bringing us the Word of God sometimes mislead us in order to advance themselves in the world. Such religious leaders and people of letters are very dangerous. They attract seekers with promises and sweet words but have nothing to offer. The **Koran** says, "And who is more wicked than the man who invents a falsehood about God when called upon to submit to Him? God does not guide the wrongdoers. They seek to extinguish the light of God with their mouths; but God will perfect His light, much as the unbelievers may dislike it" (Koran 61:8). Their actions lead us away from spiritual wisdom and divert us from our true paths. The **Hebrew Bible** says:

> Therefore,
> behold,
> I *am* against the prophets,
> saith the Lord,
> that steal my words every one from his neighbour.

Behold,
I *am* against the prophets,
saith the Lord,
that use their tongues,
and say,
He saith.

Behold,
I *am* against them that prophesy false dreams,
saith the Lord,
and do tell them,
and cause my people to err by their lies,
and by their lightness;
yet I sent them not,
nor commanded them:
therefore they shall not profit this people at all,
saith the Lord.
(Jeremiah 23:30-32)

God is against false prophets and teachers. In the end they will not profit. The **Hebrew Bible** tells us, "And the key of the house of David will lay upon his shoulder; so he shall open, and none shall shut; and he shall shut, and none shall open" (Isaiah 22:22). Ultimately, God is key as He is the only one that can really guide us to spiritual wisdom. The **Upanishad** says:

How difficult for man, though meditating much,
To know Him from the lips of vulgar men:
[Yet] unless another tells of Him,
the way to Him is barred,
For than all subtleties of reason He's more subtle, —
Logic He defies.
(Katha Upanishad 2:0)

God will not reveal Himself through vulgar men. As seekers, we dearly need other seekers to mix and associate with to give us strength and a sense of community. As we often tend to cherish and protect our childlike innocence, we can easily be confused by the subtleties in spiritual wisdom that defy conventional logic. How can we determine who are the vulgar men among the authentic leaders and scholars? The **Koran** says, "When Our revelations are recited to them in all their clarity, you will note denial in the faces of the unbelievers. Barely can they restrain themselves from assaulting those who recite Our revelations" (Koran 22:72). The **Diamond Sutra** tells us to look carefully to find the false ones. When we study their actions, we will see that they cherish the ego, the personality, and the separate individuality. They are not concerned with being a true messenger and do not live God's message. Seekers will know them by their actions and deeds. The following passage explains:

> At the time Subhuti addressed Buddha, saying: "World-Honored One, if good men and good women seek the consummation of incomparable enlightenment, by what criteria should they abide and how should they control their thoughts?"
>
> Buddha replied to Subhuti: "Good men and good women seeking the consummation of incomparable enlightenment must create this resolved attitude of mind: 'I must liberate all living beings; yet when all have been liberated, verily not anyone is liberated.' Wherefore? If a bodhisattva cherishes the idea of an ego entity, a personality, a being, or a separated individuality, he is consequently not a bodhisattva, Subhuti. This is because in reality there is no formula that gives rise to the consummation of incomparable enlightenment.
>
> "Subhuti, what do you think? When the Tathagata was with Dipamkara Buddha, was there any formula [dharma] for the attainment of the consummation of incomparable enlightenment?"
>
> "No, World-Honored One, as I understand Buddha's meaning, there was no formula by which the Tathagata attained the consummation of incomparable enlightenment."
>
> Buddha said: "You are right, Subhuti! Verily there was no formula by which the Tathagata attained the consummation of incomparable enlightenment. Subhuti, had there been any such formula, Dipamkara Buddha would not have predicted concerning me: 'In the ages of the future you will come to be a buddha called Shakyamuni;' but Dipamkara Buddha made that prediction concerning me because there is actually no formula for the attainment of the consummation of incomparable

enlightenment. The reason herein is that *Tathagata* is a signification implying all formulas. In case anyone says that the Tathagata attained the consummation of incomparable enlightenment, I tell you truly, Subhuti, that there is no formula by which the Buddha attained it. Subhuti, the basis of the Tathagata's attainment of the consummation of incomparable enlightenment is wholly *beyond*; it is neither real nor unreal. Hence I say that the whole realm of formulations is not really such, therefore it is called 'realm of formulations.'

"Subhuti, a comparison may be made with [the idea of] a gigantic human frame."

The Subhuti said: "The World-Honored One has declared that such is not a great body; 'a great body' is just the name given to it."

"Subhuti, it is the same concerning bodhisattvas. If a bodhisattva announces, 'I will liberate all living creatures,' he is not rightly called a bodhisattva. Wherefore? Because, Subhuti, there is really no such condition as that called bodhisattvaship, because Buddha teaches that all things are devoid of selfhood, devoid of personality, devoid of entity, and devoid of separate individuality. Subhuti, if a bodhisattva announces, 'I will set forth majestic buddha-lands,' one does not call him a bodhisattva, because the Tathagata has declared that the setting forth of majestic buddha-lands is not really such: 'a majestic setting forth' is just the name given to it.

"Subhuti, bodhisattvas who are wholly devoid of any conception of separate selfhood are truthfully called bodhisattvas." (The Diamond Sutra 17)

This spiritual wisdom provides us with an important warning. No one else can liberate us. We must liberate ourselves through our discipline, prayers, and meditations; and we must beware of anyone who would make such tempting promises as to do it for us. Certainly some individuals would deny us our progress toward the spiritual wisdom while refusing to receive it themselves. Sometimes the very ones who claim to love God the most are the ones who use God for their own advantages. With God's help we can see past those who would mislead us so that we can find the truth. "Be as shrewd as snakes and as innocent as doves." Firstly, we must realize and recognize that misdirections exist. Secondly, we need to understand what motivates them. Thirdly, we should try to realize that innocence and purity motivates the true messengers.

There is no one test or formula to detect the absolute truth, but we can detect the fraud. God, Himself, takes the ultimate responsibility for communicating the Word of the Light to us, because God is revealed to each of us privately in our hearts. We should listen for His word as it is there for each of us to hear. We must always remember that mere robes or apparent vocation are not a guarantee of validity. We must take great care in whom we take as a teacher, as the ultimate responsibility for the decision rests in each of us, because only we can choose the path to Oneness with God. We must decide wisely.

The Kingdom of God Apprenticeship

◆

SOURCE OF SPIRITUAL WISDOM

Question:
What is the source of spiritual wisdom?

Brief Answer:
God is the only source.

from the *Gospel of Thomas*

40. Jesus said, "A grapevine has been planted outside the father. And because it is not sound, it will be plucked out by the root and will perish."
(See Layton, p. 387.)

Longer Answer:

The plain and simple truth is that the source of spiritual wisdom is God. The **New Testament** says, "But he answered and said, Every plant, which my heavenly Father hath not planted, shall be rooted up" (Matthew 15:13). Although the source is God, spiritual wisdom must develop inside the heart of each seeker. We must live in God and then God will reveal Himself in us. The **Koran** says:

> Give them this parable. Once there were two men, to one of whom We gave two vineyards set about with palm-trees and watered by a running stream, with a cornfield lying in between. Each of the vineyards yielded an abundant crop, and when their owner had gathered in the harvest, he said to his companion while conversing with him: "I am richer than you, and my clan is mightier than yours."
>
> And when, having thus wronged his soul, he entered his vineyard, he said: "Surely this will never perish! Nor do I believe that the Hour of Doom will ever come. Even if I returned to my Lord, I should surely find a better place than this."
>
> His companion replied, while still conversing with him: "Have you no faith in Him who created you from dust, from a little germ, and fashioned you into a man? As for myself, God is my Lord. I will associate none with my Lord. When you entered your garden, why did you not say: 'What God has ordained must surely come to pass: There is not strength except in God?' Though you see me poorer than yourself and blessed with fewer children, yet my Lord may give me a garden better than yours, and send down thunderbolt from heaven upon your vineyard, turning it into a barren waste, or drain its water deep into the earth so that you will find none of it."
>
> His fruit were destroyed, and he wrung his hands with grief at all that he had spent on the garden: for the vines had tumbled down upon their trellises. "Would that I had served no other gods besides my Lord!" he cried. He had none to help him besides God, nor was he able to defend himself. (Koran 18:31-40)

This parable helps us understand that our strength emanates from God because of His spiritual wisdom. We must not judge ourselves by the standards of man. We must live according to the standards of God, that is, in Oneness. Often we fail to comprehend the strength of the source. The

Upanishad says:

> Higher than the senses is the mind,
> Higher than mind the soul,
> Higher than soul,
> the SELF,
> the "great,"
> Higher than [this] "great" the Unmanifest.
> (Katha Upanishad 6:7)

In this ancient scale of greatness, our senses rank the lowest and God ranks the highest. Yet we use the lowest to judge our worth, our success, and even God. The **Hebrew Bible** says, "Woe is me! for I am as when they have gathered the summer fruits, as the grape gleanings of the vintage: *there is* no cluster to eat: my soul desired the firstripe (sic) fruit. The good *man* is perished out of the earth: and *there is* none upright among men: they all lie in wait for blood; they hunt every man his brother with a net" (Micah 7:1-2). Humankind continually confuses the order of priority. The **Dhammapada** says, "The fragrance of aloe wood and sandalwood is but slight; the fragrance of virtuous people is supreme, reaching even to the gods" (Dhammapada 4:13). We seek after and pay dearly for the fashionable symbols of wealth and the luxuries of the day. Yet, we ignore and even mock those who choose to be virtuous. The **New Testament** is blunt on this point. It says, "I am the vine, ye *are* the branches: He that abideth in me, and I in him, the same bringeth forth much fruit: for without me ye can do nothing. If a man abide not in me, he is cast forth as a branch, and is withered; and men gather them, and cast *them* into the fire, and they are burned" (John 15:5-6). As we grow with inner knowledge from spiritual wisdom, our priorities shift and we move up the ancient scale of the **Upanishad** closer to the "great Unmanifest."

A frequently used metaphor in spiritual wisdom is the grapevine. This metaphor helps us understand that just as the nourishment for the grape comes from the soil, spiritual nourishment comes from the Word of the Light. Our inner life needs the support of spiritual wisdom or we will not grow strong. God gives us life and even continuing life, but this opportunity is finite. Without enlightenment, we will not reach Oneness with Him. If we stray too far from the source of our support, the light within us will not grow strong and, in fact, will grow weaker until we give up seeking altogether.

SPIRITUAL WISDOM GROWS

Question:
Will spiritual wisdom always grow?

Brief Answer:
No, God always guides us in growing our spiritual wisdom within us; but if we reject it, eventually the opportunities for spiritual growth will be fewer and fewer.

from the *Gospel of Thomas*

41. Jesus said, "Whoever has something in hand will be given more, and whoever has nothing will be deprived of even the little that person has."

Longer Answer:

God cultivates spiritual wisdom to grow within us through His guidance. The **Hebrew Bible** says, "For God giveth to a man that *is* good in his sight wisdom, and knowledge, and joy: but to the sinner he giveth travail, to gather and to heap up, that he may give to *him that is* good before God. This also *is* vanity and vexation of spirit" (Ecclesiastes 2:26). He provides wisdom, knowledge, and joy to all. The **New Testament** says, "For whosoever hath, to him shall be given and he shall have more abundance: but whosoever hath not, from him shall be taken away even that he hath" (Matthew 13:12; similar Luke 19:26 and Luke 8:18).

God gives us unlimited experiences and opportunities to grow. If we value and cherish these gifts, He will give us more. But if we do not value and cherish them, we will lose what little we had. The **Dhammapada** says, "Vigilance is the realm of immortality: negligence is the realm of death. People who are vigilant do not die; people who are negligent are as if dead"

(Dhammapada 2:1). The growth of spiritual wisdom within each of us depends on our vigilance and enthusiasm. Conversely, our permanent death is our denial and neglect of the gifts God gives us. The **Koran** says, "As for those who follow the right path, He will increase their guidance and show them the way to righteousness" (Koran 47:17). We must decide for ourselves to follow the right path. We must decide what we value and give it the highest priority. These are choices that each individual must make.

Spiritual wisdom bears a warning. The **New Testament** says, "And he said unto them, Take heed what ye hear: with what measure ye mete, it shall be measured to you: and unto you that hear shall more be given. For he that hath, to him shall be given: and he that hath not, from him shall be taken even that which he hath" (Mark 4:24-25; similar Matthew 25:29). In the following quote, the **Upanishad** clarifies that the lessons of our lives reveal to us all that we can grow into by using the inner light of spiritual wisdom:

> This SELF is Brahman indeed: it consists of understanding, mind, breath, sight and hearing; of earth, water, wind and space, light and darkness, desire and desirelessness, anger and the lack of it, right and wrong: it consists of all things. This is what is meant by saying: "It consists of this: it consists of that."
>
> As a man acts, as he behaves, so does he become. Whoso does good, becomes good: whoso does evil, becomes evil. By good works a man becomes holy, by evil works he becomes evil.
>
> But some have said: "This 'person' consists of desire alone. As is his desire, so will his will be; as is his will, so will he act; as he acts, so will he attain." (Brihadaranyaka Upanishad 4,4:5)

BE IN THE KINGDOM OF MAN, BUT NOT OF IT

Question:
How should we live in this world given all its pitfalls?

Brief Answer:
We must maintain our focus on our spiritual growth and view life in its larger context.

from the *Gospel of Thomas*
42. Jesus said, "Be passersby."

Longer Answer:

The world is only a sideshow to the main event — reaching Oneness with God. The **Koran** tells us, "The life of this world is but a sport and a pastime. Surely better is the life to come for those that fear God. Will you not understand?" (Koran 6:32). The Kingdom of Man is the world we must live in, but although we are in it, we need not be of it. The **Dhammapada** says, "Just as the bee takes the nectar and leaves without damaging the color or scent of the flowers, so should the sage act in a village" (Dhammapada 4:6). Like the bees who get their nourishment from the flowers without taking on the color or scent, we get our spiritual nourishment from our own life's experiences without taking on the world's darkness and greed. The **New Testament** says:

> Love not the world,
> neither the things *that are* in the world.
> If any man love the world,
> the love of the Father is not in him.

> For all that *is* in the world,
> the lust of the flesh,
> and the lust of the eyes,
> and the pride of life,

is not of the Father,
but is of the world.

And the world passeth away,
and the lust thereof:
but he that doeth the will of God abideth for ever.
(John 1,2:15-17)

In the previous quote, we are specifically told not to be drawn into the world and all its desires. If the material gain of the world attracts us, then inevitably we will learn to participate in its affairs and soon will become entangled and dominated by it. Although we must live in this world because this is where we can spiritually grow, we must not allow desire to capture and enslave us. We must never allow ourselves to be detracted from our pursuit of spiritual love and Oneness. If we can treat the world as a passer-by, we will avoid many such difficulties. The **Hebrew Bible** says, "When thou passest through the waters, I *will be* with thee; and through the rivers, they shall not overflow thee: when thou walkest through the fire, thou shalt not be burned; neither shall the flame kindle upon thee" (Isaiah 43:2). As we pass through life, God is with each of us to love, guide, and inspire us. Buddha says:

> THE SEVENTH REALIZATION is that the five categories of desire (that is being wealthy, being beautiful, being ambitious, finding pleasure in eating, being lazy) lead to difficulties. Although we are in the world, we should try not to be caught up in worldly matters. A monk, for example, has in his possession only three robes and one bowl. He lives simply in order to practice the Way. His precepts keep him free of attachment to worldly things, and he treats everyone equally and with compassion. (The Sutra on the Eight Realizations of the Great Beings 7)

The world is composed of desire upon desire that only lead us into difficulties. Our purpose in life should be to live in the Kingdom of God without attachment to worldly things. God presents goodness to us in many forms. The **Hebrew Bible** says, "And he said, I will make all my goodness pass before thee, and I will proclaim the name of the Lord before thee; and will be gracious to whom I will be gracious, and will shew mercy on whom I will shew mercy" (Exodus 33:19). God presents spiritual wisdom directly to us but we must choose to recognize it and accept it. The **Upanishad** says:

Hence the man who thus knows will be at peace, tamed, quietly con-
tented, long-suffering, recollected, for he will see the SELF in [him]self:
he will see all things as the SELF. Evil does not touch him: all evil he
shrugs off. Evil does not torment him: all evil he burns out. Free from
evil, free from doubt, immaculate, he becomes a Brahman (in very truth,
for Brahman now indwells him). This, sire, is the Brahman-world, (this
the state of being which is Brahman). This it is that has been granted
you. (Brihadaranyaka Upanishad 4,4:23b)

If we accept the spiritual wisdom that God directly presents to us on our
path of life, we will see all things in this world from the perspective of SELF,
that is, from the point of view of Oneness. If we do not, the **Koran** warns:
"Avoid those that treat their faith as a sport and a pastime and are seduced by
the life of this world. Admonish them with this lest their souls be damned by
their own sins. They have no guardian or intercessor besides God: and
though they offer every ransom, it shall not be accepted from them. Such are
those that are damned by their own sins. They shall drink scalding water and
be sternly punished for their unbelief" (Koran 6:70). Faith is not a pastime or
sport, it is the manifestation of our relationship of trust. The spiritual wisdom
tells us that we have no greater challenge nor gift than our faith.

If we fix our focus in life upon the temporal, we are making a big mistake.
We will always want more and be eternally disappointed with what we have.
Thus, we would be wiser to be simply a "passer-by" to what we have.
Another expression found in spiritual wisdom is "Be in the world, but not of
it." We should keep our focus squarely on God and not on the temporal ebb
and flow of life. This is not to say that the temporal is to be ignored entirely, but it should not be the focus of life. The physical world should be like the
storm on the ocean surface that whips up giant waves and causes significant
turbulence. Our focus should be finding the calm deeper water of the spiritual life. We need to be detached about our daily worldly activities as we
focus our concerns and attention on the spiritual growth represented by the
calmer deep waters that remain always under the surface storms. Success in
following the guidance in Thomas 42 will result in peace, contentment,
endurance, and reconciliation to life.

WE MUST LOVE GOD AND
THE GIFTS OF GOD

Question:
What must be done?

Brief Answer:
Love God and all His gifts.

from the *Gospel of Thomas*

43. His followers said to him, "Who are you to say these things to us?"
    "You do not know who I am from what I say to you. Rather, you have become
    like the Jewish people, for they love the tree but hate its fruit, or they love the fruit
    but hate the tree."

Longer Answer:

When asked by His followers to identify Himself, Jesus answered that
we should know Him from what He does or from the fruits of His
labors. We are what we do. Jesus's elaboration gives us an important insight. Jesus, who is a Jew, is talking to His followers who are also Jews.
Jesus says His followers are like the Jewish people. They either love God but
hate His gifts or they love His gifts but hate God. The same is true today of
many so-called religious people. Some of us love God but ignore His spiritual wisdom. Others of us love to quote selective scriptures (often endlessly), but
disregard God by not embracing His full wisdom and reflecting it in our lives.
The **Hebrew Bible** explains the problem as follows:

> And God spake all these words, saying,
> I *am* the Lord thy God,
> which have brought thee out of the land of Egypt,
> out of the house of bondage.

Thou shalt have no other gods before me.

Thou shalt not make unto thee any graven image,
or any likeness *of any thing* that *is* in heaven above,
or that *is* in the earth beneath,
or that *is* in the water under the earth:
(Exodus 20:1-4)

And when the people saw
that Moses delayed to come down out of the mount,
the people gathered themselves together unto Aaron,
and said unto him,
Up,
make us gods,
which shall go before us;
for *as for* this Moses,
the man that brought us up out of the land of Egypt,
we wot (sic) not what is become of him.
(Exodus 32:1)

And it came to pass,
as soon as he came nigh unto the camp,
that he saw the calf,
and the dancing:
and Moses' anger waxed hot,
and he cast the tables out of his hands,
and brake them beneath the mount.

And he took the calf which they had made,
and burnt *it* in the fire,
and ground *it* to powder,
and strewed *it* upon the water,
and made the children of Israel drink *of it.*

And Moses said unto Aaron,
What did this people unto thee,
that thou hast brought so great a sin upon them?

And Aaron said,
Let not the anger of my lord wax hot:
thou knowest the people,
that they *are set* on mischief.

For they said unto me,
Make us gods,
which shall go before us:
for *as for* this Moses,
the man that brought us up out of the land of Egypt,
we wot (sic) not what is become of him.

And I said unto them,
Whosoever hath any gold,
let them break *it* off.

So they gave *it* me:
then I cast it into the fire,
and there came out this calf.

And when Moses saw that the people *were* naked;
for Aaron had made them naked unto their shame among their enemies:

Then Moses stood in the gate of the camp,
and said.
Who *is* on the Lord's side?
let him come unto me.
And all the sons of Levi gathered themselves together unto him.

And he said unto them,
Thus saith the Lord God of Israel,
Put every man his sword by his side,
and go in and out from gate to gate throughout the camp,
and slay every man his brother,
and every man his companion,
and every man his neighbour.

And the children of Levi did according to the word of Moses:
and there fell of the people that day about three thousand men.
(Exodus 32:19-28)

When these quotes from the **Hebrew Bible** are reflected upon carefully, note that God gave His sweet fruit (message) directly to His people. Through Moses, He gave humankind a code of conduct for living His spiritual wisdom in the tablets of the ten commandments. When Moses returned with the tablets, he found the rest of the people dancing in a celebration, loving God but not following the message He had just given them. On seeing his people behaving improperly, according to God's own message, Moses, in an act of rage, not only flung God's precious gift of the tablets down, destroying them, he also ordered the death of many of his own people by the hands of the sons of Levi — the priestly tribe. This is honoring the message but not honoring the unconditional love of God. Both types of believers are described in this quote.

In spiritual wisdom, "fruit" is an important metaphor. The **New Testament** says, "For a good tree bringeth not forth corrupt fruit; neither doth a corrupt tree bring forth good fruit" (Luke 6:43). Jesus is saying good begets good; in contrast, corruption begets corruption. In other words, karma exists: we live the consequences of our actions. Its concept is captured in the phrase: "As we sow, so will we reap." The **New Testament** also says, "Either make the tree good, and his fruit good; or else make the tree corrupt, and his fruit corrupt: for the tree is known by *his* fruit" (Matthew 12:33). In life we always have choices. If we choose to truly live in the Kingdom of God, then our actions will reflect our choices and we will be known by our actions as good. The **New Testament** also says:

> Ye shall know them by their fruits.
> Do men gather grapes of thorns,
> or figs of thistles?
>
> Even so every good tree bringeth forth good fruit;
> but a corrupt tree bring forth evil fruit.
>
> A good tree cannot bring forth evil fruit,
> neither *can* a corrupt tree bring forth good fruit.

> Every tree that bringeth not forth good fruit is hewn down,
> and cast into the fire.
> Wherefore by their fruits ye shall know them.
> (Matthew 7:16-20)

In life the choices we make reflect what is inside us. If we are living in Oneness, then our actions will be good. If only the desires of the Kingdom of Man are inside us, then our actions will be limited and flawed. This simple interrelationship is fundamental in spiritual wisdom. The **Upanishad** says, "In this word *satiyam*, 'Reality and Truth', there are three syllables: *sat*, which means 'immortal", *ti*, which means 'mortal', and *yam*, which means 'by this the two are held together.' Because the two are held together by this [element, it is called] yam (yam, meaning to 'control' or 'hold together'). Whoever understands it in this way day in and day out, goes to the heavenly world" (Chandogya Upanishad 8,3:5). The **Dhammapada** tells us, "In the priestly one who has gone to the goal in two principles, in the knowing one, all bonds come to an end" (Dhammapada 26:2). By knowing, we grow into the knowing one called enlightenment. Once enlightened, there is nothing to tie us down. In contrast, the **Hebrew Bible** says, "Therefore my people are gone into captivity, because *they have* no knowledge: and their honourable men *are* famished, and their multitude dried up with thirst" (Isaiah 5:13). If we do not have a thirst for spiritual wisdom, we will remain ignorant, living only in the world of desire, and eventually we will die.

In spiritual wisdom, knowing is critical. But how do we know that we know? The **Upanishad** presents the following dialogue:

> [The pupil:] "Sir, tell me the secret doctrine. [The teacher:] "You have been told the secret doctrine. We ourselves have told you the secret doctrine concerning Brahman."
> "Its basis is ascetic practice, self-restraint, and works, the Vedas and all the treatises that depend on them. Truth is [its] dwelling-place.
> "Whoever knows this [doctrine] in this way will vanquish evil and find his home in the infinite, unconquerable world of heaven — [there] will he find his home." (Kena Upanishad 4:7-9)

What should we know? We should learn spiritual wisdom from all the
sources available to us including the holy scriptures. We must develop self-
control, work at learning, and become the fruit of the learning. The **Koran**
tells us to, "Say: 'We believe in God and that which is revealed to us; in what
was revealed to Abraham, Ishmael, Isaac, Jacob, and the tribes; to Moses and
Jesus and the other prophets by their Lord. We make no distinction among
any of them, and to God we have surrendered ourselves'" (Koran 2:137).
Spiritual wisdom cuts across all faiths. We must choose of our own free will
to surrender ourselves to God, learn His spiritual wisdom, and live His spiritual wisdom.

Saying 43 communicates this important spiritual wisdom. When asked by
His followers to identify Himself, Jesus answers that they should know Him by
His teaching. That nonrecognition is significant because we commonly do not
realize that there is a direct relationship between our Oneness and our actions.
God's spiritual wisdom is His constant gift that represents the sweet fruit of
His eternal trees. However, for us to use the sweet fruit requires our heartfelt
work and actions to manifest God within us. Because we are sometimes tired,
lazy, or afraid to make the effort, we fail to work with all our minds and hearts
to embody the light given us. Thus, we do not grow and radiate the Kingdom
of God in our actions. If we love His fruit without understanding and loving
God, we charge off in absolutely the wrong direction. If we simply love God
and ignore His wisdom or fruit, we are equally misguided. Inner growth does
not come from rote action but individual heartfelt work with the constant ebb
and flow of praxis and reflection.

THE KEY TO ENLIGHTENMENT

Question:
How do we reach enlightenment?

Brief Answer:
By listening to God.

from the *Gospel of Thomas*

44. Jesus said, "Whoever blasphemes against the father will be forgiven, and whoever blasphemes against the son will be forgiven, but whoever blasphemes against the holy spirit will not be forgiven, either on earth or in heaven."

Longer Answer:

God has given us the necessary means by which to grow spiritually. God is within each of us, although the various traditions use different names to denote that presence. In Saying 44, Jesus says that whoever damns or denounces the father and the son will be forgiven, but he that damns the Holy Spirit will not be forgiven. The Holy Spirit is within each of us. Therefore, if we deny the Holy Spirit, we are condemning our personal link to God. The **Dhammapada** says, "I will endure abusive words like the elephant in battle endures the arrow shot from the bow; for many people are ill-behaved" (Dhammapada 23:1). God knows us well and realizes that although many of us are basically good, we are sometimes ill-behaved and will rail against Him from time to time.

However, we must not destroy the connection to Him. The **New Testament** says, "Wherefore I say unto you, All manner of sin and blasphemy shall be forgiven unto men: but the blasphemy *against* the *Holy Ghost* shall not be forgiven unto men. And whosoever speaketh a word against the Son of man, it shall be forgiven him: but whosoever speaketh against the Holy Ghost, it shall not be forgiven him, neither in this world, neither in the *world* to come" (Matthew 12:31-32; similar Luke 12:10 and Mark 3:28-29). This essentially repeats the **Gospel of Thomas**. The **Upanishad** says,

[Like] light and shade [there are] two [selves]:
[One] here on earth imbibes the law of his own deeds;
[The other,] though hidden in the secret places [of the heart],
[Dwells] in the uttermost beyond.
So say [the seers] who Brahman know,
The owner of five fires and three Naciketa fires.
(Katha Upanishad 3:1)

The foolishness of denouncing God is a flirtation with disaster. The **Koran** warns, "Do not make God, when you swear by Him, a means to prevent you from dealing justly, from guarding yourselves against evil, and from making peace among men. God knows all and hears all. God will not call you to account for that which is inadvertent in your oaths. But He will take you to task for that which is intended in your hearts. God is forgiving and lenient" (Koran 2:226). Fortunately for us, God is forgiving and looks beyond our foolishness into our hearts. Thus, although damning and denouncing God reflects bad taste, such action, in itself, is not going to deny us a place in the Kingdom of God. The danger of the flirtation is that it creates a negative and hostile attitude within us toward God and thus our hearts are not focused on Oneness. Dangerous language can easily become a dangerous heart. When we deny God within us — the Holy Spirit — then we have broken the vital link between ourselves and God. This is what is not forgiven. The **Hebrew Bible** and the **Koran** agree. The **Hebrew Bible**'s poetry says:

Create in me a clean heart, O God;
and renew a right spirit within me.

Cast me not always away from thy presence;
and take not thy holy spirit from me.

Restore unto me the joy of thy salvation;
and uphold me *with thy* free spirit.
(Psalms 51:10-12)

The right spirit within us is vital in our quest for enlightenment. The **Koran** tells us to pray by telling us to, "Say: 'The Holy Spirit brought it down from your Lord in truth to reassure the faithful, and to give guidance and good news to those that surrender themselves'" (Koran 16:102). The Holy Spirit is from God and is within each of us. The Holy Spirit gives us guidance along the sacred path of spiritual learning we call our life. Spiritual wisdom is often expressed in poetry. The **Upanishad** tells us why SELF is so important as follows:

[Thus] did he discourse:

Mark well,
it is not for the love of a husband that a husband is dearly loved.
Rather it is for the love of the SELF that a husband is dearly loved.

Mark well,
it is not for the love a wife that a wife is dearly loved.
Rather it is for the love of the SELF that a wife is dearly loved.

Mark well,
it is not for the love of sons that sons are dearly loved.
Rather it is for the love of the SELF that sons are dearly loved.

Mark well,
it is not for the love of riches that riches are dearly loved.
Rather it is for the love of the SELF that riches are dearly loved.

Mark well,
it is not for the love of the Brahman class that the Brahman class is dearly loved.
Rather it is for the love of the SELF that the Brahman class is dearly loved.

Mark well,
it is not for the love of the princely class that the princely class is dearly loved.
Rather it is for the love of the SELF that the princely class is dearly loved.

Mark well,
it is not for the love of the worlds that the worlds are dearly loved.
Rather it is for the love of the SELF that the worlds are dearly loved.

Mark well,
it is not for the love of the gods that the gods are dearly loved.
Rather it is for the love of the SELF that the gods are dearly loved.

Mark well,
it is not for the love of contingent beings that contingent beings are dearly loved.
Rather it is for the love of the SELF that contingent beings are dearly loved.

Mark well,
it is not for the love of the All that the All is dearly loved.
Rather it is for the love of the SELF that the All is dearly loved.

Mark well,
it is the SELF that should be seen, [the SELF] that should be heard,
[the SELF] that should be thought on and deeply pondered,
Maitreyi.

Mark well,
by seeing the SELF and hearing It,
by thinking of It and knowing It,
this whole [universe] is known."
(Brihadaranyaka Upanishad 2,4:5)

As we start our journey in life, God gives us the necessary means to grow spiritually. That necessary gift is the SELF, the Holy Ghost, the Spirit, a portion of the Supreme. The Spirit awakens us and guides us along the path to enlightenment and eventually Oneness because the Spirit is the lamp that lightens our journey and guides us back to the God. Thus, the Spirit is valuable in every respect. God can easily forgive foolishness, poor choices, or mistakes. The only real mistake we can make is to ignore or deny the Spirit within us.

ENLIGHTENMENT COMES FROM THE RIGHTEOUS HEART

Question:

Does God give each of us the knowledge?

Brief Answer:

God gives us His guidance but we must learn through the heart.

from the *Gospel of Thomas*

45. Jesus said, "Grapes are not harvested from thorn trees, nor are figs gathered from thistles, for they yield no fruit. A good person brings forth good from the storehouse; a bad person brings forth evil things from the corrupt storehouse in the heart and says evil things. For from the abundance of the heart this person brings forth evil things."

Longer Answer:

Spiritual wisdom tells us that the heart is the key to learning spiritual wisdom. Righteousness is, in turn, the key to developing the heart so that we can be enlightened. The **Hebrew Bible** says, "To appoint unto them that mourn in Zion, to give unto them beauty for ashes, the oil of joy for mourning, the garment of praise for the spirit of heaviness; that they might be called trees of righteousness, the planting of the Lord, that he might be glorified" (Isaiah 61:3). Our hearts must become the trees of righteousness that are planted by God. The **Bhagavad-Gita** says:

> Men who put no faith
> In this law of righteousness,
> Fail to reach Me and must return
> To the road of recurring death.
> (Bhagavad-Gita 9:3)

Without righteousness we cannot reach the Kingdom of God. What is a righteous heart? The poetry of the **Dhammapada** says:

One who does evil sorrows in this world and after death,
sorrowful in both.
Seeing the pollution of one's own actions,
one is tormented by sorrow and grief.

One who does good is happy in this world and after death,
happy in both.
Seeing the purity of one's own actions,
one is happy,
most joyful.

One who does evil suffers regret in this world and after death,
suffering regret in both.
One suffers regret knowing one has done wrong,
and suffers even more when gone to a state of misery.

One who does good rejoices in this world and after death,
joyful in both.
One rejoices knowing one has done good,
and rejoices even more when gone to a state of felicity.
(Dhammapada 1:15-18)

We must allow God to create within each of us a righteous heart. The **New Testament** says, "Either make the tree good, and his fruit good; or else make the tree corrupt, and his fruit corrupt: for the tree is known by *his* fruit. . . . A good man out of the good treasure of the heart bringeth forth good things: and an evil man out of the evil treasure bringeth forth evil things (Matthew 12:33,35). A person's deeds reflect a righteous heart. The **New Testament** says, "For every tree is known by his own fruit. For of thorns men do not gather figs, nor of a bramble bush gather they grapes. A good man out of the good treasure of his heart bringeth forth that which is good; and an evil man out of the evil treasure of his heart bringeth forth that which is evil; for of the abundance of the heart his mouth speaketh" (Luke 6:44-45). The **Koran** also tells us, "The true believers are those whose hearts are filled with awe at the mention of God, and whose faith grows stronger as they listen to His revelations. They are those who put their trust in their Lord, pray steadfastly, and bestow in alms from that which We have given them. Such are the true believers. They will be exalted and forgiven by their Lord, and generous provisions shall be made for them" (Koran 8:2).

A righteous heart comes from loving and serving God and from a faith that grows with spiritual wisdom. The **New Testament** warns us that there are false prophets who will instruct us incorrectly. As discussed in Thomas 39, their actions and deeds are easily detected. The **New Testament** says:

Beware of false prophets,
which come to you in sheep's clothing,
but inwardly they are ravening wolves.

Ye shall know them by their fruits.
Do men gather grapes of thorns,
or figs or thistles?

Even so every good tree bringeth forth good fruit;
but a corrupt tree bringeth forth evil fruit.

A good tree cannot bring forth evil fruit,
neither *can* a corrupt tree bring forth good fruit.

Every tree that bringeth not forth good fruit is hewn down,
and cast into the fire.

Wherefore by their fruits ye shall know them.
(Matthew 7:15-20)

This saying tells us that the heart is important. If the storehouse of light in our hearts is filled with spiritual wisdom, then our actions will be good. If there is no light in the storehouse, then our actions and the impact of our actions will reflect that darkness. Whatever we cultivate in our hearts is what we ultimately are. If people have good will, they radiate peace and harmony. If people have anger and jealousy in their heart, they exude hatred and aggression. Thus, spiritual wisdom is telling us to continuously choose how to prepare our hearts. Such cultivation may take time and effort to be successful, but with a positive orientation and attitude we can alter our hearts. Righteousness is a glorification of God because it transforms darkness into light. Righteousness converts ashes to beauty, mourning to joy, heaviness of spirit to praise. Without righteousness, we will fail to reach Oneness with God.

BE RIGHTEOUS AND CHILDLIKE

Question:
If we are righteous, we will be enlightened by God?

Brief Answer:
We must also become sweet and childlike.

from the *Gospel of Thomas*

46. Jesus said, "From Adam to John the Baptist, there has been none among the off-spring of women who has been more exalted than John the Baptist, so that such a person's eyes might be broken. But I have said that whoever among you becomes a little one will become acquainted with the kingdom and will become more exalted than John."
(See Layton, p. 388.)

Longer Answer:

No one between the time of Adam and John the Baptist was greater than John. To Jesus, John the Baptist was a remarkably righteous man. "That such a person's eyes might be broken" is a idiom denoting deep respect. However, as discussed in Thomas 4, to reach the Kingdom of God each of us must also become a child. The **New Testament** says, "And said, Verily I say unto you, Except ye be converted, and become as little children, ye shall not enter into the kingdom of heaven. Whosoever therefore shall humble himself as this little child, the same is greatest in the kingdom of heaven" (Matthew 18:3-4). Purity, innocence, and humility are required virtues. If we can develop them, we can end suffering as noted by Buddha:

> This is the Noble Truth of the Cessation of suffering: such was the vision . . . "This Cessation of suffering, as a noble truth, should be realized: such was the vision, . . . "This Cessation of suffering, as a noble truth, has been realized: such was the vision, . . . with regard to things not heard before. (The First Sermon of the Buddha 10)

God guides us to righteousness by His inspiration and His word. The **Koran** says, "Thus have We inspired you (Muhammad) with a spirit of Our will when you knew nothing of faith or scriptures, and made it a light whereby We guide those of Our servants whom We please. You will surely guide them to a straight path: the path of God, to whom belongs all that the heavens and the earth contain. Surely to God all things shall in the end return" (Koran 42:53). God guides us along our straight path to Oneness with Him.

Righteousness delivers the soul but a childlike innocence is also essential to enter the Kingdom of Heaven. The **Hebrew Bible** says, "Though these three men, Noah, Daniel, and Job, were in it, they should deliver *but* their own souls by their righteousness, saith the Lord God" (Ezekiel 14:14). The **Upanishad** clarifies childlike life as follows:

> So let a Brahman put away learning with disgust
> and lead a childlike life.
> Let him then put away both the childlike life and learning with disgust,
> and [become] a silent sage.
> Let him then put away both silence and its opposite with disgust,
> and [become a true] Brahman (a man who really knows Brahman).
>
> And what is it that makes him a Brahman?
>
> Whatever really makes him such.
> What is other than [the SELF] suffers.
> (Brihadaranyaka Upanishad 3,5)

The Kingdom of God is not a place but an evolving mind-set that guides our behavior and in which we are always increasing our spiritual wisdom. The **New Testament** says, "For I say unto you, Among those that are born of women there is not a greater prophet than John the Baptist: but he that is least in the kingdom of God is greater than he" (Luke 7:28). No greater prophet existed prior to John the Baptist. Yet, when we attain the Kingdom of God, we will be greater than John the Baptist. We must liberate ourselves from the body so that its needs and desires are not the driving force within us. We must liberate the bondage of the heart by freeing the mind. Thus, becoming free and happy, we are as little children.

GOD WISHES OUR UNDIVIDED LOVE

Question:
If I love my family and I am a good person, will I be in the Kingdom of God?

Brief Answer:
We must become totally One with God.

from the *Gospel of Thomas*

47. Jesus said, "A person cannot mount two horses or bend two bows. And a servant cannot serve two masters, or that servant will honor the one and offend the other. No person drinks aged wine and immediately desires to drink new wine. New wine is not poured into aged wineskins, or they might break, and aged wine is not poured into a new wineskin, or it might spoil. An old patch is not sewn onto a new garment, for there would be a tear."

Longer Answer:

We must reject dualism and seek only Oneness with God. In this Thomas saying, dualism is presented in such a way that we can understand it as foolishness. Living in both Oneness and dualism is not a possible option, as Oneness is clearly superior. For example, wise wine drinkers know that they can not enjoy new wine after drinking aged wine. A person skilled in sewing knows that sewing an old patch on a new garment is foolish because the strength of the new fabric will immediately tear the old fabric. In other words, dualism is foolish. A person cannot have a life devoted to seeking both vital desires and spiritual goals. We must make a decisive choice, as even a nondecision has consequences and constitutes a choice.

Spiritual wisdom requires us to reject the Kingdom of Man and accept only the Kingdom of God. The **Bhagavad-Gita** says:

> Do works for Me,
> make Me thy highest goal,
> Be loyal in love to Me,
> Cast off [all other] attachments,
> Have no hatred for any being at all:
> For all who do thus shall come to Me.
> (Bhagavad-Gita 11:55)

We must work for the Kingdom of God and make Oneness our highest goal. When God is first in our life, all joy and fulfillment follows. This means being loyal and loving God. This also means shedding our worldly attachments without hatred or contempt toward them. True love of God requires us to reject division. The **Hebrew Bible** says:

> And the king said,
> Divide the living child in two,
> and give half to the one,
> and half to the other.

> Then spake the woman whose the living child *was* unto the king,
> for her bowels yearned upon her son,
> and she said,
> O my lord,
> give her the living child,
> and in no wise slay it.

> But the other said,
> Let it be neither mine nor thine,
> *but* divide *it*.

> Then the king answered and said,
> Give the living child,
> and in no wise slay it:
> she *is* the mother thereof.

And all Israel heard of the judgment which the king had judged;
and they feared the king:
for they saw that the wisdom of God *was* in him,
to do judgment.
(Kings 1,3:25-28)

A difficult concept to understand in spiritual wisdom is that of emotional neutrality towards attachments to the Kingdom of Man. We should feel neither positive nor negative feelings toward those attachments. The **Dhammapada** explains the neutrality as, "Those whose senses are tranquil, like a horse well controlled by a charioteer, who are free from pride and have no compulsion, are the envy of even the gods" (Dhammapada 7:5). We should strive to control our emotions, thus freeing ourselves of our egos and desires. The **New Testament** says, "No servant can serve two masters: for either he will hate the one, and love the other; or else he will hold to the one, and despise the other. Ye cannot serve God and mammon" (Matthew 6:24, similar Luke 16:13).

Emotional neutrality is not easy, but it is necessary to accomplish. Unless we achieve it, our progress, at times, will seem like we are taking one step forward but two steps backward, because emotional neutrality is indispensable for us to escape living in dualism. Emotional neutrality is not indifference to the plight of others, but it is protecting our inner life so that it is not influenced by life's events. The **New Testament** also says: "No man putteth a piece of new cloth unto an old garment, for that which is put in to fill it up taketh from the garment, and the rent is made worse. Neither do men put new wine into old bottles: else the bottles break, and the wine runneth out, and the bottles perish: but they put new wine into new bottles, and both are preserved (Matthew 9:16-17; similar Mark 2:21-22 and Luke 5:36-39). Trying to live in the dualism of the Kingdom of Man and the Kingdom of God is foolish and in fact impossible, since when we try to serve the needs of one, we neglect the needs of the other. The **Koran** says, "God is the Patron of the faithful. He leads them from darkness to the light. As for the unbelievers, their patrons are false gods, who lead them from light to darkness. They are the heirs of the Fire and shall abide in it for ever" (Koran 2:257). God is our patron; therefore, we should give God our loyalty and love.

ACCEPT ONENESS

Question:

How do we identify only with God and be emotionally neutral toward the events of life?

Brief Answer:

We must make peace with ourselves and others.

from the *Gospel of Thomas*

48. Jesus said, "If two make peace with one another within a single house, they will say to a mountain, 'Go elsewhere,' and it will go elsewhere."
(See Layton, p. 389.)

Longer Answer:

Spiritual wisdom uses the metaphor "say to a mountain, 'Go elsewhere,' and it will go elsewhere" to indicate that the impossible can be done. This is demonstrated by the following **New Testament** quote, "And Jesus said unto them, Because of your unbelief: for verily I say unto you. If ye have faith as a grain of mustard seed, ye shall say unto this mountain, Remove hence to yonder place; and it shall remove; and nothing shall be impossible unto you" (Matthew 17:20). In the **Gospel of Thomas** saying, keeping peace even in a single house is obviously difficult; but if we can achieve that peace, its strength alone can do the impossible. In other words, we need to make peace with both ourselves and with others around us. The **New Testament** clarifies, "Again I say unto you, That if two of you shall agree on earth as touching any thing that they shall ask, it shall be done for them of my Father which is in heaven. For where two or three are gathered together in my name, there am I in the midst of them" (Matthew 18:19-20). To Jesus, the single house in this Thomas saying is the Kingdom of God.

Spiritual wisdom stresses that God alone can reward us with true peace. The **Hebrew Bible** says, "God *is* our refuge and strength, a very present help in trouble. Therefore will not we fear, through the earth be removed, and though the mountains be carried into the midst of the sea; *Though* the waters thereof roar *and* be troubled, *though* the mountains shake with the swelling thereof" (Psalms 46:1-3). What we often fail to realize is that peace is a mind-set. Emotional neutrality gives us that peace or inner tranquility. The **Dhammapada** says, "One who has attained completion, is fearless, dispassionate, and unattached, has broken the stakes of existence and is in the final body" (Dhammapada 24:18). If we attain the Kingdom of God, we have found both inner and outer peace. The lesson is taught as follows in the **Bhagavad-Gita**:

> [First learn to] treat pleasure and pain as things equivalent,
> Then profit and loss,
> victory and defeat;
> Then gird thyself for battle.
> Thus wilt thou bring no evil on thyself.
> (Bhagavad-Gita 2:38)

Our peace largely is due to the Grace of God. The **New Testament** says, "Jesus answered and said unto them, Verily I say unto you, If ye have faith and doubt not, ye shall not only do this *which is done* to the fig tree, but also if ye shall say unto this mountain, Be thou removed, and be thou cast into the sea; it shall be done. And all things, whatsoever ye shall ask in prayer, believing, ye shall receive" (Matthew 21:21-22). Spiritual wisdom stresses the need for our abiding faith and its relationship to God's Grace. The **Koran** says, "And even if there be a Koran that could move mountains, rend the earth asunder, and make the dead speak, surely all things are subject to God's will. Are the faithful unaware that, had He pleased, God could have guided all mankind?" (Koran 13:31). Everything is subject to God's will. God guides the faithful and He ignores the others. Why? Because they freely choose not to be guided.

Saying 48 stresses the importance of rejecting dualism and accepting Oneness. Emotional neutrality does not mean a person lacks feelings but rather has transformed their feelings. For example, the love one feels is universal love and a person's compassion exists for the whole of God's creation. Entering into Oneness transforms ordinary happiness into a profound eternal jubilation. Jesus is saying that once we become One there is absolutely nothing we cannot do or accomplish. We all need to make peace with ourselves. However, we must do more; we must be One with God. This means loving all His creation. With that change of heart, there is nothing that is impossible. When we love all humanity and join together in Oneness and divine love, the strength that exudes from such a bond can move mountains and withstand any adversity. When we unite in common goodwill for one another, the power in us increases exponentially. The energy in us grows with love and moves the world forward collectively. Together, we stand; divided we fall. We are only weakened by our divisiveness and duality.

BUILDING SPIRITUAL WISDOM

Question:
If all the previous instructions are followed, will we find the Kingdom of God?

Brief Answer:
Once the process is started, then it continues to build continually as long as we wish to be engaged.

from the *Gospel of Thomas*

49. Jesus said, "Blessed are the solitaires and the elect person, for you will find the kingdom; for since you have come from it you shall return to it."
(See Layton, p. 389.)

Longer Answer:

Spiritual wisdom builds upon itself. As we have discussed before, Hindus and Buddhists believe in reincarnation, that is, being born again and again. The **Upanishad** says, "This self of his is given good works to do. Then this second self of his (the son), once he has performed his duty and reached [his appointed] age, passes on. Having passed on from here, he is really born again. This is his third birth" (Aitareya Upanishad 4:4). In each life, we do our good works and make spiritual progress by building upon the accumulated spiritual development of our past lives. The **New Testament** says:

> Howbeit that *was* not first which is spiritual,
> but that which is natural;
> and afterward that which is spiritual.
>
> The first man *is* of the earth,
> earthy;
> the second man *is* the Lord from heaven.
>
> As *is* the earthy,
> such *are* they also that are earthy;
> and as *is* the heavenly,
> such *are* they also that are heavenly.
>
> And as we have borne the image of the earthy,
> we shall also bear the image of the heavenly.
> (Corinthians 1,15:46-49)

Once we start the process, we are moving along on our own path to the Kingdom of God. Regardless if there is only one or if there are many lifetimes, once we have found spiritual wisdom and acted accordingly, then we are acting in the heavenly image of God. Once we have found Oneness, we will return there again, according to the **Gospel of Thomas**. This spiritual wisdom is perhaps best stated by the following quote from the **Diamond Sutra**:

"Furthermore, Subhuti, if it be that good men and good women who receive and retain this discourse are downtrodden, their evil destiny is the inevitable retributive results of sins committed in their past mortal lives. By virtue of their present misfortunes the reacting effects of their past will be thereby worked out, and they will be in a position to attain the consummation of incomparable enlightenment.

"Subhuti, I remember the infinitely remote past before Dipamkara Buddha. There were eighty-four thousand myriads of multimillions of buddhas, and to all these I made offerings; yes, all these I served without the least trace of fault. Nevertheless, if anyone is able to receive, retain, study, and recite this discourse at the end of the last [five-hundred-year] period he will gain such a merit that mine in the service of all the buddhas could not be reckoned as one-hundredth part of it, not even one-thousandth part of it, not even one-thousand-myriad-multimillionth part of it — indeed, no such comparison is possible.

"Subhuti, if I fully detailed the merit gained by good men and good women coming to receive, retain, study, and recite this discourse in the last period, my hearers would be filled with doubt and might become disordered in mind, suspicious and unbelieving. You should know, Subhuti, that the significance of this discourse is beyond conception; likewise the fruit of its rewards is beyond conception." (The Diamond Sutra 16)

In being born again, God is giving us a remarkable opportunity to cultivate His spiritual wisdom in our hearts over many lifetimes. Thus, each of us have an increased chance to reach Oneness with God. Although most religious leaders in Islam do not subscribe to reincarnation, we believe that the **Koran** can be interpreted to say otherwise. The **Koran** says, "It is God who splits the seed and the fruit-stone. He brings forth the living from the dead, and the dead from the living. Such is God. How then can you turn away?" (Koran 6:95). God brings forth the living from the dead. The **Koran** also says, "Can the dead man whom We have raised to life, and given a light to walk with among men, be compared to him who is in darkness from which he will never emerge? Thus do their deeds seem fair to the unbelievers" (Koran 6:122). God raises the dead to life. This can be interpreted figuratively or literally, but in either case, are not such people blessed? The **Koran** continues, "You sometimes see the earth dry and barren: but no sooner do We send the water down upon it than it begins to stir and swell, putting forth every kind of radiant bloom. This is because God is Truth: He resurrects the dead and has power over all things" (Koran 22:6). If we believe God can and does do any-thing, including resurrecting the dead, why not believe this can be done over many lifetimes?

What possible reason can there be for being born again? The **Hebrew Bible** says, "Blessed *is* the nation whose God *is* the Lord; *and* the people *whom* he hath chosen for his own inheritance" (Psalms 33:12). Being reborn means that people are given many opportunities to chose a spiritual life. The **Hebrew Bible** also says, "Behold, the righteous shall be recompensed in the earth: much more the wicked and the sinner" (Proverbs 11:31). What better way to compensate those that try to be righteous than to give them addition-al opportunities for eternal life? The **Dhammapada** perhaps explains being reborn best as follows: "Some are born in the womb; evildoers go to hell. People whose conduct is good go to heaven; people who are free from com-pulsion attain nirvana" (Dhammapada 9:11). In part, the Kingdom of God is a mind-set for those growing with spiritual wisdom. Without that mind-set, we remain lost in darkness. With that mind-set, we have the opportunity for greater spiritual wisdom including attaining nirvana. The **Upanishad** says,

> This wise one is not born nor dies;
> From nowhere has He [sprung] nor has he anyone become;
> Unborn is He,
> eternal,
> everlasting and primeval, —
> He is not slain when the body is slain.
> (Katha Upanishad 2:18)

In summary, making the free choice to be One with God is made within ourselves and we must make that decision based on our inner growth. Spiritual wisdom tells us that because of rebirth, we can continue to build on our soul's previous inner growth, due to the continuum of the spiritual evolu-tionary process, through repeated lives until we reach Oneness with God. This is an extended opportunity given to us by God out of His love for us. Spiritual growth arises within individuals because they choose to be righteous. They have chosen to walk the path to Oneness with God.

By being reborn, we have a repeated opportunities to lift the veils and fil-ters of our minds that blind us. This growth is a natural incremental process of spiritual enlightenment or realization. At the beginning, the soul is earthbound and grounded in the desires of the world. After several cycles of rebirth, spiritual growth begins; and eventually after many cycles, we come ever closer to Oneness with God. Our conduct determines our karma and our fate. Thus, our destiny is the inevitable result of our good and bad deeds committed in our present and past mortal lives. The cumulative positive lessons from karma taken to heart bring us rewards beyond our understanding. For some, the lessons from karma are preposterous; for some others they are difficult to understand; but for a few, they will be a wondrous awakening to God's love.

CHILDREN OF THE LIGHT

Question:
When we are in the Kingdom of God, who are we?

Brief Answer:
At those times, we are children of the light.

from the *Gospel of Thomas*

50. Jesus said, "If they say to you, 'Where are you from?' say to them, 'It is from the light that we have come — from the place where light, on its own accord alone, came into existence and [stood at rest]. And it has been shown forth in their images. If they say to you, 'Is it you?' say, 'We are its offspring, and we are the chosen of the living father.' If they ask you, 'What is the sign of your father within you?' say to them, 'It is movement and repose.'"
(See Layton, p. 389.)

Longer Answer:

Spiritual wisdom maintains that those who have faith in Him are God's chosen people. They have received His Grace. The **Hebrew Bible** says, "And God said, Let there be light: and there was light" (Genesis 1:3). As we have previously discussed, light is a metaphor for spiritual wisdom that allows us to grow spiritually. The **Koran** tells us:

Say:
"Think!
If God should enshroud you in perpetual night till the Day of Resurrection,
what other god could give you light?
Will you not hear?"

Say:
"Think!
If God should give you perpetual day until the Day of Resurrection,
what other god could bring you the night to rest in?
Will you not see?

Of His mercy He has given you the night that you may rest in it,
and the day that you may seek His bounty and give thanks."
(Koran 28:71)

Darkness is the opposite metaphor and represents spiritual ignorance. This quote from the **Koran** is a cry to us to use our minds to understand that God gave us both light and darkness for a reason. With light or spiritual wisdom, we seek God's bounty and we give thanks for His rich gifts. However, spiritual evolution moves slowly and takes a great deal of time and enormous effort. Thus, we often "rest" in the night (darkness), sometimes at new and somewhat more advanced plateaus of evolution, because we must digest or assimilate the lessons just learned. This spiritual wisdom is stated another way as follows:

In the beginning was the Word,
and the Word was with God,
and the Word was God.

The same was in the beginning with God.

All things were made by him;
and without him was not any thing made that was made.

In him was life;
and the life was the light of men.

And the light shineth in darkness;
and the darkness comprehended it not.
(John1:1-5)

That was the true Light,
which lighteth every man that cometh into the world.
(John1:9)

And the Word was made flesh,
and dwelt among us,
(and we beheld his glory,
the glory as of the only begotten of the Father,)
full of grace and truth.
(John 1:14)

In the beginning was the Word or spiritual wisdom. It was God. God made all things knowing what would occur. The **Hebrew Bible** says, "And God blessed them and God said unto them, Be fruitful, and multiply, and replenish the earth, and subdue it: and have dominion over the fish of the sea, and over the fowl of the air, and over every living thing that moveth upon the earth" (Genesis 1:28). God gave us life for an expressed purpose because God is the potential that is in man. The **Hebrew Bible** also says, "And on the seventh day, God ended his work which he had made; and he rested on the seventh day from all his work which he had made" (Genesis 2:2). God knows the value of rest. There is a specific sequence involving action, reflection, rest, and praxis (that is, embodying the lessons learned through our actions).

Motion and rest are important metaphors in spiritual wisdom. The **Upanishad** says, "Assuredly there are two forms of Brahman, the formed and the unformed, the mortal and immortal, the static and the moving, the actual and the beyond" (Brihadaranyaka Upanishad 2,3:1). There are two forms of God: One is static and the other is in motion. Possibly, we can learn more from the poetry of the **Upanishad** as follows:

It moves.
It moves not.
It is far,
yet It is near:
It is within this whole universe,
And yet It is without it.

Those who see all beings in the SELF,
And the SELF in all beings
Will never doubt It.

When once one understands that in oneself
The SELF's become all beings,
When once one's seen the unity,
What room is there for sorrow?
What room for perplexity?
(Isa Upanishad 5-7)

Brahman or God is motion and rest. God is immortal, constant, the beyond, far away, and outside the universe. However, God is also mortal, moving, actual, near, and within the whole universe. Spiritual wisdom tells us God is SELF and God is One. God is patient and realizes that we need time to grow spiritually . However, spiritual wisdom also tells us there is an eventual end to the process. The **Dhammapada** says, "Knowing the body is like froth, realizing it is insubstantial, breaking the flowery arrow of the Killer, one goes to a realm invisible to the King of Death" (Dhammapada 4:3). Our bodies are insubstantial and we must use knowledge to break through to the permanent Kingdom of God. The **Hebrew Bible** says:

For thus saith the Lord God,
the Holy One of Israel;
In returning and rest shall ye be saved;
in quietness and in confidence shall be your strength:
and ye would not.

But ye said,
No;

for we will flee upon horses;
therefore shall ye flee:
and,
We will ride upon the swift;
therefore shall they that pursue you be swift.
(Isaiah 30:15-16)

Although we have a multitude of opportunities within the perspective of many lives, we must not squander those opportunities through procrastination. Spiritual wisdom stresses that we need to use all the time we have to evolve as children of the light. Perhaps the value of time left is best expressed by the **New Testament** as follows:

Then Jesus said unto them,
Yet a little while is the light with you.
Walk while ye have the light,
lest darkness come upon you:
for he that walketh in darkness knoweth not whither he goeth.

While ye have light,
believe in the light,
that ye may be the children of light.

These things spake Jesus,
and departed,
and did hide himself from them.
(John 12:35-36)

On the path, we recognize that we must try to have an open mind and have a pure heart. We must continually try to be receptacles of God's spiritual wisdom and grow as a direct result of the light given to us. As we grow in and with the light, we more clearly resemble the true image of God. Make no mistake! We are what we are and we will become One with God only because of His Grace. We are properly called the chosen ones, but *we* are also the ones that must do the choosing. What is the proof? The SELF is the motion which propels us along our path. If we can quiet the mind and hear the proof, we will hear our inner voice, which is the voice of the SELF. The ultimate proof of truth is in God's word.

As we grow spiritually, we change only subtly at first, but in time the change will become discernable to others. As our light increases, people around us will take notice and inquire about not only the change of our physical appearance but also about our obvious new peacefulness. When honestly asked, we must acknowledge openly and with frankness the source of our light, power, strength, and wisdom. Some will believe us, and others will doubt and demand proof. Tell them that the proof is there to be seen in our actions as we transcend our limited past. God wants us to subdue the world and have dominion over it. However, we misunderstand the message due to our worldly-oriented minds, because the outer world is not our real existence. We must subdue our inner world in order to have dominion over everything that affects us. We will have dominion over the world in terms of learning from it and being its trustee.

God rested after His work to reflect. He is telling us to work on finding our spiritual path and then rest to reflect on what we have done and learned. In both work and rest, God will save us. The word or spiritual wisdom is key. God gives His spiritual wisdom to us individually and privately so that each of us can make our fastest progress possible and then have a time for rest to reflect, grow, and move along our path to Oneness. Each individual has to hear and see God for themselves and choose their path. In turn, God will choose the right moment to reveal Himself to each of us.

JUDGMENT DAY HAS BEGUN

Question:
When will the Kingdom of God begin?

Brief Answer:
It has already begun.

from the *Gospel of Thomas*

51. His disciples said to him, "When will the repose for the dead come to pass, and
when will the new world come?"
He said to them, "That repose which you are waiting for has come, but for your
part you do not recognize it."
(See Layton, p. 389.)

Longer Answer:

Even though it may sound contradictory, spiritual wisdom tells us that God
is both the absolute and the relative. The **Hebrew Bible** says:

> But the Lord shall endure for ever:
> he hath prepared his throne for judgment.
>
> And he shall judge the world in righteousness,
> he shall minister judgment to the people in uprightness.
>
> The Lord also will be a refuge for the oppressed,
> a refuge in time of trouble.
>
> And they that know thy name will put their trust in thee:
> for thou,
> Lord,
> hast not forsaken them that seek thee.
> (Psalms 9:7-10)

Although we cannot fully comprehend God, we can comprehend what we
need to know so that we can grow spiritually. We can comprehend that we
need to leave worldly consciousness and acquire the divine consciousness of

the Kingdom of God. We can comprehend that with the latter mind-set, we can transcend and grow into Oneness with God. That transcending process can be called the positive judgment of God because it only takes place with His guidance and Grace. The **Upanishad** says:

> [This SELF] cannot be apprehended
> By voice or mind or eye:
> How,
> then,
> can He be understood,
> Unless we say
> — HE IS?
>
> HE IS
> — so must we understand Him,
> And as the true essence of the two (the absolute and the relative).
> HE IS
> — when once we understand Him thus,
> The nature of his essence is limpidly shown forth.
>
> When all desires that shelter in the heart
> Of [mortal] man are cast aside,
> The mortal puts on immortality, —
> Thence to Brahman he attains.
>
> When here [and now] the knots [of doubt]
> Are all cut out from the heart,
> Mortal puts on immortality:
> Thus far the teaching goes.
> (Katha Upanishad 6:12-15)

God invented time as an aid to guide us in His way. The **Hebrew Bible** says, "I said in mine heart, God shall judge the righteous and the wicked: for *there is* a time there for every purpose and for every work" (Ecclesiastes 3:17). As we gain spiritual wisdom, we grow more aware of the Kingdom of God and the passage from the temporary to the permanent. The **New Testament** explains as follows:

> Verily,
> verily,

I say unto you,

He that heareth my word,

and believeth on him that sent me,

hath everlasting life,

and shall not come into condemnation;

but is passed from death unto life.

Verily,

verily,

I say unto you,

The hour is coming,

and now is,

when the dead shall hear the voice of the Son of God:

and they that hear shall live.

For as the Father hath life in himself;

so hath he given to the Son to have life in himself;

And hath given him authority to execute judgment also,

because he is the Son of man.

Marvel not at this:

for the hour is coming,

in the (sic) which all that are in the graves shall hear his voice.

And shall come forth;

they that have done good unto the resurrection of life;

and they that have done evil,

unto the resurrection of damnation.

I can of mine own self do nothing:

as I hear,

I judge:

and my judgment is just;

because I seek not mine own will,

but the will of the Father which hath sent me.

(John 5:24-30)

Saying 51 says that the final days have begun for those who have heard His word. Once we begin our spiritual journey, we are on our way out of the finite world and into the eternal. It may take many lifetimes, but we are on our way at last. That new world will be Oneness for all with God. Turmoil and struggle are merely learning opportunities for us. They are lessons so that we can transcend like the metamorphosis of the caterpillar into a butterfly. Union with God gives us peace. In contrast, the world cannot give us anything except an opportunity to learn. However, God's Grace is not given to us on our own terms. We must want to meet His terms, understand His terms, and change ourselves until our metamorphosis is complete and we are One with Him. In this period, we are given opportunities to gain in spiritual wisdom. If we make the choice to begin the spiritual learning process, God's Grace will guide us during this period. If, by our actions, we do not choose spiritual wisdom, He will simply withdraw from us. God's judgment is very real.

If we seek our own will over that of God's will, then we have rejected God. The **Dhammapada** says, "Cut down the forest, not the tree; danger comes from the forest. Having cut down the forest and craving as well, you will attain nirvana" (Dhammapada 20:11). If we choose to live in the Kingdom of God, we have chosen a mind-set that will influence all our actions and God will use those actions to teach us more. We must choose to live in the Kingdom of God. The **Koran** says, "We have revealed it thus so that We may strengthen our faith. We have imparted it to us by gradual revelation. No sooner will they come to you with an argument than We shall reveal to you the truth and properly explain it. Those who will be dragged headlong into Hell shall have an evil place to dwell in, for they have strayed far from the right path" (Koran 25:33). During this period, God slowly reveals more and more of His spiritual wisdom to those trying to live in His divine consciousness so that our faith is strengthened and our progress is swift. Also during this period, impostors will attempt to mislead us, but God will always reveal the truth to us individually, personally, and directly to our hearts.

Transcending into the divine consciousness of God is not easy. First, our minds cannot comprehend the SELF by voice, mind, or eye. Faith helps but it is not enough. The mind must undergo a transformation that occurs only when all the desires for wordly gain that are sheltered in the hearts are cast aside. We need to cut the knots of doubt. God is our refuge not only in times of trouble but always. We must put our unconditional trust in Him because He does everything for the purpose of strengthening our faith and because He is acting out of His infinite love for each of us. Therefore, we should also act out of our unconditional love for Him.

Few Will Succeed
But All Can

THE LIVING MESSAGE
IS IN OUR PRESENCE

Question:
Where is God when I need him?

Brief Answer:
He is always in our presence and always speaking to us directly,
only we do not permit ourselves to hear Him.

from the *Gospel of Thomas*

52. His followers said to him, "Twenty-four prophets have spoken in Israel, and they
all spoke of you."

He said to them, "You have disregarded the living one who is in your presence and have spoken of the dead."

Longer Answer:

God is living and is constantly in our presence. Spiritual wisdom tells us God is always speaking to us directly but privately in our hearts. The SELF is within us and God is everywhere. Jesus Christ is alive. Buddha is alive. Muhammad is alive. Each brought God's eternal spiritual wisdom to us. As they and we live those words, they and we will always be alive. However, we must open our eyes and let our hearts grow. In that way, we will see and feel God in our presence. The **Upanishad** says:

> Take up [thy] bow,
> the Upanishad,
> a mighty weapon!
> Fit in [thine] arrow sharpened by devotion!
> Stretch it on thought allied to determination!
> The Imperishable!
> This is the target,
> friend:
> [so] pierce it.
> (Mundaka Upanishad 2,2:3)

We should pick up and use the words of God as He reveals them to us. They are our means to discover spiritual wisdom and sharpen our devotion so we can pierce the ignorance of the Kingdom of Man. If we stretch the mind with determination, the goal of the eternal Kingdom of God is won. God's very words are always there for us, regardless of our background or circumstance. The **Hebrew Bible** says, "The Lord thy God will raise up unto thee a Prophet from the midst of thee, of thy brethren, like unto me; unto him ye shall hearken" (Deuteronomy 18:15). There is always another person nearby to help us with spiritual wisdom, because light and love draw like-minded seekers to us like magnets. The **Dhammapada** says, "One who has understood the truth taught by the perfectly enlightened Buddha should be honored as the priest honors the ceremonial fire" (Dhammapada 26:10). We should honor the ones that possess and share their spiritual wisdom with us. The **New Testament** says:

But I have greater witness than *that* of John:
for the works which the Father hath given me to finish,
the same works that I do,
bear witness of me,
that the Father hath sent me.

And the Father himself,
which hath sent me,
hath borne witness of me.
Ye have neither heard his voice at any time,
nor seen his shape.

And ye have not his word abiding in you:
for whom he hath sent,
him ye believe not.

Search the scriptures:
for in them ye think ye have eternal life:
and they are they which testify of me.

And ye will not come to me,
that ye might have life.

I receive not honour from men.
(John 5:36-41)

If we cannot hear the voice of God nor see Him in our lives, then we are not allowing spiritual wisdom to grow within us. We exist in the Kingdom of God by allowing spiritual wisdom to grow first in our hearts and then in our minds. When we do that, we know we are hearing God's voice and we are seeing God's face when we look at any face, including our own. When we read spiritual wisdom, we are hearing the words of God speaking directly to our hearts. If we wish to honor Jesus or any other spiritual messenger or master who brings the word to us, we do so by living in God's consciousness and thus in His Kingdom.

Many are blind to God. The **Koran** tells us, "They also say: 'How is it that this apostle eats and walks about the market-squares? Why has no angel been sent down with him to warn us? Why has no treasure been given him, no garden to provide his sustenance?'" (Koran 25:7). There are messengers from God living and walking among us every day. God has not announced them to us, but they are here nevertheless. Every encounter we have, including chance meetings, contain hidden divine messages for us. Therefore, we must be watchful and thoughtful in order to find the messages. The **Koran** says, "Nothing can prevent men from having faith and seeking forgiveness of their Lord, now that guidance has been revealed to them: unless they are waiting for the fate of the ancients to overtake them or to behold the scourge with their own eyes" (Koran 18:55).

Spiritual wisdom tells us that there is nothing at all preventing us from reaching our goal at this very moment except ourselves. The **Koran** says, "Men, you have received clear evidence from your Lord. We have sent down to you a glorious light. Those that believe in God and hold fast to Him He will admit to His mercy and His grace; He will guide them to Him along a straight path" (Koran 4:174). God has given us all spiritual wisdom, but we must want it and use it. If we seek it, God will welcome us into His Kingdom with love.

He will individually guide us to Him along our own path. If we seek Him, God will make our path to him a direct one without detours or undue difficulties. The **New Testament** says:

> For Moses truly said unto the fathers,
> A prophet shall the Lord your God raise up unto you of your brethren,
> like unto me;
> him shall ye hear in all things whatsoever he shall say unto you.

> And it shall come to pass,
> *that* every soul,
> which will not hear that prophet shall be destroyed from among the people.

> Yea,
> and all the prophets from Samuel and those that follow after,
> as many as have spoken,
> have likewise foretold of these days.

Ye are the children of the prophets,
and of the covenant which God made with our fathers,
saying unto Abraham,
And in thy seed shall all the kindreds of the earth be blessed.

Unto you first God,
having raised up his Son Jesus,
sent him to bless you,
in turning away every one of you from his iniquities.
(The Acts 3:22-26)

God has sent us many "prophets" like Himself. They have learned spiritual wisdom well and are willing to teach it to us. If we refuse to hear them by our own choosing, we slow our progress down and increase our chances of failing to reach our goal. God has been sending His prophets with spiritual wisdom since the beginning of time to help us confront the desires of the world and grow into Oneness with Him. We must not allow the noise and chatter of our temporal lives to distract us, because God wants us to contact Him directly through prayer and also through silent meditation. In these ways, we allow His knowledge and light to grow within us.

THE IMPORTANCE OF THE HOLY SPIRIT

Question:
What is the most important key in finding enlightenment?

Brief Answer:
The key to finding enlightenment is discovering the portion of God that is already within us.

from the *Gospel of Thomas*

53. His followers said to him, "Is circumcision useful or not?"

He said to them, "If it were useful, children's fathers would produce them already circumcised from their mothers. Rather, the true circumcision in spirit has become valuable in every respect."

Longer Answer:

Spiritual wisdom uses various names to describe that part of us that is Godly. SELF, spirit, Holy Ghost, and Holy Spirit are important ones and are often used. The **Upanishad** says:

> Know this:
> The SELF is the owner of the chariot,
> The chariot is the body,
> Soul is the [body's] charioteer,
> Mind the reins [that curb it].
> (Katha Upanishad 3:3)

We may think that we possess our own bodies but really we do not. The **Upanishad** says, "This [SELF] is dearer than a son, dearer than wealth, dearer than all else, for the SELF is what is most inward. Were one to speak of a man who says that there is some other thing dearer than the SELF, [and say]: 'He will weep for what he holds dear,' he would very likely do so. So, let a man revere the SELF as dear. For one who reveres the SELF alone as dear, what he holds dear will never perish" (Brihadaranyaka Upanishad 1:4).

Deep within us is the Holy Spirit. The **Hebrew Bible** says, "The burden of the word of the Lord for Israel, saith the Lord, which stretcheth forth the heavens, and layeth the foundation of the earth, and formeth the spirit of man within him" (Zechariah 12:1). God placed the Holy Spirit within us so that we might grow spiritually. Why is it essential? The **Dhammapada** says, "By day the sun shines, the moon illumines the night; the warrior shines in armor, the priestly one shines in meditation. But the Buddha shines with radiant energy day and night." (Dhammapada 26:5). Reaching liberation by ourselves is very difficult, which is why He provides us with teachers. The **Koran** says, "God does not love harsh words, except when uttered by a man who is truly wronged. God hears all and knows all. Whether you do good openly or in private, whether you forgive an injustice — God is forgiving and all-powerful" (Koran 4:148). God hears all and knows all because His presence is within us. The **New Testament** says:

> For circumcision verily profiteth,
> if thou keep the law:
> but if thou be a breaker of the law,
> thy circumcision is made uncircumcision.

> Therefore if the uncircumcision keep the righteousness of the law,
> shall not his uncircumcision be counted for circumcision?

> And shall not uncircumcision which is by nature,
> if it fulfil the law,
> judge thee,
> who by the letter and circumcision doest transgress the law?

> For he is not a Jew,
> which is one outwardly;
> neither *is that* circumcision,
> which is outward in the flesh:

> But he *is* a Jew,
> which is one inwardly;
> and circumcision *is that* of the heart,
> in the spirit,
> *and* not in the letter;
> whose praise *is* not of men,
> but of God.
> (Romans 2:25-29)

True faith exists in the heart, and the Holy Spirit or SELF makes that happen by awakening us, bringing us forward, and guiding us along our path toward enlightenment. It lightens our journey and guides our footsteps to God. As we start our journey in life, God gives us the necessary means to grow spiritually. That gift goes by various names including the SELF, the Holy Ghost, the Spirit, and a portion of the Supreme. Thus, it is invaluable and is hidden in the secret places of the heart.

---◆---

HARDSHIP AS A TEACHER

Question:

Do the hardships of life help us spiritually grow?

Brief Answer:

Yes, because through hardship we are more likely to dig deeper within ourselves, and in that effort we often more easily understand the importance of God.

from the *Gospel of Thomas*

54. Jesus said, "Fortunate are the poor, for yours is heaven's kingdom."

Longer Answer:

Spiritual wisdom recognizes the special role played by hardship in everyone's lives. The **Hebrew Bible says,** "He raiseth up the poor out of the dust, *and* lifteth up the beggar from the dunghill, to set *them* among princes, and to make them inherit the throne of glory: for the pillars of the earth *are* the Lord's and he hath set the world upon them" (Samuel 1, 2:8). The **New Testament** says, "And he lifted up his eyes on his disciples, and said, Blessed *be ye* poor; for yours is the kingdom of God" (Luke 6:20). Although there is no special virtue in poverty, God has a very special regard for those who suffer. Buddha says, "THE SIXTH REALIZATION is the awareness that poverty creates hatred and anger, which creates a vicious cycle of negative thoughts and activity. When practicing generosity, bodhisattvas consider everyone, friends and enemies alike, as equal. They do not condemn anyone's past wrongdoings, nor do they hate those who are presently causing harm" (The Sutra on the Eight Realizations of the Great Beings 6). For

although some poverty and deprivation can lead to greater spiritual awareness, it can also create hatred and anger in a vicious cycle of negative thoughts
and deeds brought against others.

Regardless, the **New Testament** says, "Blessed *are* the poor in spirit: for
theirs is the kingdom of heaven" (Matthew 5:3). The Spirit is strong in the
poor, thus the Kingdom of God can be easier for them to attain. The
Hebrew Bible says, "For he shall deliver the needy when he crieth; the poor
also, and *him* that hath no helper. He shall spare the poor and needy, and shall
save the souls of the needy" (Psalms 72:12-13).

God cares for the needy and the poor but in matters and ways that are truly
important. Why? The **Koran** says, "To endure with fortitude and to forgive is
a duty incumbent on all. He whom God confounds has none to protect him"
(Koran 42:43). When there is no one else to ask for assistance, there is always
God. Adversity can be a lesson that strengthens the faith of the heart, but we
can also misunderstand the lesson and weaken our faith. The poor often endure
with great fortitude, forgiving those who oppress them and offering whatever
they have to those even more needy than themselves, because in their hearts
they understand God's message. The **Koran** says, "For every community We
have ordained a ritual, that they may pronounce the name of God over the cattle which He has given them for food. Your God is one God; to Him surrender
yourselves. Give good news to the humble, whose hearts are filled with awe at
the mention of God; who endure adversity with fortitude, attend to their
prayers, and bestow in charity of that which We have given them" (Koran
22:33). God also appreciates the humble. The **Bhagavad-Gita** says:

> Work alone is thy proper business,
> Never the fruits [it may produce];
> Let not your motive be the fruit of work,
> Nor your attachment to [mere] worklessness.
>
> Stand fast in Yoga,
> surrendering attachment;
> In success and failure be the same,
> And then get busy with thy works.
> Yoga means "sameness" and "indifference."

For lower far is the [path of] active work [for its own sake]
Than the Yoga of the soul.
Seek refuge in the soul!
[How] pitiful are they whose motive is the fruit [of works]!
(Bhagavad-Gita 2:47-49)

People often only see the hardship of their labor and not its fruits. When
their work becomes their offering to God, it is no longer a hardship but a privilege. When the poor perform their work as an offering, we can learn great
lessons from those examples. We all need to surrender our attachments to the
fruits of our work and offer our labors to God with our love. Too often such
behavior is rare among the well-off, because their financial successes and fail-
ures are driven by the Kingdom of Man. Work for its own sake drives people
in the Kingdom of God. The desire for wealth, power, and earthly fame
makes achieving spiritual success very difficult for anyone to attain. Most of
us tend to learn our spiritual lessons more easily from a life of hardships than
from a life of ease. A life of comfort tends to direct us toward fulfilling the
desires of the physical world, rather than encouraging our inner spiritual
growth. Confronting difficulties makes us aware of the Supreme's importance
in our lives.

The extreme danger in relentless deprivation is that it often creates in many
of us hatred or anger, resulting in vicious and desperate negative thoughts and
actions that can drive us to despair. From this dark place, we can often not see
any light at all, including the spiritual lesson of our experience. Those of us in
poverty or other adverse circumstances must always proceed with caution, transcend our circumstances, and, especially, forgive our oppressors. Conditions do
not make seekers but attitude does. Therefore, we must embrace our conditions and let them help us grow spiritually. Poverty will only defeat us if we
let it keep us in a dark and angry place. In contrast, worldly wealth only leads
us away from spiritual growth.

REJECT ALL DUALISM

Question:

Is a loving family a high priority in the search for Oneness with God?

Brief Answer:

We must reject all dualism and single-mindedly focus on the Kingdom of God.

from the *Gospel of Thomas*

55. Jesus said, "Those who do not hate their fathers and mothers cannot be disciples of me, and those who do not hate their brothers and their sisters and take up their cross like me will not become equal to me."
(See Layton, p. 390.)

Longer Answer:

Although difficult, spiritual wisdom eventually requires emotional detachment from all things having to do with the Kingdom of Man. Jesus states this reality in harsh language for the few that choose to listen. The **New Testament** says, "If any *man* come to me, and hate not his father, and mother, and wife, and children, and brethren, and sisters, yea, and his own life also, he cannot be my disciple. And whosoever doth not bear his cross, and come after me, cannot be my disciple" (Luke 14:26-27). These words tell us something very significant that goes beyond the concept of prioritization.

If we wish to live in the Kingdom of God, then we must try to become equal to Him. We must transcend our present finite self, which is driven by the desires and attachments of the Kingdom of Man, to reach the unlimitedness, infinity, and singleness of God. The **Dhammapada** says, "Killing mother and father, and two learned kings, killing five eminent men, the priestly one goes untroubled" (Dhammapada 21:6). If we truly love God, all things and people are important but only in the context of God. The **New Testament** is very clear as the following demonstrates:

For I am come to set a man at variance against his father,
and the daughter against her mother,
and the daughter-in-law against her mother-in-law.

And a man's foes *shall be* they of his own household.

He that loveth father or mother more than me is not worthy of me:
and he that loveth son or daughter more than me is not worthy of me.

And he that taketh not his cross,
and followeth after me,
is not worthy of me.
(Matthew 10:35-38)

How do we achieve such a high standard? The **Bhagavad-Gita** says,

To be detached and not to cling
To sons,
wives,
houses and the like,
A constant equal-mindedness
Whatever happens,
pleasing or unpleasing.
(Bhagavad-Gita 13:9)

The key is detachment from the values of the Kingdom of Man, except as a tool to learn God's lessons. In life, we must achieve a constant equal-mindedness or detachment, regardless if what happens is pleasing or not. Why? The **Koran** says, "But when the dread blast is sounded, on that day each man will forsake his brother, his mother and his father, his wife and his children: for each one of them will on that day have enough sorrow of his own" (Koran 80:41). A lesson from lifesaving training for swimming is to not place your own life in jeopardy when trying to save someone else. Often if that lesson is not followed, two people drown. When we can safely help others without endangering our own spiritual lives, we should eagerly extend ourselves to them as long as they are truly seeking help.

The **Hebrew Bible** says, "Honour thy father and thy mother, as the Lord thy God hath commanded thee; that thy days may be prolonged, and that it may go well with thee, in the land which the Lord thy God giveth thee" (Deuteronomy 5:16). This quote seems to be inconsistent with the other quotes. When reading spiritual wisdom, we must always notice the contexts in which the insight is given. First and foremost, the larger context is that we must always live in the Kingdom of God. If that is done, then we should, of course, always honor our parents and family just as we should honor all of God's creation Unfortunately, many of us forget the larger context and love our family first and then, maybe, we "love" God. Although the difference may be hard to understand, our love must be placed first and completely with God, as loving Him sets the proper context for understanding the significance of everything else. All our other relationships flow from Him.

Jesus is telling us to single-mindedly focus on being One with the Supreme. If being with the family is not consistent with being One with God, then they, too, must be rejected. In seeking Oneness with God, often those professing to love us the most will try the hardest to keep us from our spiritual path. Why? They believe such seeking will cause an unreconcilable change in our relationship to them so that we will not address their needs and desires. Ironically, if they themselves chose their path to God, they would find Oneness with us and we would all move a step closer to the goal together. However, the Oneness would be on God's terms and not theirs or ours. Once we are awakened, we must follow our own individual spiritual path to Oneness in an unconditional and unrestricted way.

THE KINGDOM OF MAN IS WORTHLESS

Question:

What could be more important than the family?

Brief Answer:

God is more important than anyone or anything. If the world or any of its parts are not understood in the larger context of the Kingdom of God, we will remain ignorant.

from the *Gospel of Thomas*

56. Jesus said, "Whoever has become acquainted with the world has found a corpse, and the world is not worthy of the one who has found the corpse." (See Layton, p. 390.)

Longer Answer:

Spiritual wisdom is extremely demanding and not many will be able or interested in seeking it, because it requires the total rejection of the values and desires of the Kingdom of Man and surrendered acceptance of the values of the Kingdom of God. The Buddha says, "Bhikkhus, these two extremes ought not to be practiced by one who has gone forth from the household life. What are the two? There is devotion to the indulgence of sense-pleasures, which is low, common, the way of ordinary people, unworthy and unprofitable; and there is devotion to self-mortification, which is painful, unworthy and unprofitable" (The First Sermon of the Buddha). Neither extreme of self-indulgence or self-denial will bring us closer to understanding spiritual wisdom. It is not captured by acting excessively, but rather is realized over time through our conscious and constant cry for Oneness and the application of the gentle but consistent discipline of the senses. The **Hebrew Bible** says, "The earth *is* the Lord's, and the fulness thereof; the world, and they that dwell therein" (Psalms 24:1).

Do not think we own anything on earth or that we are the masters of our own fate. God "owns" all aspects of the universe and He permits us to dwell here so that we can make progress. The **Koran** says, "If We sent the angels down to them, and caused the dead to speak with them, and ranged all things in front of them, they would still not believe, unless God willed otherwise. But most of them are ignorant men" (Koran 6:112).

We must not underestimate the importance of God's omnipotent power. The **Hebrew Bible** says, "He hath made every *thing* beautiful in his time: also he hath set the world in their heart, so that no man can find out the work that God maketh from the beginning to the end" (Ecclesiastes 3:11). As long as we cling to the Kingdom of Man or any part of it in our hearts, we cannot live in complete surrender to the Kingdom of God. The **Dhammapada** says, "The world is blind; few can see here. Few go to heaven, like birds escaped from a net" (Dhammapada 13:8). As much as we intellectually understand our spiritual ignorance, we find that purging ourselves of the desires of the world is remarkably difficult. That is why it takes lifetimes to perfect our spiritual development.

The **Upanishad** says:

> The breath of life is greater than hope. For just as the spokes [of a wheel] are fixed in the hub, so is everything fixed in this breath of life. But life does life [itself] go on: life gives life, — gives [it back] to life. Life is father, life mother, life brother and sister, life the teacher and life the Brahman.
>
> [And so,] if a man, showing even a little harshness, answers back his father or mother, brother or sister, teacher of a Brahman, people will say to him: "A curse on you, you have killed your father," or "You have killed your mother," — or your brother or sister or teacher or a Brahman.
>
> But if, when the breath of life has left such as he, someone were [to strike them] with a stake, cast them aside and burn them up completely, no one would say to him: "You have killed your father," or "You have killed your mother," — or your brother or sister or teacher or a Brahman.
>
> For truly the breath of life is all these things; and the man who sees that this is so, has it thus in mind and understands that it is so, becomes a master of dialectic. Should people say to him, "You are a master of dialectic," and he should reply, "That is perfectly true." He should not deny it. (Chandogya Upanishad 7,15)

God gave us the breath of life and because of that gift we can solve all of God's mysteries. With the breath of life we can fully reach the Kingdom of

God, because with it we can surpass ourselves by treasuring not the temporary but the eternal. The **New Testament** says:

> For which cause we faint not;
> but though our outward man perish,
> yet the inward *man* is renewed day by day.

> For our light affliction,
> which is but for a moment,
> worketh for us a far more exceeding and eternal weight of glory;

> While we look not at the things which are seen,
> but at the things which are not seen:
> for the things which are seen *are* temporal;
> but the things which are not seen *are* eternal.
> (Corinthians 2,4:16-18)

We must center ourselves in God's consciousness each and every day with
our prayers and meditations. There we will find help and strength. The
Upanishad says, "He continued: 'I am the breath of life, the SELF that consists of consciousness: reverence me as life and immortality. Life is breath and
breath is life. The breath of life, he said, 'is immortality. For so long as the
breath remains in this body, so long is there life. For by this breath [of life] a
man attains immortality in the other world, by consciousness, true conception.
Whoso reverence me as life and immortality, wins all [his allotted] life in this
world and immortality and indestructibility in the heavenly world'"
(Kaushitaki Upanishad 3:2). Because we have the spirit or the SELF, we can
create in our hearts what Christians call the Christ Consciousness. As students, we must apply ourselves to learning; as a teacher, God gives us the
opportunities, the assistance, and the lessons to transfer our worldly experiences into divine wisdom. However, as so many of the Thomas quotes have
pointed out, the choice is always ours to make. We must want to learn and
want to reach His goal.

This **Gospel of Thomas** saying cited in this section needs to be read in
the context of idioms used in the time of Jesus. The Jewish expression used
by Jesus "the world is not worthy of the one" connotes extreme praise of an
individual. Finding a corpse connotes finding the desolate aspects of life.

Thus, a worthy person knows that the world is filled with negative and lifeless aspects and that they have nothing whatsoever to offer a seeker. There is a parallel between the concept of evolution and the concept of spiritual growth of the soul through reincarnation. The birth-death-rebirth cycle of the human body called evolution permits humankind over time to adapt slowly and evolve to be better suited to our environment. The birth-death-rebirth cycle for the soul permits it over time to slowly adapt to a closer relationship with God. Adaptation is slow and requires many cycles, but in both situations, it can be accelerated by God's Grace.

WEEDS ARE AMONG US

Question:
If friends and family do not think this way, are they wrong?

Brief Answer:
They are not so much wrong as unaware.

from the *Gospel of Thomas*
57. Jesus said, "The father's kingdom is like a person who had [good] seed. His enemy came at night and sowed weeds among the good seed. The person did not let them pull up the weeds, and said to them, 'No, or you might go to pull up the weeds and pull up the wheat along with them.' For on the day of the harvest the weeds will be conspicuous and will be pulled up and burned."

Longer Answer:

As many of the previous quotes have noted, the Kingdom of God exists not as a place but a process of continual evolution toward the Oneness with God. God alone carves out each person's spiritual path. For each of us our path is like the labyrinth but not like the maze. There are no deliberate dead ends, hidden passages, or tricks, as there is only one sure path.

Nevertheless, there are many unexpected twists and turns with only a single narrow path into the center representing enlightenment. When we travel it, we will see others in the labyrinth moving at their own pace and being at different places on their path. If we take our eyes off our footsteps on our own path to see where others are, we easily lose our way and get off our path. The **Hebrew Bible** says, "Truly my soul waiteth upon God: From him *cometh* my salvation" (Psalms 62:1). The soul evolves and awaits His decisions on their progress and the next lesson that each individual should learn. Nothing occurs by chance as every individual experience is another step along our singular paths.

From our perspective on the path, this learning process appears as a series of mysteries that slowly unravel. The **Upanishad** says:

> This is the great wheel of Brahman
> Giving life and livelihood to all,
> Subsist in all:
> In it the swan [of the soul] is hither and thither tossed.
> One is the SELF, another
> He who impels to action,
> So thinking,
> a man rejoices:
> Hence and hereby he passes on to immortality.
> (Svetasvatara Upanishad 1:6)

God gives us life and livelihood. He sets the stage, determines our path, calls us to action, and loves us unconditionally. His greatest gift to us is free choice; we must use it to decide if we want to travel our assigned path or not. We must not be fooled or tempted by those who would lead us away from God's path by following only desire. The **Koran** says, "If you obeyed the greater part of mankind, they would lead you away from God's path. They follow nothing but idle fancies and preach nothing but falsehoods. God best knows the men who stray from His path, as He best knows the rightly guided" (Koran 6:116). Our only guide is God Himself. The **New Testament** repeats the **Gospel of Thomas** parable as follows:

> Another parable put he forth unto them,
> saying,
> The kingdom of heaven is likened unto a man
> which sowed good seed in his field:

But while men slept,
his enemy came and sowed tares among the wheat,
and went his way.

But when the blade was sprung up and brought forth fruit,
then appeared the tares also.

So the servants of the householder came and said unto him,
Sir,
didst not thou sow good seed in the field?
from whence then hath it tares?

He said unto them, An enemy hath done this.
The servants said unto him,
Wilt thou then that we go and gather them up?

But he said,
Nay;
lest while ye gather up the tares,
ye root up also the wheat with them.

Let both grow together until the harvest:
and in the time of harvest I will say to the reapers,
Gather ye together first the tares,
and bind them in bundles to burn them:
but gather the wheat into my barn.
(Matthew 13:24-30)

The distractions around us will always be there as we move along our path. In time, God will resolve all our problems and difficulties in His own way. Spiritual wisdom tells us to be gentle but consistent about controlling our desires in the Kingdom of Man. The **Dhammapada** says, "I will tell all of you gathered here something good. Uproot craving entirely, as the seeker of a fragrant root digs out the grass above, so the Killer may not destroy you over and over again, as a torrent destroys reeds" (Dhammapada 24:4). We must be ever vigilant not to let the true "killer" — our own desires — destroy us. The **New Testament** explains the earlier parable as follows:

> Then Jesus sent the multitude away,
> and went into the house:
> and his disciples came unto him,
> saying,
> Declare unto us the parable of the tares of the field.
>
> He answered and said unto them,
> He that soweth the good seed is the Son of man;
> The field is the world;
> the good seed are the children of the kingdom;
> but the tares are the children of the wicked *one;*
> The enemy that sowed them is the devil;
> the harvest is the end of the world;
> and the reapers are the angels.
>
> As therefore the tares are gathered and burned in the fire;
> so shall it be in the end of this world.
>
> The Son of man shall send forth his angels,
> and they shall gather out of his kingdom all things that offend,
> and them which do iniquity;
> And shall cast them into a furnace of fire:
> there shall be wailing and gnashing of teeth.
>
> Then shall the righteous shine forth
> as the sun in the kingdom of their Father.
> Who hath ears to hear,
> let him hear.
> (Matthew 13:36-43)

We are the seeds God sows in the world. Then, He gives us opportunities to mature correctly. However, hazards do exist — the distractions and temptations referred to as weeds — such as human passion, hatred, folly, and desire. By avoiding the weeds with our free will, we can assist our spiritual maturity. With our free will, we can help God by increasing His crop yield. He has the power to kill the weeds as they arise, but that would interfere with His most sacred gift to us, our free will. God knows at the precise moment when He can easily harvest just the wheat, leaving the weeds behind. Until we draw our last breath, each of us can make progress in growing our spiritual wisdom. God's love gives us remarkable chances to make mistakes and recover and learn from those errors. With its extended opportunities, reincarnation not only helps us appreciate that life and all its lessons are gifts of love from God, but also that His love for us is indeed remarkable.

WE MUST WORK HARD

Question:
Is being in the Kingdom of God hard work?

Brief Answer:
Yes. Our spiritual growth requires both will power and concentration.

from the *Gospel of Thomas*
58. Jesus said, "Fortunate is the person who has worked hard and has found life."

Longer Answer:

Spiritual wisdom tells us self-control and concentration are essential. The **Upanishad** says, "Now, man is possessed of an active will. As is his will in this world, so does he, on departing hence, become. Let a man exercise his will" (Chandogya Upanishad 3,14:2). Will power determines our success. The **Dhammapada** says, "Though one defeats a million men in battle, one who overcomes the self alone is in fact the highest victor" (Dhammapada 8:4). Our greatest enemy in life is always ourselves, because we let the Kingdom of Man consciousness get the better of us. We must defeat that consciousness with our self-control and mental focus. The **New Testament** says:

And when they had found him on the other side of the sea,
they said unto him,
Rabbi,
when camest thou hither?

Jesus answered them and said,
Verily,
verily,
I say unto you,
Ye seek me,
not because ye saw the miracles,
but because ye did eat of the loaves,
and were filled.

Labour not for the meat which perisheth,
but for the meat which endureth unto everlasting life,
which the Son of man shall give unto you:
for him hath God the Father sealed.
(John 6:25-27)

We seek spiritual wisdom not because of any advantage that it might give us in the world or afterlife, but rather out of our desire and longing to be One with God. He makes it possible for us to succeed. The **Hebrew Bible** says, "And I have filled him with the spirit of God, in wisdom, and in understanding, and in knowledge, and in all manner of workmanship" (Exodus 31:3). Each of us has the Holy Spirit of God within us.

Spiritual wisdom is in front of us right now. However, we must work to develop our ability to see and understand it. The **Koran** says, "Truly, none will take heed but the wise: those who keep faith with God and do not break their pledge; who join together what God has bidden to be united; who fear their Lord and dread the terrors of an evil reckoning; who for the sake of God endure with fortitude, attend to their prayers, and give alms in private and in public; and ward off evil with good. These shall have a blissful end. They shall enter the gardens of Eden, together with the righteous among their fathers, their wives, and their descendants. From every gate the angels will come to them, saying: 'Peace be to you for all that you have steadfastly endured. Blessed is the reward of Paradise'" (Koran 13:20). The committed seeker will hear and act on spiritual wisdom as they will see the universal message and long to be One with it. The **Koran** says, "As for those who have faith and do good works, their Lord will admit them into His mercy. That shall be the glorious triumph" (Koran 45:30). Those who have faith in God and act with love toward all of His creation will proceed through the cycles of reincarnation and reach enlightenment and Oneness.

In this, Jesus applauds those who, through hard work, understand the purpose of life. We must first choose to take the right path and then remain on it to reach Oneness with the Supreme. Choosing it in the first place may be greatly assisted by Grace. Remaining on it requires our hard work and unwavering determination, because transcendence demands an active, dynamic effort that reflects self-discipline, endurance, patience, and dedication to the goal. Selecting and staying on the path also requires the SELF or the spirit of God. On our part, such dedication takes strong will power, wisdom, understanding, knowledge, and "all manner of workmanship." Overcoming the ego alone is our highest victory in life. Inner progress is often not defined by the fruits of our physical labor. We need to understand that it may take a long time before we see a measurable difference in our spiritual lives from our efforts. In all instances, our work must be an offering of love to God and reflect our lack of concern for worldly outcomes or recognition, since any outer achievement we may realize is unimportant to our spiritual growth. Spiritual achievement is found in the sincerity of our effort and our offering. Therefore, we need to surrender ourselves to God by performing all work with the utmost love, concern, and dedication, because the work itself is our offering of devotion.

FOCUS ON GOD IN OUR LIVES

Question:
How is spiritual wisdom acquired?

Brief Answer:
We acquire it by focusing on God throughout our lives.

from the Gospel of Thomas

59. Jesus said, "Look to the living one as long as you live, or you might die and then try to see the living one, and you will be unable to see."

Longer Answer:

We acquire spiritual wisdom by focusing our lives on God. The **Koran** says to us, "Say: 'God's guidance is the only guidance. We are commanded to surrender ourselves to the Lord of the Universe, to pray, and to fear Him. Before Him you shall all be assembled'" (Koran 6:72). We lovingly surrender our will to God's will and guidance. The **Dhammapada** says, "Uproot self-love, as you would an autumn lily by hand; cherish the path to peace, to nirvana taught by the Felicitous one" (Dhammapada 20:13). We grow into Oneness with God when we leave behind us the ego-centered desires of the world. The **Hebrew Bible** says, "But I *am* like a green olive tree in the house of God: I trust in the mercy of God for ever and ever" (Psalms 52:8). God wants us to exist in Him.

We must always let the fruit of our actions manifest our trust in the love and compassion of God. The **New Testament** says:

> Little children,
> yet a little while I am with you.
> Ye shall seek me:
> and as I said unto the Jews,
> Whither I go,
> ye cannot come;
> so now I say to you.
>
> A new commandment I give unto you,
> that ye love one another;

> as I have loved you,
> that ye also love one another.

> By this shall all *men* know that ye are my disciples,
> if ye have love one to another.
> (John 13:33-35)

The most important testimony of our faith in God is our love for all His creation and not the possessive and conditional love of humankind. Rather, our love needs to be the type of love demonstrated by Christ, who was and is selfless and unconditional. We should never doubt God's infinite capacity to love us. The **Upanishad** says, "For when a man finds security from fear and permanence in this invisible, insubstantial, unspecified, uncontainable [saviour], then does he achieve [full] security from [all] fear. But when he excavates a hole in it and splits it into different parts, then will he experience fear, — the fear of a man who does not think he knows" (Taittiriya Upanishad 2:7). In seeking permanence in the invisible, unsubstantial, unspecific, and uncontainable saviour, we are seeking our true state of being — we are seeking God.

We have no reason to fear anything. However, once doubt enters the mind, then fear begins. The **Koran** says, "We have sent you forth as a witness and as a bearer of good news and warnings, so that you may have faith in God and His apostle and that you may assist Him, honor Him, and praise Him morning and evening" (Koran 48:8). God provides spiritual wisdom so that we might have faith in Him and His messengers. The **Koran** also says, "Do they not see the birds that wing their flight in heaven's vault? None but God sustains them. Surely in this there are signs for true believers" (Koran 16:79). While maintaining the possibility of individual free choice, God sends us a constant stream of positive signs of His existence. Therefore, we need only look and see. For example, this **Gospel of Thomas** saying is talking to each of us directly and is telling us to seek Oneness with the Supreme because life is our opportunity to reach Oneness and only through life can we achieve Oneness. Inner progress can only take place in the body, since progress comes from achieving increasingly greater enlightenment. We cannot expect to be One with God unless and until we shed our limited temporal minds by becoming sincere seekers and by using God's spiritual wisdom to develop our individual capacities.

LOOK FOR HIS SIGNS

Question:

Is God constantly teaching us spiritual wisdom?

Brief Answer:

Yes, but we must take the time to reflect on it and embody it.

from the *Gospel of Thomas*

60.   <They saw> a Samaritan carrying a lamb as he went to Judaea.
       He said to his disciples, "This <. . .> the lamb."
       They said to him, "So that he might slaughter it and have it to eat."
       He said to them, "He will not eat it while it is alive, but rather when he has slaughtered so it becomes a carcass."
       They said, "Otherwise he cannot do it."
       He said to them, "You, too, seek for yourselves a place for repose, lest you might become a carcass and be devoured."
       (See Layton p. 391.)

Longer Answer:

This parable tells us to take the time to look around for God's lessons and reflect carefully on them. God is constantly teaching us; yet, we are largely blind to His lessons. For example, in this parable the lamb represents all seekers. Jesus may have said, "For what reason is that person carrying around the lamb?" He notes the Samaritan will not eat the lamb until the Samaritan has killed it. Jesus stated the obvious but there is a deeper lesson here. Because we have a life, we have the opportunity to learn, reflect, and know before death over takes us. However, not only must we seize every opportunity, but we must also perceive that action and reflection lead to our growth through introspection. The **Upanishad** says:

Let a wise man think upon that God,
Let him engage in spiritual exercise (yoga) related to the SELF:
[Let him think upon that God,]
so hard to see,
Deep hidden in the depths,
dwelling in a secret place,
Firm-fixed in the abyss,
primordial;
Then will he put behind him both sorrow and [unstable] joy.
(Katha Upanishad 2:12)

Yoga is a form of action and reflection designed to increase spiritual wisdom within us. Seeking is difficult because the SELF is very deep within us. Meditation helps us go deep within ourselves to find the SELF and can take many forms. The **Hebrew Bible** says, "When I remember thee upon my bed, *and* meditate on thee in the *night* watches. Because thou hast been my help, therefore in the shadow of thy wings will I rejoice. My soul followeth hard after thee: thy right hand upholdeth me" (Psalms 63:6-8). We can meditate on God anywhere and anytime. The **Hebrew Bible** says, "Blessed *is* the man that walketh not in the counsel of the ungodly, nor standeth in the way of sinners, nor sitteth in the seat of the scornful. But his delight *is* in the law of the Lord; and in his law doth he meditate day and night. And he shall be like a tree planted by the rivers of water, that bringeth forth his fruit in his season; his leaf also shall not wither; and whatsoever he doeth shall prosper" (Psalms 1:1-3).

We can meditate on the vastness and multiplicity of God as do Hindus and others, or we can meditate on His laws, creations, or silence. Regardless of the type or technique, meditation gives us nourishment, increases our spiritual wisdom, and moves us closer to Oneness with God. The alternative to reflection and learning from God is existing in the Kingdom of Man and being controlled by its desires. The **Koran** says, "Know that the life of this world is but a sport and a pastime, a show and an empty vaunt among you, a quest for greater riches and more children. It is like the plants that flourish after rain: the husbandman rejoices to see them grow; but then they wither and turn yellow, soon becoming worthless stubble. In the life to come a woeful scourge awaits you — or the forgiveness of God and His pleasure. The life of this world is but a vain provision" (Koran 57:20).

Often we find the Kingdom of Man flourishing and we delight in it. However, in time, everything in the Kingdom of Man withers, turns yellow, and decays as it is all transient. The **Dhammapada** says, "It is by oneself that evil is done, by oneself that one is afflicted. It is by oneself that evil is not done, by oneself that one is purified. Purity and impurity are individual matters; no one purifies another" (Dhammapada 12:9). We ourselves choose to walk in the light or remain in the darkness. If we select the light, then we are working to purify ourselves. The **New Testament** says, "For I tell you that many prophets and kings have desired to see those things which ye see, and have not seen *them*; and to hear those things which ye hear, and have not heard *them*" (Luke 10:24). God is talking to us directly: We can consider ourselves among the most fortunate because we have chosen to learn spiritual wisdom now. Many have desired to understand spiritual wisdom, but they could not recognize it; not comprehending it, they gave up seeking it.

Action and reflection almost naturally lead to growth and introspection, because that is the pattern of the inner life. We need to manifest our inner awareness and become One with God. When we are so busy with worldly priorities that we fail to reflect on the messages sent to our hearts, our will is weakened, we do not hear His guidance, and we fail to grow in His light. Failure to take the time to spiritually nourish ourselves means we will grow weak from inner hunger. Our inner light becomes depleted and possibly even extinguished. A wise person thinks and engages in spiritual exercise because the path is difficult and he recognizes the importance of remaining strong and fit. No one, regardless of title, can do the important inner work for another, because reaching Oneness is strictly a solitary matter.

THE GOAL IS ONENESS

Question:

What should be the ultimate goal in the process of spiritual evolution?

Brief Answer:

The only goal is achieving Oneness with God.

from the *Gospel of Thomas*

61. Jesus said, "Two will rest on a couch; one will die, one will live."

Salome said, "Who are you, mister? You have climbed onto my couch and eaten from my table as if you are from someone."

Jesus said to her, "I am the one who comes from what is whole. I was given from the things of my father."

"I am your follower."

"For this reason I say, if one is <whole>, one will be filled with light, but if one is divided, one will be filled with darkness."

Longer Answer:

In the above saving, Jesus is having a discussion with Salome. Ancient Mediterranean people often dined in a reclining position or on a couch. Evidently, this is the middle of an important conversation. Jesus is making the point that even as we are engaged in normal activities such as dining, God is selecting one person and not another. She says Jesus acts "as if you are from someone"; this Jewish idiom means Jesus acts as if He were someone special. She is questioning on whose authority is Jesus addressing such a lofty topic and who is He to offer such a remarkable opinion. He answers that He is from the whole or the Oneness.

The **New Testament** says, "Then shall two be in the field; the one shall be taken, and the other left. Two *women shall* be grinding at the mill; the one shall be taken, and the other left" (Matthew 24:40-41). The **New Testament** also says, "I tell you, in that night there shall be two *men* in one bed; the one shall be taken, and the other shall be left. Two *women* shall be grinding together; the one shall be taken, and the other left. Two *men* shall be in the field; the one shall be taken, and the other left. And they answered and said unto him, Where, Lord? And he said unto them, Wheresoever the body *is*, thither will the eagles be gathered together" (Luke 17:34-37). Grace plays an important role in determining who is chosen to seek and who succeeds on their path. If we reach the destination, then by definition we are among those chosen. At the end of our spiritual path, God will positively acknowledge us. The **Koran** says, "Thus, if he is favored, his lot will be repose and plenty, and a garden of delight. If he is one of those on the right hand, he will be greeted with, 'Peace be to you!' by those on the right hand" (Koran 56:77). Another commonly used metaphor in spiritual wisdom is "the right hand" meaning the favored side. When we reach the end of our spiritual journey, God will be well pleased with us.

The **New Testament** says, "Which is his body, the fullness of him that filleth all in all" (Ephesians 1:23). If we are One with God, then we are in the fullness of Him that has filled all. Our role is to follow the examples of the wise masters as they are the experts. The **Dhammapada** says, "The irrigation engineer guides water, the fletcher makes arrows true, the carpenter makes timber straight; the wise master themselves" (Dhammapada 6:5). On the path of spiritual growth and evolution, our job is to master ourselves — that is transcending our egos and desires. The **Hebrew Bible** says, "Behold, God will not cast away a perfect *man*, neither will he help the evildoers" (Job 8:20). God wants us to be spiritually perfected.

The same spiritual wisdom message is repeated with the following poetry:

On this there is this verse:

To what his mind [and] character are attached,
To that attached a man goes with his works.
Whatever deeds he does on earth,
Their rewards he reaps.
From the other world he comes back here, —
To the world of deed and work.

So much for the man of desire.

Now [we come to] the man without desire:

He is devoid of desire,
free from desire;

[all] his desires have been fulfilled;
the SELF [alone] is his desire.
His bodily functions do not depart when he departs this world.
Being very Brahman to Brahman does he go.

On this there is this verse:

When all desires which shelter in the heart
Detach themselves,
then does a mortal man
Become immortal:
to Brahman he wins through.
(Brihadaranyaka Upanishad 4,4:6)

The spiritually advanced person is without worldly desires and has total and unconditional love for God. At the end of the path, we become filled "all in all." In other words, we will be filled with divine consciousness and thus become One with God.

MYSTERIES ARE ONLY FOR THE FAVORED

Question:
Can spiritual wisdom be shared with loved ones?

Brief Answer:
We should not reveal our new wisdom to anyone who is not ready for that knowledge.

from the *Gospel of Thomas*

62. Jesus said, "I disclose my mysteries to those [who are worthy] of [my] mysteries. Do not let your left hand know what your right hand is doing."

Longer Answer:

We should reveal our new spiritual wisdom only to those who are ready and eager to hear it. This caution extends especially to those closest to us because we tend to want to share our inner joy with those for whom we care deeply. The **Upanishad** says:

> The face of truth is hidden
> By the golden vessel [of the sun]:
> That Person yonder in the sun,
> I in truth am He.
> (Isa Upanishad 17)

God obscures His truth until we are ready to appreciate and properly use it because He teaches each of us privately and secretly through our individual experiences with Him. Our inner knowledge is His special and sacred gift to each of us. Therefore, we need to guard it carefully. The **Hebrew Bible** says, "But he said unto her, Thou speakest as one of the foolish women speaketh. What? shall we receive good at the hand of God, and shall we not receive evil? In all this did not Job sin with his lips" (Job 2:10). We must share our inner knowledge only with those who love God totally and will respect and value the sharing. The **New Testament** says, "But when thou doest alms, let not thy left hand know what thy right hand doeth: That thine alms may be in secret: and thy Father which seeth in secret himself shall reward thee openly" (Matthew 6:3-4). When we give to others, our true charity is spiritual wisdom. We must not let those who will mock and ridicule the sacred gift of inner knowledge see it, because spiritual wisdom is given to each of us in secret by God. The **Dhammapada** says, "A wayfarer who does not find anyone better or equal should firmly go alone; there is no companionship with a fool" (Dhammapada 5:2). If we cannot find any seekers of God, then we must not share or reveal our new spiritual wisdom with anyone. The **New Testament** says, "Write the things which thou hast seen, and the things which are, and the things which shall be hereafter; The mystery of the seven stars which thou sawest in my right hand, and the seven golden candlesticks. The seven stars are the angels of the seven churches: and the seven candlesticks which thou sawest are the seven churches" (Revelations 1:19-20).

We can and should study and write about what we have learned. The **Koran** says:

> When that which is coming comes —
> and no soul shall then deny its coming —
> some shall be abased and others exalted.
>
> When the earth shakes and quivers,
> and the mountains crumble away and scatter abroad into fine dust,
> you shall be divided into three multitudes;
> those on the right (blessed shall be those on the right);
> those on the left (damned shall be those on the left);
> and those to the fore (foremost shall be those).
> Such are they that shall be brought near to their Lord
> in the gardens of delight:
> a whole multitude from the men of old,
> but only a few from the latter generations.
> (Koran 56:1)

God's mysteries can only be shared when all parties can appreciate and properly use that increased inner knowledge. However, as they grow, we can share more with them. Our sharing at inappropriate times only confounds them and might even inhibit their spiritual development. Everything has its perfect moment, which is not my time, nor your time, but God's time.

DO NOT WAIT

Question:
Will I have enough time to reach Oneness?

Brief Answer:
God does not want us to waste precious opportunities as each lifetime is a special gift from God and we should not waste a moment of it.

from the *Gospel of Thomas*

63. Jesus said, "There was a rich person who had a great deal of money. He said, 'I shall invest my money so that I may sow, reap, plant, and fill my storehouses with produce, that I may lack nothing.' These were the things he was thinking in his heart, but that very night he died. Whoever has ears should hear."

Longer Answer:

Even if we are spiritually wealthy and believe in our hearts that tomorrow we will invest even more in our quest for Oneness, we may die this very night without ever reaching our goal. We cannot waste one minute. We must try to make all the progress we can in this lifetime right now because we must always seek in the present. Even though we believe in an infinite God, we must not put off spiritual matters for a later time because too many of us get distracted and invest our precious time in the Kingdom of Man. Thus, we delay our spiritual development. For example, we think we will seek inner wisdom when we are more financially secure, or we think this is an activity we can do when we are older or when the children are grown. Thus, we neglect our inner life, we die, and we have wasted a whole lifetime of spiritual growth opportunities.

Such neglect is foolish, for we should remember that spiritual wealth is all that is everlasting. At death our heirs receive our precious worldly wealth and spend it pursuing their desires, while we depart this life without having made the spiritual progress we could and should have. What is gained from our bequest? Spiritual wisdom is true wealth and the time to devote to our inner growth is now. God tells us to seek Oneness with Him as He wants us to be truly rich and blessed. The **Upanishad** says:

Perishable is Nature;
Immortal and imperishable [the SELF]:
Both the perishable and the SELF
Doth the One God Hara rule.
By mediating on Him,
by constant striving,
By becoming what one real is,
The whole world of appearance will once again,
Be lost to sight at last.
(Svetasvatara Upanishad 1:10)

We know that the nature of the physical world is perishable, the SELF is immortal and imperishable, and God rules both the Kingdom of Man and the Kingdom of God. By constant striving, we will become One with God and be fully transcended. This is our true wealth and our only real goal. The **Hebrew Bible** says:

They spend their days in wealth,
and in a moment go down to the grave.

Therefore they say unto God,
Depart from us;
for we desire not the knowledge of thy ways.

What *is* the Almighty,
that we should serve him?
and what profit should we have,
if we pray unto him?

Lo,
their good *is* not in their hand:
the counsel of the wicked is far from me.

How oft is the candle of the wicked put out!
and *how oft* cometh their destruction upon them!
God distributeth sorrows in his anger.

They are as stubble before the wind,
and as chaff that the storm carrieth away.

God layeth up his iniquity for his children:
he rewardeth him,
and he shall know *it.*

His eyes shall see his destruction,
and he shall drink of the wrath of the Almighty.

For what pleasure *hath* he in his house after him,
when the number of his months is cut off in the midst?
(Job 21:13-21)

Spiritual wisdom tells us that we may spend our lives amassing material wealth, but in a moment it is all lost when we go to our grave. What was the point of all of our hard work? God cares nothing for material wealth, so those matters should be of little concern to us. The **Koran** tells us, "Say: 'Had you possessed the treasures of my Lord's mercy, you would have covetously hoarded them. How niggardly is man!'" (Koran 17:100). We should seek only God's love. Similarly, the **Dhammapada** says, "You have now come to the end of your life; you have arrived in the presence of Death. There is no resting place for us on the way, and we have no provisions for the journey" (Dhammapada 18:3). Our "provisions" are spiritual wisdom. If we have gathered no provisions, how can we continue our inner journey into the next life? The **Koran** says, "You shall not barter God's covenant for a trifling price. His reward is better than all your gain, if you but knew it. Your worldly riches are transitory, but God's reward is everlasting" (Koran 16:95). God is constantly offering us His eternal gifts, and we must be gracious enough to accept them. The **New Testament** says:

And he spake a parable unto them,
The ground of a certain rich man brought forth plentifully:

And he thought within himself,
saying,
What shall I do,
because I have no room where to bestow my fruits?

And he said,
This will I do:
I will pull down my barns,
and build greater:
and there will I bestow all my fruits and my goods.

And I will say to my soul,
Soul thou hast much goods laid up for many years;
take thine ease,
eat,
drink,
and be merry.

But God said unto him,
Thou fool,
this night thy soul shall be required of thee:
then whose shall those things be,
which thou hast provided?

So is he that layeth up treasure for himself,
and is not rich toward God.

And he said unto his disciples,
Therefore,
I say unto you,
Take no thought for your life,
what ye shall eat;
neither for the body,
what ye shall put on.

The life is more than meat,
and the body *is more* than raiment.

Consider the ravens:
for they neither sow nor reap;
which neither have storehouse nor barn;
and God feedeth them:
how much more are ye better than the fowls?

And which of you with taking thought can add to his stature one cubit?

If ye then be not able to do that thing which is least,
why take ye thought for the rest?

Consider the lilies how they grow:
they toil not,
they spin not;
and yet I say unto you,
that Solomon in all his glory was not arrayed like one of these.

If then God so clothe the grass,
which is to day in the field,
and to morrow is cast into the oven;
how much more *will he clothe* you,
O ye of little faith?

And seek not ye what ye shall eat,
or what ye shall drink,
neither be ye of doubtful mind.

For all these things do the nations of the world seek after:
and your Father knoweth that ye have need of these things.
(Luke 12:16-30)

This **Gospel of Luke** passage is very similar to the **Gospel of Thomas** passage. Jesus is telling us to have trust and confidence in God. He will provide all that we need.

Bringing Forth the Fruit

◆

AN INVITATION SNUBBED

Question:
Abandoning the pressing matters in life is not easy. How do we proceed?

Brief Answer:
We have been invited into His kingdom and have the free choice to decline His invitation. Nonaction is as clear a message as action.

from the *Gospel of Thomas*

64. Jesus said, "A person was receiving guests. When he had prepared the dinner, he sent his servant to invite the guests.

"The servant went to the first and said to that one, 'My master invites you.'

"That person said, 'Some merchants owe me money; they are coming to me tonight. I must go and give them instructions. Please excuse me from dinner.'

"The servant went to another and said to that one, 'My master has invited you.'

"That person said to the servant, 'I have bought a house and I have been called away for a day. I shall have no time.'

"The servant went to another and said to that one, 'My master invites you.'

"That person said to the servant, 'My friend is to be married and I am to arrange the banquet. I shall not be able to come. Please excuse me from dinner.'

"The servant went to another and said to that one, 'My master invites you.'

"That person said to the servant, 'I have bought an estate and I am going to collect the rent. I shall not be able to come. Please excuse me.'

"The servant returned and said to his master, 'The people whom you invited to dinner have asked to be excused.'

"The master said to his servant, 'Go out on the streets and bring back whomever you find to have dinner.'

"Buyers and merchants [will] not enter the places of my father."

Longer Answer:

Because of God's love for each and everyone of us, He invites us to share everything that is His. However, He fully realizes that we may reject outright or passively decline His offer by our nonaction. He knows that if we are concerned with the material wealth of the Kingdom of Man, including the duties and responsibilities of a family, that we may not accept His invitation. The **Upanishad** says:

> Two birds,
> close-linked companions,
> Cling to the selfsame tree:
> Of these the one eats of the sweet fruit
> The other,
> eating nothing,
> looks on intent.

> On [this] same tree a person [sits] plunged [in grief],
> Mourning his lack of mastery,
> perplexed:
> When he sees the Other,

the Lord rejoicing
In his magnificence,
his sorrow melts away.
(Mundaka Upanishad 3,1:1-2)

God knows that if two are exposed to the same spiritual experiences, one will embrace it wholeheartedly and "eat its sweet fruit" while the other will remain oblivious to it. God also knows that in the initial stages of seeking, our lack of mastery of desire will plague us and the numerous challenges of a spiritual life will perplex us. However, once we start understanding the magnificence of God, our concerns will melt away. If we accept His invitation, what must be done? The **Hebrew Bible** says, "And now, Israel, what doth the Lord thy God require of thee, but to fear the Lord thy God, to walk in all his ways, and to love him, and to serve the Lord thy God with all thy heart and with all thy soul. To keep the commandments of the Lord, and his statutes, which I command thee this day for thy good? (Deuteronomy 10:12-13). We must walk the path God has laid out for each of us.

We must learn to love Him, serve Him, and keep His standards. These are awesome and difficult tasks. For example, surrendering the will of the ego is very difficult. We may surrender it for a while; but when it comes back again, we are required to surrender it again. The **Koran** says, "The true believers are those that have faith in God and His apostle, and never doubt; and who fight with their wealth and their persons for the cause of God. Such are those whose faith is true" (Koran 49:15). We must carefully cultivate our unwavering faith in God and His messengers because we must never allow doubt to enter our minds or our hearts. We must pledge ourselves again and again to His service. The **Hebrew Bible** says:

And the officers shall speak unto the people,
saying,
What man *is there* that hath built a new house,
and hath not dedicated it?
Let him go and return to his house,
lest he die in the battle,
and another man dedicate it.

And what man *is he* that hath planted a vineyard,
and hath not yet eaten of it?
Let him *also* go and return unto his house,
lest he die in the battle,
and another man eat of it.

And what man *is there* that hath betrothed a wife,
and hath not taken her?
Let him go and return unto his house,
lest he die in the battle,
and another man take her.
(Deuteronomy 20:5-7)

Once we agree to His invitation for our inner life, we need to accept the importance of evolving slowly and steadily in spiritual wisdom. According to the **Dhammapada**, "Those who have no accumulation, who eat with perfect knowledge, whose sphere is emptiness, signlessness, and liberation, are hard to track, like birds in the sky" (Dhammapada 7:3). If we attend to our inner search and constantly try to gain in perfect knowledge, we become as liberated as the birds in the sky. If we decline His invitation, the **Koran** says, "On those men We bestowed the Scriptures, wisdom, and prophethood. If these are denied by this generation, We will entrust them to others who will not deny them" (Koran 6:89). If we do not accept the invitation and the gifts of God, others assuredly will and we will have missed our opportunity. The following **Gospel of Matthew** and **Gospel of Luke** provide very parallel passages to the previously cited **Gospel of Thomas**. All three gospels are saying that we should not let the world of business, family, money, or friends divert us from accepting His invitation.

And Jesus answered and spake unto them again by parables,
and said,
The kingdom of heaven is like unto a certain king,
which made a marriage for his son.

And sent forth his servants to call them that were bidden to the wedding;
and they would not come.
Again,
he sent forth other servants,
saying,
Tell them which are bidden,
Behold,
I have prepared my dinner:
my oxen and *my* fatlings *are* killed,
and all things *are* ready:
come unto the marriage.

But they made light of *it,*
and went their ways,
one to his farm,
another to his merchandise:
And the remnant took his servants,
and entreated *them* spitefully,
and slew *them.*
(Matthew 22:1-6)

Then saith he to his servants,
The wedding is ready,
but they which were bidden were not worthy.

Go ye therefore into the highways,
and as many as ye shall find,
bid to the marriage.

So those servants went out into the highways,
and gathered together all as many as they found,
both bad and good:
and the wedding was furnished with guests.
(Matthew 22:8-10)

For many are called, but few *are* chosen.
(Matthew 22:14)

Then said he unto him,
a certain man made a great supper,
and bade many:
And sent his servant at supper time to say to them that were bidden,
Come;
for all things are now ready.

And they all with one *consent* began to make excuse.
The first said unto him,
I have bought a piece of ground,
and I must needs go and see it:
I pray thee have me excused.

And another said,
I have bought five yoke of oxen,
and I go to prove them:
I pray thee have me excused.
And another said,
I have married a wife,
and therefore I cannot come.

So that servant came,
and shewed his lord these things.
Then the master of the house being angry said to his servant,
Go out quickly into the streets and lanes of the city,
and bring in hither the poor,
and the maimed,
and the halt,
and the blind.

And the servant said,
Lord,
it is done as thou hast commanded and yet there is room.

And the lord said unto the servant,
Go out into the highways and hedges,
and compel *them* to come in,
that my house may be filled.

> For I say unto you,
> That none of those men which were bidden shall taste of my supper.
> (Luke 14:3-24)

These lengthy parallel parables explain a great deal about the nature of God's love. He invites us to share everything with Him. However, God's love demands that we respond enthusiastically, that we make our choice with free will, and that we try to be worthy of His gift. If we cannot recognize the importance and significance of His offer, then the offer is rescinded and offered to others. God is willing and wants to give us everything including Oneness, but we must be willing to put aside the desires and priorities of the Kingdom of Man.

DO NOT BE NAIVE

Question:
Are we judged?

Brief Answer:
We are judged every time we are tested.

from the *Gospel of Thomas*

65. He said, "A kind man owned a vineyard, and put it in the hands of cultivators for them to cultivate, so that he might get its produce from them. He sent his slave so that the cultivators might give the produce of the vineyard to the slave. They seized, beat, and all but killed his slave, and the slave went and spoke to its owner. Its owner said, 'Perhaps they did not recognize it (the slave), and he sent another slave. The cultivators beat the other slave. Next the owner sent his son and said, 'Perhaps they will show respect for my son.' Those cultivators, since they recognized that it was he who was heir to the vineyard, seized him and killed him. Whoever has ears should listen!
(See Layton, p. 392.)

Longer Answer:

God is patient, infinitely patient. If we do not respond to His message at this moment, He will try again later. He continues to send His messages well past the time we would tolerate such poor and even improper behavior from others. God has sent prophets, messengers, and teachers like Buddha, Jesus, Muhammad, and many others with his spiritual wisdom. Humankind has not only ignored His messengers, but we have often seized, beaten, and sometimes even killed them. God has infinite patience, but our continuous refusal to accept spiritual wisdom from Him may lead him to conclude that we will not receive His message properly. A common metaphor used in spiritual wisdom to discuss patience is the vineyard. The **Hebrew Bible** says:

> Now will I sing to my well beloved
> a song of my beloved touching his vineyard.
> My well beloved hath a vineyard in a very fruitful hill:

> And he fenced it,
> and gathered out,
> the stones thereof,
> and planted it with the choicest vine,
> and built a tower in the midst of it,
> and also made a winepress therein:
> and he looked that it should bring forth grapes,
> and it brought forth wild grapes.

> And now,
> O inhabitants of Jerusalem,
> and men of Judah,
> judge,
> I pray you,
> betwixt me and my vineyard.

> What could have been done more to my vineyard,
> that I have not done in it?
> wherefore,
> when I looked that it should bring forth grapes,
> brought it forth wild grapes?

And now go to;
I will tell you what I will do to my vineyard:
I will take away the hedge thereof,
and it shall be eaten up;
and break down the wall thereof,
and it shall be trodden down:

And I will lay it waste:
it shall not be pruned,
nor digged;
but there shall come up briers and thorns:
I will also command the clouds that they rain no rain upon it.

For the vineyard of the Lord of hosts *is* the house of Israel,
and the men of Judah his pleasant plant:
and he looked for judgment,
but behold oppression;
for righteousness,
but behold a cry.
(Isaiah 5:1-7)

The vineyard represents all humankind. God cares greatly for His vineyard and wants the fruit of His vineyard to be sweet and plentiful. He knows that adversity, oppression, and suffering test our faith and our resolve. He does everything He can to give us strength and consolation to transcend these experiences in order for us to grow in His light. In spite of His best efforts, some of us will remain wild and arrogant. For most of us, our greatest challenge is to respond positively to His cultivation. God wants us to start the process of enlightenment by learning spiritual wisdom. The **Diamond Sutra** says:

"Subhuti, someone might fill innumerable worlds with the seven treasures and give all away in gifts of alms, but if any good man or any good woman awakens the thought of enlightenment and takes even only four lines from this discourse, reciting, using, receiving, retaining, and spreading them abroad and explaining them for the benefit of others, it will be far more meritorious.

"Now in what manner may he explain them to others? By detachment from appearances — abiding in real truth. So I tell you:
Thus shall ye think of all this fleeting world:
A star at dawn,
a bubble in a stream;
A flash of lightning in a summer cloud,
A flickering lamp,
a phantom,
and a dream."
When Buddha finished this discourse the venerable Subhuti, together with the *bhikshus, bhikshunis,* lay brothers and sisters, and the whole
realms of gods, men, and titans, were filled with joy by his teaching, and
taking it sincerely to heart they went their way. (The Diamond Sutra 32)

However, spiritual wisdom is not always what we might think. The
Upanishad says:

"Put this piece of salt in the water and come to me tomorrow morning."
[Svetaketu] did as he was told.
[Then his father] said to him:
"[Do you remember] that piece of salt
you put in the water yesterday evening?
Would you be good enough to bring it here?"
He groped for it but could not find it.
It had completely dissolved.
"Would you please sip it at this end?
What is it like?"
he said.
"Salt."
"Sip it in the middle.
What is it like?"
"Salt."
"Throw it away,
and then come to me."
He did as he was told;
but [that did not stop the salt from] remaining ever the same.
[His father] said to him:
"My dear child,
it is true that you cannot perceive Being here,

but it is equally true that it is here.
This finest essence,
— the whole universe has it as its SELF:
That is the Real:
That is the SELF:
That you are,
Svetaketu!"
(Chandogya Upanishad 6,13:1-3)

This simple scientific experiment demonstrates that something can physically exist and at the same time be beyond our normal perception, just as God's ways exist beyond our senses' ability to perceive their meaning. We may not see Him or hear Him or be able to reach out and touch Him, yet a seeker's entire being knows Him and knows His presence. The **Koran** says, "We know too well that what they say grieves you. It is not you that they are disbelieving; the evil-doers deny God's own revelations. Other apostles have been denied before you. But they patiently bore with disbelief and persecution until Our help came down to them: for none can change the decrees of God. You have already heard of those apostles" (Koran 6:33). God knows when we have reached the point on our paths at which we can hear His invitation; He also knows that although we can hear Him, many of us will still deny His spiritual wisdom. However, because of His Grace and compassion, He still sends additional invitations for us to hear His spiritual wisdom. God has sent His massagers time after time. The continuing question is, "When will we not only hear but respond appropriately?" Although God is infinitely patient, there comes a point when our inaction clearly means the refusal of His invitation.

The parable is repeated by the **New Testament** as follows:

Hear another parable:
There was a certain householder,
which planted a vineyard,
and hedged it round about,
and digged a winepress in it,
and built a tower,
and let it out to husbandmen,
and went into a far country:

And when the time of the fruit drew near,
he sent his servants to the husbandmen,
that they might receive the fruits of it,
And the husbandmen took his servants,
and beat one,
and killed another,
and stoned another.

Again he sent other servants more than the first:
and they did unto them likewise.

But last of all he sent unto them his son,
saying,
They will revere my son.

But when the husbandmen saw the son,
they said among themselves,
this is the heir;
come,
let us kill him,
and let us seize on his inheritance.

And they caught him,
and cast *him* out of the vineyard,
and slew *him*.

When the lord therefore of the vineyard cometh,
what will he do unto those husbandmen?
(Matthew 21:33-40; similar Luke 20:9-16)

God planted His vineyard. The ripened fruit are those that have accepted
His spiritual wisdom and have become enlightened. He sent His agents, messengers, and even His son to collect His fruit. Fortunately, God has infinite
persistence; but that does not mean that we are not accountable for our decisions. Karmic judgment applies to each of us; and for all of our actions, there
will be a reactions. Thus, there are always individual consequences, due to
our previous actions, which according to some traditions, can even follow us

from one incarnation to another. These consequences can be determining factors in the path we are on and the speed at which we travel down it.

GOD'S CHOICE AND NOT OURS

Question:
Does God ask us to do the impossible?

Brief Answer:
What God is asking may seem impossible for us, but we can achieve the impossible because of His Grace.

from the *Gospel of Thomas*

66. Jesus said, "Show me the stone that the builders rejected: That is the corner-stone."

Longer Answer:

We can all reject God but only God can select us. We can repeatedly reject God's offer of His Kingdom. However, if we accept God's offer, God alone will enable us to reach enlightenment and eventually Oneness with Him. The **Upanishad** says, "[This SELF] neither increases by good works nor diminishes by evil ones. For it is He who makes him whom He would raise up from these worlds perform good works, and it is He again who makes whom He would drag down perform evil works. He is the guardian of the worlds, sovereign of the worlds, universal Lord. Let a man know: 'He is my SELF.' Let a man know: 'He is my SELF!' " (Kaushitaki Upanishad 3:9). In this context, God determines our fate. The **Bhagavad-Gita** says:

> However evil a man's livelihood may be,
> Let him but worship Me with love and serve no other,

Then shall he be reckoned among the good indeed,
For his resolve is right.
(Bhagavad-Gita 9:30)

At a minimum, God wants love, dedication, and surrender from us. The **Dhammapada** says, "Even the gods praise a mendicant who does not despise what he has gotten, even be it a little, and whose life is pure and free from laziness" (Dhammapada 25:7). Our attitude is critical. A poor but hard-working beggar, who feels no ill will toward others in spite of his condition, is preferred to someone who is surly and ungrateful. The **Koran** says, "It was not in sport that We created the heaven and the earth and all that lies between them. Had it been Our will to find a pastime, We could have found one near at hand" (Koran 21:17). God created the Kingdom of Man and the Kingdom of God for a reason. Although that reason may remain a mystery to us, clearly He gave us choice and our exercising the gift of choice is an important part of His plan.

Another important metaphor in spiritual wisdom is the cornerstone. The **Hebrew Bible** says, "The stone *which* the builders refused is become the head *stone* of the corner" (Psalms 118:22). The **New Testament** refers to scripture quotes as follows: "And have ye not read this scripture: The stone which the builders rejected is become the head of the corner: This was the Lord's doing, and it is marvelous in our eyes?" (Mark 12:10-11; similar Luke 20:17-18). No matter what we think of ourselves or what society thinks of us, we are precious to God. God's values are not based on the same criteria used by humankind. One rejected by the Kingdom of Man can become the centerpiece of the Kingdom of God precisely because that person selected God's values. If we have the will to grow and surrender ourselves to God, He will select us. The **New Testament** makes the same comment as follows:

Jesus saith unto them,
did ye never read in the scriptures,
The stone which the builders rejected,
the same is become the head of the corner:
this is the Lord's doing,
and it is marvelous in our eyes?

Therefore say I unto you,
The kingdom of God shall be taken from you and given to a nation bringing
forth the fruits thereof.

And whosoever shall fall on this stone shall be broken:
but on whomsoever it shall fall,
it will grind him to powder.
(Matthew 21:42-44)

The **New Testament** also says, "Be it known unto you all, and to all the people of Israel, that by the name of Jesus Christ of Nazareth, whom ye crucified, whom God raised from the dead, *even* by him doth this man stand here before you whole. This is the stone which was set at nought of you builders, which is become the head of the corner" (The Acts 4:10-11). Those in the Kingdom of Man think they can determine if a person is worthy or not, but God alone decides who is worthy. God can take away His gifts from us if we stop using them to grow inwardly. In the above Matthew metaphor, fruit is the object as it was in the vineyard parable. God wants us to try and reach enlightenment and Oneness once we have chosen our path to the Kingdom of God. To remain on our inner path, we need only love and be dedicated to Him. But once on the path, we have the responsibility to mature properly as His ripe fruit. That means using His gifts wisely to continue our journey.

Spiritual wisdom helps us to mature. For example, Jesus was a model of spiritual wisdom who freely elected His choice. Although many of His people rejected Him, he matured and reached Oneness with God. God made Jesus a cornerstone of His kingdom. For those who grow weary and stumble walking their paths, Jesus remains a model of how to reach full maturity. The **New Testament** says, "Wherefore also it is contained in the scripture, Behold, I lay in Sion a chief corner stone, elect, precious: and he that believeth on him shall not be confounded. Unto you therefore which believe *he is* precious: but unto them which be disobedient, the stone which the builders disallowed, the same is made the head of the corner, And a stone of stumbling, and a rock of offense, *even to them* which stumble at the word, being disobedient: whereunto also they were appointed" (Peter 1:6-8). Mankind can reject. Individuals can reject. However, God selects. Mankind and individuals may think they make wise judgments. Yet the very fact that we think we can make such good judgments shows our arrogance and ignorance. God's judgment is based only on our capacity and our merit and not on worldly factors that cloud the temporal mind of humankind.

INNER KNOWLEDGE

Question:
Should we follow the example that Jesus and other messengers have provided?

Brief Answer:
Absolutely, for we need guides to gain complete inner knowledge.

from the *Gospel of Thomas*
67. Jesus said, "If anyone should become acquainted with the entirety and should fall short at all (?), that person falls short of the whole place."
(See Layton, p. 392. The question mark is in the translation.)

Longer Answer:
Inner knowledge is critical. Outer knowledge is centered in the mind and values such earthly attributes as doubt, criticism, suspicion, and divisiveness. In contrast, the **Upanishad** says, "Next the teaching concerning the SELF. The SELF is below, the SELF is above, the SELF is to the west, to the east, to the south, to the north. Truly the SELF is this whole universe. The man who sees and thinks and understands in this way has pleasure in the SELF, plays with the SELF, lies with the SELF and has his joy with the SELF: he becomes an independent sovereign. In all the worlds (and in every state of being) freedom of movement is his. But [all] those who understand [reality] in any way that is different from this, are subjects of another sovereign: their states of being are perishable, and in all the worlds (and states of being) they have no freedom of movement" (Chadogya Upanishad 7,25:2). We discover

inner knowledge in the heart from the SELF. It values such divine attributes as unconditional love, forgiveness, unselfishness, trust, faith, and enjoying other people, ideas, and nature. Inner knowledge is always building a larger synthesis and awareness of Oneness. How important is this inner knowledge? The **New Testament** says, "For what shall it profit a man, if he shall gain the whole world, and lose his own soul?" (Mark 8:36; similar Luke 9:25).

In the Kingdom of God, concern and compassion for others is essential. The **New Testament** also says, "And though I have *the gift of* prophecy, and understand all mysteries, and all knowledge; and though I have all faith, so that I could remove mountains, and have not charity, I am nothing" (Corinthians 1,13:2). If we have all the spiritual knowledge of enlightenment, without a concern for others we are nothing. Compassion and unselfishness are paramount to inner growth. The **Koran** says, "You are called upon to give in the cause of God. Some among you are ungenerous; yet whoever is ungenerous to this cause is ungenerous to himself. Indeed, God does not need you, but you need Him. If you pay no heed, He will replace you by others who shall bear no resemblance to yourselves" (Koran 47:38). Although we might have great insight and spiritual wisdom, we must always use it for God's purposes. Our generosity is not just of material things, but it is also a generosity of spirit, kindness, concern, and love.

Inner knowledge cannot exist within an ego. The **Diamond Sutra** quotes the Buddha as saying, "Subhuti, all the bodhisattva heroes should discipline their thoughts as follows: All living creatures of whatever class, born from eggs, from wombs, from moisture, or by transformation, whether with form or without form, whether in a state of thinking or exempt from thought necessity, or wholly beyond all thought realms — all these are caused by me to attain unbounded liberation nirvana. Yet when vast, uncountable, immeasurable numbers of beings have thus been liberated, verily no being has been liberated. Why is this, Subhuti? It is because no bodhisattva who is a real bodhisattva cherishes the idea of an ego entity, a personality, a being, or a separated individuality" (The Diamond Sutra 3). Enlightened persons of spiritual wisdom can never cherish or value their ego, their separate individuality, or a personality that is distinctive from the whole. Enlightened persons know they are One with God. Enlightened persons discern that all individual accomplishments are not the result of the sole effort of the individual but are the result of God's Grace in conjunction with our sincere effort. Thus, we can claim every victory as our own because it is God's victory, and conversely we suffer every indignity and injustice to humanity as our own because it is God's loss. Inner knowledge is of the heart. The **Hebrew Bible** says:

> *That which is* crooked cannot be made straight:
> and that which is wanting cannot be numbered.
>
> I communed with mine own heart,
> saying,
> Lo,
> I am come to great estate,
> they that have been before me in Jerusalem:
> yea,
> my heart had great experience of wisdom and knowledge.
>
> And I gave my heart to know wisdom,
> and to know madness and folly:
> I perceived that this also is vexation of spirit,
>
> For in much wisdom *is* much grief:
> and he that increaseth knowledge increaseth sorrow.
> (Ecclesiastes 1:15-18)

Outer knowledge is divisive and limited. Inner knowledge is inclusive and infinite. Quietly, privately, and patiently, we are taught inner knowledge. With that inner knowledge, we reach the highest consciousness—Oneness with God. Without knowing the SELF, we have missed the entirety.

SUFFERING TEACHES THE HEART

Question:

Does suffering really help us spiritually?

Brief Answer:

Suffering can help us make progress, because we often grow in our inner knowledge through circumstances of adversity.

from the *Gospel of Thomas*

68. Jesus said, "Blessed are you whenever they hated you and persecuted you. And wherever they have persecuted you, they will find no place." (See Layton, p. 392.)

Longer Answer:

Experiencing hatred and persecution can be a valuable experience if we gain inner knowledge and grow spiritually from that event. The **New Testament** says, "Blessed *are ye* that hunger now: for ye shall be filled. Blessed *are ye* that weep now: for ye shall laugh" (Luke 6:21). A story about Buddha may help in understanding this statement. An anguished woman once asked Buddha to restore the life of her son. He did not say he would or would not. Instead, he told her to go to her village and find one household that death had not visited. She did as she was told and failed to find one household that death had not visited. She then understood. The **Koran** says, "We shall test your steadfastness with fear and famine, with loss of property and life and crops. Give good news to those who endure with fortitude; who in adversity say: 'We belong to God, and to Him we shall return.' On such men will be God's blessing and mercy; such men are rightly guided" (Koran 2:156). The **Koran** also says, "Did you suppose that you would go to Paradise untouched by the suffering which was endured by those before you? Affliction and adversity befell them; and so battered were they that each apostle, and those who shared his faith, cried out: 'When will God's help come?' God's help is ever near" (Koran 2:214). Adversity often helps our spiritual growth because it forces us to delve deep inside ourselves to find strength. In searching within ourselves, we find more than strength; we find the SELF.

However, in order for adversity to be a positive inner experience for us, we must dissociate ourselves from its worldly pain and pleasure. The **Bhagavad-Gita** says:

> By contacts with the world outside
> Give rise to heat and cold,
> pleasure and pain:
> They come and go,
> impermanent;
> Arjuna,
> put up with them!
>
> For wise men there are,
> The same in pleasure as in pain
> Whom these [contacts] leave undaunted:
> Such are conformed to immortality.
> (Bhagavad-Gita 2:14-15)

The outer world gives us only sensations: heat and cold, pleasure and pain. We must train ourselves to not be bewitched by pleasure nor destroyed by pain. In time we learn to see both pleasure and pain as merely experiences that provide us with spiritual lessons. Buddha said, "The Noble Truth of suffering is this: Birth is suffering; aging is suffering; sickness is suffering; death is suffering; sorrow and lamentation, pain, grief and despair are suffering; association with the unpleasant is suffering; dissociation from the pleasant is suffering; not to get what one wants is suffering — in brief, the five aggregates of attachment are suffering" (The First Sermon of the Buddha). In other words, the very nature of the human condition is to suffer in some form from the moment of birth until the instant of our death. To transcend the suffering we must detach ourselves mentally and physically from the results of both pain and pleasure. Through suffering we can gain understanding in our hearts.

One form of suffering is wickedness. The **Hebrew Bible** says, "The wicked in *his* pride doth persecute the poor: let them be taken in the devices that they have imagined. For the wicked boasteth of his heart's desire, and blesseth the covetous, *whom* the Lord abhorreth" (Psalms 10:2-3). We see and experience wickedness in the physical world almost daily because evil exists and we understand it as evil. Through our suffering from it we can gain important lessons of the heart; but unless taken with detachment, those lessons can also spiritually hurt us. The **Dhammapada** says, "'He reviled me; he injured me; he defeated me; he deprived me.' In those who harbor such grudges, hatred never ceases. 'He reviled me; he injured me; he defeated me; he deprived me.' In those who do not harbor such grudges, hatred eventually ceases" (Dhammapada 1:3-4). If we condemn those who hurt us in anger, keep grudges, and feel sorry for our unfortunate condition, then we will never learn the important lessons presented to us. To transcend the tragic effects of suffering, we must detach our minds and hearts from the negative, surrender to the experience, and learn to look always for the positive inner lesson.

Other reasons for suffering are fear, loss, and persecution. The **Hebrew Bible** says, "Because that he remembered not to shew mercy, but persecuted the poor and needy man, that he might even slay the broken in heart" (Psalms 109:16). Lack of compassion is also a form of suffering we can experience and we must understand it as such. By cultivating a loving merciful heart, we can at least conquer one source of pain in our lives. The **Hebrew Bible** says:

> Be merciful unto me,
> O God:
> for man would swallow me up;
> he fighting daily oppresseth me.
>
> Mine enemies would daily swallow *me* up:
> for *they be* many that fight against me,
> O thou most High.
>
> What time I am afraid,
> I will trust in thee.
>
> In God I will praise his word,
> in God I have put my trust;
> I will not fear what flesh can do unto me.
>
> Every day they wrest my words;
> all their thoughts *are* against me for evil.
> (Psalms 56:1-5)

We often see and experience fear but we need to understand it as a potential spiritual lesson because through experiencing fear and overcoming it we can gain another lesson in the heart. The **Koran** says, "Those that fled their homes or were expelled from them and those that suffered persecution for My sake and fought and were slain: I shall forgive them their sins and admit them to gardens watered by running streams, as a reward from God; God holds the richest recompense" (Koran 3:195). Whether or not the loss is ours or someone else's, when we identify with it, we find a positive inner lesson and grow with it. Given the potentially long cycles of birth, death, and being born again, some sort of suffering is an inherent condition of our total human existence. Suffering permits us to learn and grow from seemingly negative experiences just as we grow best from critical commentaries on our performance in a job or at school. If we do not embrace our suffering but instead grow angry because of it, we fail to seize the opportunity to grow spiritually. By realizing that suffering is an inseparable aspect of our physical existence, we can embrace suffering and gain from its lessons.

PERSECUTION AND HUNGER

Question:
Can even persecution help us gain inner knowledge?

Brief Answer:
Yes, if we appreciate and gain from the experience.

from the *Gospel of Thomas*

69. Jesus said, "Fortunate are those who have been persecuted in their hearts: They are the ones who have truly come to know the father. Fortunate are they who are hungry, that the stomach of the person in what may be filled."

Longer Answer:

In the world that Jesus lived, persecution of the heart was common, for He lived in an occupied land where the Roman Empire and its surrogates deliberately broke the will of the people so that they would cooperate with their conquerors. Spiritual wisdom tells us that this type of persecution can help us to grow spiritually but we need to have the correct attitude in order to gain inwardly from such an otherwise devastating experience. The **Upanishad** says, "Again the heart, Your Majesty," said he. "Of all contingent beings, sire, the support is the heart: all contingent beings are established on the heart. The heart it is, sire, that is the highest Brahman. [And] the heart does not forsake the man who, thus knowing, reveres it; all beings flow into him. He becomes a god and goes to the gods" (Brihadaranyaka Upanishad 4,1:7). In order to find the positive inner lesson in these so-called negative experiences, we are required to recognize and understand that this is just another passing experience. We must trust that whatever the challenge we face, God has already given us the capacity to meet it.

We must establish ourselves in the Kingdom of God with the inner knowledge of the heart. The **Hebrew Bible** says, "For he satisfieth the longing soul, and filleth the hungry soul with goodness" (Psalms 107:9). The heart is the essential instrument in transcending the Kingdom of Man. The **Hebrew Bible** says, "Sorrow *is* better than laughter: for by the sadness of the countenance the heart is made better. The heart of the wise *is* in the house of mourning; but the heart of fools *is* in the house of mirth" (Ecclesiastes 7:3-4). Sadness and sorrow can bring us to spiritual growth because they cause us to enter into our inmost being to find strength and answers to our burning questions. The **Dhammapada** says, "Hatreds do not ever cease in this world by hating, but by not hating; this is an eternal truth" (Dhammapada 1:5). Returning hate for hate is an action of the Kingdom of Man, whereas transcending hate is an act of the divine. Only by rising above the destructive forces of anger and hate can we really find the profound peace we seek. The **New Testament** says, "Blessed *are* they which are persecuted for righteousness' sake; for theirs is the kingdom of the heaven" (Matthew 5:10). If we are righteous and others persecute us simply because of our righteousness, then God has given us an important lesson on our path to spiritual maturity.

We must trust in God. The **Koran** says, "But those who were endowed with knowledge said: 'Alas for you! Better is the reward of God for him that has faith and does good works; but none shall attain it save those who have endured with fortitude'" (Koran 28:80). We must have the courage and conviction to live our faith with our deeds and actions. The **Hebrew Bible** says:

Thou tellest my wanderings:
put thou my tears into thy bottle:
are they not in thy book?

When I cry *unto thee*,
then shall mine enemies turn back:
this I know;
for God *is* for me.

In God will I praise *his* word:
in the Lord will I praise *his* word.

In God have I put my trust:
I will not be afraid what man can do unto me.

Thy vows *are* upon me,
O God:
I will render praises unto thee.

For thou hast delivered my soul from death:
wilt not *thou deliver* my feet from falling,
that I may walk before God in the light of the living?
(Psalms 56:8-13)

This passage helps us understand the critical importance of our mental outlook and attitude, especially when we have suffered. We can put our tears into "the bottle" — that is, put away our grief and try to learn the spiritual lesson from the experience. We can be grateful for the new insight, because the gift of the experience has allowed us to further transcend into the Kingdom of God. If we are really hungry for spiritual growth, the Supreme will fill our inner cup with all kinds of experiences, good and bad, joyful and sad. The mind is an important instrument too, but we grow internally from the heart. With the heart we search for meaning, comfort, and understanding. The very act of looking inward is the act of discovery of our inner life.

With the spirit within, the thirst and hunger for a greater inner knowledge awaken and help us transcend the darkness of our ignorance. With persecution of the heart, we are made to cry and turn toward God. We learn to put our implicit trust in Him and He satisfies our souls.

◆

MANIFEST THE SPIRITUAL WISDOM WITHIN US

Question:
What does transcending mean?

Brief Answer:
Transcending is internalizing spiritual wisdom so that it becomes part of us. In that way, we can manifest God in the world we live.

from the *Gospel of Thomas*

70. Jesus said, "If you bring forth what is within you, what you have will save you. If you do not have that within you, what you do not have within you [will] kill you."

Longer Answer:

The ultimate goal is always Oneness. The **Upanishad** says, "Then this deep serenity which, rising up from this body, attains the highest light, reveals itself in its own [true] form; this is the SELF." So said he. "This is the immortal, [this] freedom from fear: this is Brahman. And the name of Brahman is this, — Reality: [and Reality is Truth]" (Chandogya Upanishad 8,3:4). We are always striving to attain the highest light which means the deepest spiritual wisdom. God guides us and reveals to us gradually that His truth is the only true reality. The **Upanishad** also says:

> As oil in sesame,
> as butter in cream,
> As water in river beds,
> as fire between the fire-sticks,
> So is the SELF to be grasped with the self
> [Of him] who by austerity beholds Him in [very] truth, —
> (Svetasvatara Upanishad 1:15)

Spiritual wisdom is all that is God. Therefore, spiritual wisdom cannot be grasped fully without understanding God. The **Hebrew Bible** says, "Yea, the light of the wicked shall be put out, and the spark of his fire shall not shine. The light shall be dark in his tabernacle, and his candle shall be put out with him" (Job 18:5-6). Without spiritual wisdom, we remain in the dark; and the further from God we drift, the weaker our inner light becomes. The **Hebrew Bible** also says, "But the path of the just *is* as the shining light, that shineth more and more unto the perfect day. The way of the wicked *is* as darkness: they know not at what they stumble" (Proverbs 4:18-19). If we are following our own shining path, we should not be afraid because God has taken us as His apprentices to teach us His spiritual wisdom until our final days. Those who choose to stay in the Kingdom of Man are unaware that they have missed anything. When we finally come to embody spiritual wisdom, our actions define our very beings because true enlightenment comes from transcending our earthbound thoughts and desires. The Buddha says:

> As long as my vision of true knowledge was not fully clear in these three aspects, in these twelve ways, regarding the Four Noble Truths, I did not claim to have realized the perfect Enlightenment that is supreme in the world with its gods, with its Maras and Brahmans, in this world with its recluses and brahmans, with its princes and men. But when my vision of true knowledge was fully clear in these three aspects, in these twelve ways, regarding the Four Noble Truths, then I claimed to have realized the perfect Enlightenment that is supreme in the world with its gods, its Maras and Brahmans, in this world with its recluses and brahmans, with its princes and men. And a vision of true knowledge arose in me thus: My heart's deliverance is unassailable. This is the last birth. Now there is no more rebecoming (rebirth). (The First Sermon of the Buddha 12)

We need to understand and try to live spiritual wisdom as we learn it because our apprenticeships in the Kingdom of God will not be complete until it is entirely learned and lived. The **Dhammapada** says, "Let the intelligent one get rid of the impurity of the self gradually, little by little, moment to moment, as a metal worker removes impurity from silver" (Dhammapada 18:5). Our apprenticeships will no doubt continue until God removes all of our limitations and imperfections. Because God must remove them little by little and moment by moment, our patience and diligence are also essential. The **Koran** says, "Who will grant God a generous loan? He will repay him many times over. It is God who enriches and makes poor. To Him you shall return" (Koran 2:245). When we lend God our time, He gives us His spiritual lessons that will allow us eventually to return to Oneness with Him. The **New Testament** says:

> There is nothing from without a man,
> that entering into him can defile him:
> but the things which come out of him,
> those are they that defile the man.

> If any have ears to hear, let him hear.

> And when he was entered into the house from the people,
> his disciples asked him concerning the parable.

> And he saith unto them,
> Are ye so without understanding also?
> Do ye not perceive,
> that whatsoever thing from without entereth into the man,
> *it* cannot defile him;
> Because it entereth not into his heart,
> but into the belly,
> and goeth out into the draught,
> purging all meats?

> And he said,
> That which cometh out of the man,
> that defileth the man.

For from within,
out of the heart of men,
proceed evil thoughts,
adulteries,
fornications,
murders,
Thefts,
covetousness,
wickedness,
deceit,
lasciviousness,
and evil eye,
blasphemy,
pride,
foolishness:
All these evil things come from within,
and defile the man.
(Mark 7:15-23)

Nothing happens to us without purpose because everything is part of God's effort to guide us to the goal of Oneness. However, we can cause ourselves to fail by not living the lessons we learn. With enlightenment, we take the light within us and manifest it through our actions. Jesus warns us that without inner light, we are doomed, because only the awareness of the soul and commitment to the spiritual path will turn us toward the light and give us God's joy. Ignorance of both the soul and the importance of the inner life dooms us to the earthly life with its ultimate desire, pain, and suffering. God tells us eagerly about the highest light where the SELF gives us freedom from fear and confidence in the reality that is called truth. Spiritual wisdom is the path to God and is the shining light that grows brighter with every step. In contrast, those that live in darkness cannot see the path, so they stumble. Spiritual wisdom brings enlightenment because it brings a clarity of vision of the true knowledge. Once enlightenment is reached, reincarnation is no longer necessary and the endless cycle of birth, death, and rebirth is broken. God is gradually ridding us of worldly impurities little by little, patiently, and diligently, like a metalworker removing impurities from silver.

Discerning what is significant is paramount because nothing from outside of us can disturb us if we are centered in our inner existence. We need to be concerned about what exists in our hearts and not what goes on around us, because our worldly thoughts and our desires are what drag us down and prevent us from ever following our paths. We must want to give all that we have to God by giving of ourselves from our hearts.

DO NOT PROCRASTINATE

Question:

Is complete surrender to God overwhelming?

Brief Answer:

Yes, but we can begin immediately and proceed gently and continually, as every moment is a precious opportunity.

from the *Gospel of Thomas*

71. Jesus said, "I shall destroy [this] house, and no one will be able to build it [...]."

Longer Answer:

Procrastination is the thief of time and not recognizing the thief is too often our cruel reality. The **Upanishad** says, "This is the Lord of all. This the omniscient. This is the Inner Controller: This is the source of all, for it is both the origin and the end of contingent beings" (Mandukya Upanishad 6). God is omniscient and He orchestrates everything. The **Hebrew Bible** says, "For I will not contend for ever, neither will I be always wroth: for the spirit should fail before me, and the souls *which* I have made" (Isaiah 57:16). If we procrastinate in following our inner direction, we are wasting God's Grace and therefore wasting God's precious gifts to us. The **Hebrew Bible** also says, "Remember how short my time is: wherefore hast thou made all men in vain?" (Psalms 89:47). Even though we may have many lifetimes and therefore many opportunities, we do not have time to waste because each lifetime is a special gift that we must not squander senselessly.

On our journey through life, our provisions are spiritual wisdom lessons. God equips us with everything we could possibly need for our spiritual journey, but we must decide to take the "equipment" with us and use it. The **Dhammapada** says, "You are now like a withered leaf; the very heralds of Death have come near to you. You stand at the door of departure, but you have no provisions for the journey" (Dhammapada 18:1). If we have not maximized the lessons of our current lifetime, we will be even less equipped for the next one. To delude ourselves into thinking that because we may have many lifetimes we can dilly-dally in this one is the ultimate folly, because each lifetime's progress is contingent upon the amount of progress realized in the previous life experience. Therefore, each lifetime wasted increases our losses exponentially; and conversely, each lifetime of full progress likewise increases our headway exponentially.

The **Dhammapada** also says, "You have now come to the end of your life; you have arrived in the presence of Death. There is no resting place for you on the way, and you have no provisions for the journey" (Dhammapada 18:3). There is no place to rest now or later because the cycle of birth, death, and rebirth is as relentless as the wheel of time. If God generously provides all we need and more for our spiritual journey, we are indeed stupid if we do not take at least what is essential. The **Dhammapada** says, "A man whose mind is obsessed with children and chattels is carried away by death like a sleeping village by a flood. Children are no protection, nor father, for yet kin: there is no refuge in relatives, for one overtaken by death. Realizing the meaning of this, the wise one guarded in conduct should quickly clear the path that goes to nirvana" (Dhammapada 20:15-17). As we walk, march, run along our spiritual paths, the accomplishments, trappings, and desires of the Kingdom of Man become heavy burdens to carry with us, because they weigh us down and slow our pace. We can lighten our load and clear the path for the purpose of reaching the Kingdom of God.

There are serious consequences to procrastination. The **New Testament** says, "In flaming fire taking vengeance on them that know not God, and that obey not the gospel of our Lord Jesus Christ: Who shall be punished with everlasting destruction from the presence of the Lord, and from the glory of his power" (Thessalonians 2,1:8-9). Continual separation from God is the real consequence of postponing our spiritual journey. To many, such a separation does not sound like a serious matter, especially because they have never stepped out of the darkness. How can we can know what we are missing if we have never experienced it? However, some have caught a glimpse of the divine yet still decide to procrastinate a while to enjoy worldly pleasures. To have God's eternal peace, light, joy, and delight attainable and then refuse to even try to achieve them is a tragic loss. The **Koran** says, "Let those who hoard the wealth which God has bestowed on them out of His bounty never think it good for them: it is nothing but evil. The riches they have hoarded shall become their fetters on the Day of Resurrection. It is God who will inherit the heavens and the earth. God is cognizant of all your actions" (Koran 3:180).

God knows our every action; therefore, there is no escaping the consequences of our choices. The **Koran** says, "Rich is the reward of those that obey God. But those that disobey Him — if they possessed all the earth contains, and as much besides, they would gladly offer it for their ransom. Theirs shall be an evil reckoning. Hell shall be their home, a dismal resting-place" (Koran 13:18). The **Koran** also says, "Therefore stand firm in your devotion to the true Faith before that day arrives which none may put off against the will of God. On that day mankind will be parted in two. The unbelievers will answer for their unbelief, while the righteous will make ready for their blissful home: for they know He will of His bounty reward those who have embraced the Faith and done good works. He does not love the unbelievers" (Koran 30:43).

We must be smart and stand firm in our devotion to God because good intentions to seek enlightenment mean nothing if we do not act in a timely manner. The adage "The road to hell is paved with good intentions" is most applicable here because, without our active participation, our extended opportunities will become fewer and fewer. Our individual challenge is to reach enlightenment as quickly as we can, but without second-guessing God and His timetable. We do know that each moment of time is a gift of opportunity that may end abruptly, and therefore we must use each lifetime of opportunity wisely. We must keep nothing in reserve. We must love God totally, and unconditionally seek our enlightenment.

GOD WANTS UNITY, NOT DIVISION

Question:
Will God divide us?

> *Brief Answer:*
> God only wants unity and will not divide us.

from the *Gospel of Thomas*

72. A [person said] to him, "Tell my brothers to divide my father's possessions with me."
    He said to the person, "Mister, who made me a divider?"
    He turned to his disciples and said to them, "I am not a divider, am I?"

Longer Answer:

Spiritual wisdom tells us that God is not a divider but humankind is. The **Upanishad** says, "Now, when people say, 'Sacrifice to this [god], sacrifice to that [god],' — one god after another, they mean this creation of his; for he himself is all the gods" (Brihadaranyaka Upanishad 1,4:6). In trying to comprehend the infinite, we commonly make the mistake of thinking of God as ourselves—finite. For example, the bounded nature of humankind leads us to declare that God exists only for our particular religious group and not for others. By dividing Him like possessive little children, we define God in our human image and in the process easily misunderstand His vastness. He is omnificent, omniscient, omnipresent, and omnipotent. The **Hebrew Bible** says, "Behold, how good and how pleasant *it is* for brethren to dwell together in unity!" (Psalms 133:1). He tells us that we are foolish not to be united, but history tells us that, throughout the centuries, humankind is not known for its wisdom. Spiritual wisdom tells us that giving us the choice between unity and division is part of God's lesson for us. In God's educational process, we are always free to make bad choices, especially if we are determined, because that is part of discerning the meaning of Oneness. The **New Testament** says, "And one of the company said unto him, Master, speak to my brother, that he divide the inheritance with me. And he said unto him, Man, who made me a judge or a divider over you?" (Luke 12:13-

14). However, God will not divide us because He wants Oneness. The **Koran** says:

> Have you heard the story of the two litigants
> who entered his chamber by climbing over the wall?

> When they went in to David and saw that he was alarmed,
> they said:

> "Have no fear.
> We are two litigants,
> one of whom has wronged the other.
> Judge rightly between us and do not be unjust;
> guide us to the right path.

> "My brother here has ninety-nine ewes,
> but I have only one ewe.
> He demanded that I should entrust it to him,
> and got the better of me in the dispute."

> David replied:

> "He has certainly wronged you in seeking to add your ewe to his flock.
> Many partners are unjust to one another;
> but not so those that have faith and do good works,
> and they are few indeed."

> David realized that this was a test for him.

> He sought forgiveness of his Lord and fell down penitently on his knees.

> We forgave him his sin,
> and in the world to come he shall be honored and well received.
> (Koran 38:21-25)

David failed his test, but he immediately recognized his mistake. In the metaphor, the sheep represents the collective humanity. David failed because he tried to guide the two litigants into division. God guides us in His own manner but He does not divide us. With our own free will, He lets us separate ourselves from Him and others. However, God's hand has guided us throughout our many lifetimes toward uniting us with Him and *all* His creation, because God wants Oneness in His whole creation. The **Koran** says, "Apostles! Eat of that which is wholesome, and do good works: I have knowledge of all your actions. Your religion is but one religion, and I am your only Lord: therefore fear me. Yet men have divided themselves into factions, each rejoicing in its own doctrines. Leave them in their error till a time appointed" (Koran 23:51). All who know Him are connected.

Today, our minds see the illusion of division caused by differences in style, dress, custom, tradition, and cultural myths because we have not yet shaken off the mind-set of the Kingdom of Man. When we do, we will hear God's words that we are all One and there is but One. We must seek unity and Oneness with God. Why? Spiritual wisdom provides the answer. The **Dhammapada** says, "Victory breeds hatred; the defeated sleeps in misery. One who has calmed down sleeps in comfort, having given up victory and defeat" (Dhammapada 15:5). In the Kingdom of God, one does not seek victory over another because we understand there can be no winner or loser. There is only God's vast consciousness, and separation is just an illusion because unity is our genuine actuality.

God has had, has now, and will always have just one message: *Oneness*. Everything lives in His Oneness including love, compassion, joy, and light, because they all exist under, and are a part of, the umbrella of His Oneness. God's greatest hope for us is unity, love, sharing, forgiveness, mercy, compassion, and all else that constitutes and brings about our Oneness with Him. The path to God Himself is Oneness because we are all connected and unified. Because the mind is often not developed by the heart, it sees the illusion of difference, just as some of us see a glass as half full of water and others see it as half empty. In contrast, God wants us to seek out harmony and unity and replace estrangement and hostility with the vision of wholeness. Our cognizance of total interdependence and thus our Oneness with all His creation is most important because by acknowledging all differences as merely important contributions to the whole we extend our hand to others in Oneness. Accepting another's truth only affirms our own truth even if, at first impression, such an approbation appears to be an inconsistency. The differences need to be perceived as merely contributions to the larger whole, just as a blend of spices create a wonderful soup.

GOD'S WORK REQUIRES HELPERS

Question:
Is unity a large undertaking?

Brief Answer:
Yes, and God wants our active participation

from the *Gospel of Thomas*

73. Jesus said, "The harvest is plentiful but the workers are few. So plead with the lord to dispatch workers for the harvest."
(See Layton, p. 393.)

Longer Answer:
The challenge of achieving Oneness with God is huge. The **Bhagavad-Gita** says:

> In works done and works undone
> On earth what interest has He?
> What interest in all contingent beings?
> On none of them does he depend.

> And so, detached, perform unceasingly
> The works that must be done
> For the man detached who labours on,
> To the Highest must win through.

> For only by working on (karma) did Janaka
> And his like attain perfection.
> Or if again for the welfare of the world thou carest,
> Then shouldst thou work [and act].

> For whatever the noblest does,
> That too will others do:

The standard that he sets
All the world will follow.
(Bhagavad-Gita 3:18-21)

Certainly, God is not dependent on us. Why should God be concerned with any of us? Yet, spiritual wisdom tells us that we are all precious to Him. He created each of us. Like an artist, He will not be finished with us until we are perfect in His sight. He has labored long over each of us and He knows us each intimately. He wants us to succeed, and He knows if we labor enough that we will reach Oneness. If we care about Oneness in the world as God does, then we should be His helpers. If we use His standard, others will follow and our efforts will cascade.

Seekers need to be God's helpers. The **Koran** says, "Believers, be God's helpers. When Jesus the son of Mary said to the disciples: 'Who will come with me to the help of God?' the disciples replied: '*We* are God's helpers'" (Koran 61:14). If we hear the call and see what needs to be done, then we need to act decisively. The **New Testament** says, "Therefore said he unto them, The harvest truly *is* great, but the labourers *are* few: pray ye therefore the Lord of the harvest, that he would send forth labourers into his harvest. Go your ways: behold, I send you forth as lambs among wolves" (Luke 10:2-3). We must always be in the Kingdom of God in our hearts and our actions, realizing that those around us may not be. The **Dhammapada** says, "But one who takes refuge in the enlightened, the teaching, and the community, sees the four noble truths with accurate insight: misery, the origin of misery, and the overcoming of misery; and the noble eightfold path that leads to cessation of misery" (Dhammapada 14:12-13). We may face difficult challenges, including many opposing forces in our efforts to manifest God's Oneness, but we can take refuge in our spiritual wisdom.

Jesus is a model for us. The **New Testament** says, "But when He saw the multitudes, he was moved with compassion on them, because they fainted, and were scattered abroad, as sheep having no shepherd. Then saith he unto his disciples, The harvest truly *is* plenteous, but the labourers *are* few; Pray ye therefore the Lord of the harvest, that he will send forth labourers into his harvest" (Matthew 9:36-38). We must also perceive that all of humanity is God's creation, and their situations and sufferings must always move us with compassion. The **Hebrew Bible** says, "Behold, I will send for many fishers, saith the Lord, and they shall fish them; and after will I send for many hunters, and they shall hunt them from every mountain, and from every hill, and out of the holes of the rocks" (Jeremiah 16:16). We should pray for His assistance when the odds seem against us. God will answer our prayers.

MANY SEEKERS BUT SPIRITUAL WISDOM IS LACKING

Question:

Given so much interest in God, why is spiritual wisdom a topic of such little interest today?

Brief Answer:

Although there are many seekers, manifesting spiritual wisdom is difficult.

from the *Gospel of Thomas*

74. He said, "Master, there are many around the drinking trough, but there is nothing in the well."

Longer Answer:

There are many people who believe in God but have difficulty finding spiritual wisdom. The **Upanishad** says, "Meditation is greater than thought. The earth seems to meditate; atmosphere and sky seem to meditate; the waters and the mountains seem to meditate, as do gods and men. That is why whenever men achieve greatness on earth they may be said to have received their [due] portion of the fruits of meditation. So, while small men are quarrelsome, slanderous gossips, the great may be said to have received their [due] portion of the fruits of meditation. Revere meditation. Whoso reveres meditation as Brahman gains freedom of movement in the whole sphere of meditation, — whoso reveres meditation as Brahman"

(Chandogya Upanishad 7,6:1-2). One way we can receive God's message is through meditation because it stills the mind long enough for us to hear our inner voice and develop our inner knowledge, both of which strengthen us as seekers.

The **Hebrew Bible** says, "The sun shall be no more thy light by day; neither for brightness shall the moon give light unto thee: but the Lord shall be unto thee an everlasting light, and thy God thy glory. Thy sun shall no more go down; neither shall thy moon withdraw itself: for the Lord shall be thine everlasting light, and the days of thy mourning shall be ended" (Isaiah 60:19-20). God gives us spiritual wisdom because He is our everlasting source and our means of attaining full realization. The **Dhammapada** says, "The wise, with thorough knowledge of vigilance, enjoy being vigilant and delight in the realm of the noble" (Dhammapada 2:2). Because meditation is a gradual process, gaining spiritual wisdom from it requires vigilant practice. However, the reward of such vigilance and determination is the Kingdom of God itself. The **New Testament** says:

> The woman saith unto him,
> Sir,
> thou hast nothing to draw with,
> and the well is deep:
> from whence then hast thou that living water?
>
> Art thou greater than our father Jacob,
> which gave us the well,
> and drank thereof himself,
> and his children,
> and his cattle?
>
> Jesus answered and said unto her,
> Whosoever drinketh of this water shall thirst again:
> But whosoever drinketh of the water that I shall give him shall never thirst;
> but the water that I shall give him shall be in him a well of water springing into
> everlasting life.
> (John 4:11-14)

Many seekers have a well of tradition from their religion, but this source of spiritual wisdom sometimes lacks depth and can result in leaving them still thirsty. However, if we drink from the true source of spiritual wisdom, which is the entire Word of the Light, then we will never be thirsty again. The **Koran** says:

> But the unbelievers' hearts are blind to all this;
> their deeds are of a different sort,
> and they are bent on doing them.
> But when We visit Our scourge upon those of them that live in comfort,
> they will cry out for help.
> We shall say:
> "Do not howl this day,
> for from Us you shall receive no help.
> My revelations were recited to you many a time,
> but you turned your backs in scorn,
> and passed the nights reviling them."
>
> Should they not heed the Word?
>
> Was anything revealed to them that had not been revealed to their forefathers?
> (Koran 23:63)

Although some will remain blind to the Light, we should not worry about them. Even if they turned their backs in scorn and ranted against spiritual wisdom, God will awaken them and deal with them in His own way at the correct moment for them. We must just concentrate on our own task of inner progress and not become diverted by them. Like the water in a deep well, the essential ingredient of life is deep within us.

GOD ALONE GIVES GUIDANCE

Question:

Does God want us to proselytize and preach to the nonbelievers?

Brief Answer:

No, because God alone gives us His guidance.

from the *Gospel of Thomas*

75. Jesus said, "There are many standing at the door, but those who are alone will enter the wedding chamber."

Longer Answer:

Another common metaphor in spiritual wisdom, the wedding chamber represents a transition point, a new beginning, a major joyous occasion, a new natural stage in evolution. The **Upanishad** says:

> Let a man hear this and understand,
> Let him take hold upon this subtle [God],
> Let him uproot all things of law,
> — rejoice,
> For he has won That in which [alone] he should find joy:
> A house wide open is Naciketas [now],
> I see.
> (Katha Upanishad 2:13)

Although we now know God is subtle, the joy of understanding His spiritual wisdom and wanting to share that joy with others can overwhelm us. In our lives, we perceive a new era has begun for us and in our excitement we often want to uproot the old by opening the minds of others around us. The **Upanishad** says:

> This SELF cannot be won by preaching [Him],
> Not by sacrifice or much more heard;
> By him alone can He be won whom He elects:

To him This SELF reveals his own [true] form.
(Katha Upanishad 2:23)

We know that no one can reach their inner SELF but themselves, but our joy still leads us to want to do what we must not do for others. We should not preach, give offerings including prayers, or make a spectacle of ourselves to convert others. God reveals Himself to each person at the proper time and in the appropriate way for that person. We must remember that God Himself guides each of us and only He can give us or anyone else guidance. The **Hebrew Bible** says, "What man *is* he that feareth the Lord? him shall he teach in the way *that* he shall choose. His soul shall dwell at ease; and his seed shall inherit the earth. The secret of the Lord *is* with them that fear him; and he will shew them his covenant" (Psalms 25:12-14).

Another common metaphor in spiritual wisdom is "fear God." It denotes a true believer or seeker of God. Those seeking to live in the Kingdom of God must not interfere with God's relationship with others. This does not mean that we cannot help others. Just as parents should not interfere with a master teacher's instruction, they can and should assist the teacher at home when asked to do so. We must let God teach each person in His way, not our way. However, if asked, we have an obligation to share what we know, but we are not to force God's Word on anyone. The **Dhammapada** says, "A noble person is hard to find; one is not born everywhere. Wherever such a wise one is born, that family attains felicity. Felicitous is the emergence of the enlightened, felicitous is the teaching of truth. Felicitous is harmony in the community, felicitous the austerity of those in harmony" (Dhammapada 14:15-16). Spiritually advanced seekers are rare and they bring the emergence of their enlightenment. Such people produce a valued harmony but also the associated discipline and dedication. We should respect their accomplishment and their status as special helpers of God because we can learn much from them.

We must carry the responsibility of our own spiritual maturation. The **New Testament** says, "But let every man prove his own work, and then shall he have rejoicing in himself alone, and not in another. For every man shall bear his own burden" (Galatians 6:4-5). We probe and prompt our own spiritual development and find joy in our own spiritual achievements. The **Koran** says, "It is not for you to guide them. God gives guidance to whom He will" (Koran 2:272). The message is clear. We are not to proselytize, coerce, or cajole anyone. The **Koran** says, "Believers, you are accountable for none but yourselves; he that goes astray cannot harm you if you are on the right path. To God you shall all return, and he will declare to you what you have done" (Koran 5:105). We are accountable only for our own spiritual development. The **Gospel of Thomas** agrees and says that many are at the beginning point of spiritual wisdom, but each of them must evolve themselves.

Only an individual as an individual can choose to take the spiritual path to Oneness with the Supreme. Others can assist in terms of suggestions, support, love, and encouragement; but God wants each person to exercise their own free will and grow into enlightenment through their own efforts, using their own capacity. Occasionally, our enthusiasm to share our overwhelming joy of discovery with others we care about is misconstrued as proselytizing. Therefore, we must exercise great care that we only share with sincere seekers who willingly want the knowledge and are ready to receive it. If those conditions are not met, we only create resentment and anger in others, regardless of their relationship to us, and probably do more harm than good. We must allow ourselves to be guided only by God's Grace and not by our feeling of joy at our discovery of His spiritual wisdom.

Join God

GOD'S TREASURE

Question:

What is the best way we can help God develop spiritual wisdom within humankind?

Brief Answer:

The best way is to cultivate it within ourselves.

from the *Gospel of Thomas*

76. Jesus said, "The father's kingdom is like a merchant who had a supply of merchandise and then found a pearl. That merchant was prudent; he sold the merchandise and bought the single pearl for himself. So also with you, seek his treasure that is unfailing, that is enduring, where no moth comes to devour and no worm destroys."

Longer Answer:

We must focus ourselves on what is truly valuable. The **Upanishad** says, "Just as a man, closely embraced by his loving wife, knows nothing without, nothing within, does this 'person,' closely embraced by the SELF that consists of wisdom, know nothing without, nothing within. That is his [true] form in which [all] his desires are fulfilled, in which SELF is his desire, in which he has no desire, no sorrow" (Brihadaranyaka Upanishad 4,3:21). God wants only what is best for each of us. The **Hebrew Bible** says, "My soul, wait thou only upon God; for my expectation *is* from him. He only *is* my rock and my salvation: *he is* my defence; I shall not be moved" (Psalms 62:5-6). We should focus on what God wants for us and follow His guidance. The **Dhammapada** says, "One who was formerly negligent, then later becomes vigilant, lights up the world like an unclouded moon" (Dhammapada 13:6). If a seeker has neglected their spiritual life but now is once again a serious student of inner knowledge, then that student is very likely to gain significant insight because we never lose our spiritual wisdom. However, we can and often do forget it temporarily while we are distracted by worldly desires.

The **New Testament** says, "Lay not up for yourselves treasurers upon earth, where moth and rust doth corrupt, and where thieves break through and steal: But lay up for yourselves treasures in heaven, where neither moth nor rust doth corrupt, and where thieves do not break through nor steal: For where your treasure is, there will your heart be also" (Matthew 6:19-21). We should not worry about materialism but instead concentrate on building spirituality through the heart where the true treasure exists. The **New Testament** says, "Again, the kingdom of heaven is like unto a merchant man, seeking goodly pearls: Who, when he had found one pearl of great price, went and sold all that he had, and bought it" (Matthew 13:45-46). We should not concern ourselves with converting those around as our first priority is to let God build up the treasure within us. The **New Testament** also says, "Sell that ye have, and give alms; provide yourselves bags which wax not old, a treasure in the heavens that faileth not, where no thief approacheth, neither moth corrupteth" (Luke 12:33). No one can take our inner treasure from us.

The **Koran** says, "His light is found in temples which God has sanctioned to be built for the remembrance of His name. In them, morning and evening, His praise is sung by men whom neither trade nor profit can divert from remembering Him, from offering prayers, or from giving alms; who dread the day when men's hearts and eyes shall writhe with anguish; who hope that God will requite them for their noblest deeds and lavish His grace upon them. God gives without measure to whom He will" (Koran 24:37). Out of His love for us God will fan the smallest flame within a person into the fullest spiritual wisdom. Given our orientation to the Kingdom of Man, we mistakenly value that which cannot endure. By appreciating the enduring, unfailing, and valuable gifts of God, we grow to not only appreciate those gifts, but also treasure them for their remarkable worth. Nothing He gives us in our inner life can spoil, rot, or fade away. We must accept His gifts with our heartfelt gratitude. When we do, His gifts multiply. Our desires are fulfilled only in the context of God's wishes. God is without ego, desire, and sorrow; and having Oneness with Him, we share His bounty. God's treasure is absolute and can be ours, too, regardless of our past thoughts and actions.

BECOME EVERYTHING

Question:
Once we begin to evolve spiritually, what happens next?

Brief Answer:
We become One with God.

from the *Gospel of Thomas*

77. Jesus said, "It is I who am the light (that presides) over all. It is I who am the entirety: it is from me that the entirety has come, and to me that the entirety goes. Split a piece of wood: I am there. Lift a stone, and you will find me there." (See Layton, p. 394.)

Longer Answer:

As a role model of living spiritual wisdom, the actions of Jesus point the way and show us what to do and how to conduct our lives. The **Upanishad** says, "He knew that he was [the whole of] the emanation, for he had brought it all forth. Hence he became [all] creation. Whoso thus knows comes to be in that creation of his" (Brihadaranyaka Upanishad 1,4:5). God is the whole of creation. Once we understand that completely, we can also become One with God as Jesus did. The **Hebrew Bible** says:

Whither shall I go from thy spirit?
or whither shall I flee from thy presence?
If I ascend up into heaven,
thou *art* there:
if I make my bed in hell,
behold,
thou *art there*.
If I take the wings of the morning,
and dwell in the uttermost parts of the sea;
Even there shall thy hand lead me,
and thy right hand shall hold me.
If I say,
Surely the darkness shall cover me;
even the night shall be light about me.
Yea,
the darkness hideth not from thee;
but the night shineth as the day:
the darkness and the light *are* both alike *to thee*.
(Psalms 139:7-12)

God is the entirety and more. He is the One, the All. The **New Testament** says, "But to us *there is but* one God, the Father, of whom *are* all things, and we in him; and one Lord Jesus Christ, by whom *are* all things, and we by him" (Corinthians 1,8:6). God's fervent desire is we be One with Him just as Jesus is. God gives us guidance and nurtures us. Every experience in life is also a lesson about the Kingdom of God. The **Dhammapada** says, "I have overcome all, I know all, I am unaffected by all things. Leaving everything behind, having ended craving, I am freed. Having understood on my own, to whom should I attribute it?" (Dhammapada 24:20). We can reach full spiritual wisdom by resisting the desires of the Kingdom of Man and understanding that all our experiences are only lessons for the greater purpose. God is everyplace and knows everything. The **Koran** tells us, "His is all that the heavens and the earth contain. God is the Self-sufficient, the Glorious One" (Koran 22:64). The **Koran** also says:

God knows what every female bears:
He knows of every change within her womb.
For everything He has a finite measure.
He knows the unknown and the manifest.
He is the Supreme One,
the Most High.
It is the same whether you speak in secret or aloud,
whether you hide under the cloak of night
or walk about in the light of day.
Each has guardian angels before him and behind him,
who watch him by God's command.
(Koran 13:7-9)

Nothing is so small or seemingly unimportant that it escapes His notice, because God is infinite and eternal. Each revelation of spiritual wisdom we acquire is directly from God as everything grows from Him. Everyplace we cast our eyes we will see Him. The Supreme is omnipresent, omniscient, and omnipotent. He is everywhere, knows all, and is all. Because Jesus Christ is One with God, He correctly can claim all of the attributes of God. Our challenge with our limited consciousness is to recognize the meaning of Oneness. Possibly the words of the *Martyrdom of Peter 10* can clarify: "You are what is and there is nothing else that is except you alone. You are all and all is in you." (Meyer, p. 98).

THE IGNORANT CANNOT UNDERSTAND THE TRUTH

Question:
Does God fool the ignorant?

Brief Answer:
No. God lets the ignorant fool themselves.

from the *Gospel of Thomas*

78. Jesus said, "Why have you come out to the countryside? To see a reed shaken
by the wind? And to see a person dressed in soft clothes, [like your] rulers and
your powerful ones? They are dressed in soft clothes, and they cannot understand truth."

Longer Answer:

God lets the ignorant be ignorant as that is their free choice; thus, the ignorant doom themselves. For example, by merely leaving the nonseekers in
darkness, God has let them choose and even seal their fate by their own
actions and beliefs. The **Upanishad** says:

"Look at [your]selves in a dish of water,
and report to me anything you do not understand about [your]selves."

So the two of them looked into a dish of water;
and Prajapati said to them:
"What do you see?"

And they said:
"We see all of it,
good sir,
— a self corresponding exactly [to our own bodies] right up the hairs
on our bodies and the finger-nails."

And Prajapati said to them:
"Attire yourselves gorgeously,
put on fine raiment,
adorn yourselves and then look [again] into the dish of water."
And so did they do.

And Prajapati said to them:
"What did you see?"

And they said:
"Just as we ourselves here,
good sir,
are gorgeously attired,

clad in fine raiment and [richly] adorned,
so are they gorgeously attired,
clad in fine raiment and [richly] adorned."

"This is the SELF,"
said he:
"this the immortal,
[this] the free from fear:
this is Brahman."

And the two of them,
their hearts at peace,
went their way.

And Prajapatik gazing after them,
said:
"There they go,
understanding nothing and without having discovered the SELF.
All who hold such a doctrine,
be they gods or demons,
can but go down to defeat."

And Virocana,
his heart at peace,
returned to the demons and preached to them this doctrine:
"Let [one]self be magnified!
Let [one]self be carefully tended!
Whoso magnifies [him]self and carefully tends him]self here and now,
wins the two worlds,
both this one and the next."

That is why even now men say on earth [when they run across] a man who gives
no alms,
has no faith,
and offers no sacrifice:
"Oh!
what a demon!"
for such is the doctrine of the demons.

They deck out the body of the dead with what they have begged,
[adorning it] with clothes and ornaments,
— for that is what they call them, —
thinking that they will win the next world thereby.
(Chandogya Upanishad 8,8:1-5)

God lets the nonseekers and false believers fool themselves with their own character flaws such as vanity, greed, and avarice. The **Hebrew Bible** says, "They that trust in their wealth, and boast themselves in the multitude of their riches; None *of them* can by any means redeem his brother, nor give to God a ransom for him: (For the redemption of their soul *is* precious, and it ceaseth for ever:)" (Psalms 49:6-8). Those that live the worldly consciousness full of ego and desire are left in the darkness of their own making. One reason nonseekers remain ignorant is because they cannot detached themselves from their endless cravings and desires. The **Diamond Sutra** says:

> "Furthermore, Subhuti, in the practice of charity a bodhisattva should be detached. That is to say, he should practice charity without regard to appearances — without regard to sound, odor, touch, flavor, or any quality. Subhuti, thus should the bodhisattva practice charity without attachment. Wherefore? In such a case his merit is incalculable.
> "Subhuti, what do you think? Can you measure all the space extending eastward?"
> "No, World-Honored One, I cannot."
> "Then can you, Subhuti, measure all the space extending southward, westward, northward, or in any other direction, including nadir and zenith?"
> "No, World-Honored One, I cannot."
> "Well, Subhuti, equally incalculable is the merit of the bodhisattva who practices charity without any attachment of appearances. Subhuti, bodhisattvas should persevere one-pointedly in this instruction." (The Diamond Sutra 4)

We must be able to perform the correct action for no other reason than it is the right thing to do, and not because there is some benefit in doing the action nor some punishment for not doing it. To gain spiritual knowledge we need to be detached not only from the actions about us, but also from the values of those actions. The moment we have an expectation of the fruits of our actions, even when those expectations are lofty in nature, we are doomed to frustration and attachment and perhaps resentment. If we approach an act of kindness with the attitude of doing good, we will feel frustrated if the recipients of our action are not grateful enough, or respectful enough, or do not change their behavior in some fashion that is agreeable to us.

Another good example of such values is the outer manifestations of religious ritual and how it influences us. Our actions must come from the heart and sincerity must motivate us. Not even missionary zeal is appropriate. The **Dhammapada** says, "Neither nudism nor matted hair, nor wearing mud nor fasting, nor lying on hard ground, nor dust and dirt, nor squatting motionless will purify a mortal who has not gotten over doubt and desire" (Dhammapada 10:13). Everything from opulant finery to puritan deprivation are creations of our minds and not our hearts. For some, nudism, wearing matted hair, and wearing mud are regarded as great finery, just as much as the most elegant clothes are considered badges of honor that publicly display status and ego.

A sign of spiritual ignorance is an inability to perceive the signs correctly. The **New Testament** says, "And when the messengers of John were departed, he began to speak unto the people concerning John, What went ye out into the wilderness for to see? A reed shaken with the wind? But what went ye out for to see? A man clothed in soft raiment? Behold, they which are gorgeously apparelled, and live delicately, are in kings' courts" (Luke 7:24-25). In any age, there will be those that live in the halls of power with all the trappings of the Kingdom of Man. However, those values make seeing the greatness of the universe beyond their physical world almost impossible. Perhaps the **Koran** explains it best. It says, "Those that desire the life of this world with all its finery shall be rewarded for their deeds in their own lifetime: nothing shall be denied them. These are the men who in the world to come shall have nothing but Hell-fire. Fruitless are their deeds, and vain are all their works" (Koran 11:15). This is the irony of karma.

REMOVE THE FALSE PERCEPTION

Question:

Can we be misdirected?

Brief Answer:

Yes, we certainly can be led astray.

from the *Gospel of Thomas*

79. A woman in the crowd said to him, "Fortunate are the womb that bore you and the breasts that fed you."

He said to [her], "Fortunate are those who have heard the word of the father and have truly kept it. For there will be days when you will say, 'Fortunate are the womb that has not conceived and the beasts that have not given milk.'"

Longer Answer:

To be guided by God, we need to recognize the false values of the Kingdom of Man. The **New Testament** says, "And it came to pass, as he spake these things, a certain woman of the company lifted up her voice, and said unto him, Blessed *is* the womb that bare thee, and the paps which thou hast sucked. But he said, yea rather, blessed are they that hear the word of God, and keep it" (Luke 11:27-28). This woman was thinking in terms of the Kingdom of Man and imposing her worldly value scheme on Jesus' life. He answered her in terms of the Kingdom of God explaining what experiences can really give the most value to a life. The **Upanishad** tells us, "This is what the men of old knew well, [and knowing it,] they had no wish for offspring. 'What should we do with offspring?' [so they said,] 'for we possess this SELF, — this [immortal] state of being.' Rising above their desire for sons, their desire for riches, their desire for [exalted] states of being, they wander forth to lead a beggar's life. For there is no difference between a desire for sons and a desire for riches; and there is no difference between a desire for riches and a desire for [exalted] states of being: all of them are nothing more than desire" (Brihadaranyaka Upanishad 4,4:22). Desire for children, wealth, and high social standing are characteristics of the Kingdom of Man. In contrast, seeking spiritual wisdom is a characteristic of the Kingdom of God.

Avoiding misdirection is difficult, for the realities of the world and its associated values are so dominant in the minds of most. The process of spiritual growth takes so long and there are no shortcuts. The **Hebrew Bible** states, "Also, *that* the soul *be* without knowledge, *it is* not good; and he that hasteth with *his* feet sinneth" (Proverbs 19:2). We must gain our spiritual knowledge slowly and carefully in a deliberate maturation process. If we are only in kindergarten, we cannot understand the lessons of graduate school. Each step must be in the right order for us to fully understand each lesson. The **Dhammapada** says, "When truth is correctly explained, those who follow truth will go beyond the domain of death, which is so hard to cross over" (Dhammapada 6:11).

Over time God speaks to us through many messengers. The **New Testament**, "Verily, verily, I say unto you, He that receiveth whosoever I send receiveth me; and he that receiveth me receiveth him that sent me" (John 13:20). By receiving spiritual wisdom from God's messengers, we are also receiving spiritual wisdom from God Himself. The **Koran** says, "People of the Book! Our apostle has come to reveal to you much of what you have hidden of the Scriptures, and to forgive you much. A light has come to you from God and a glorious Book, with which God will guide to the paths of peace those that seek to please Him; He will lead them by His will from darkness to the light; He will guide them to a straight path" (Koran 5:15).

Our progress can be faster but the individual must decide how fast they wish to travel and if they are ready to learn each lesson. We can be like a marathon runner, we can march, or we can stroll, because the pace of our progress is a function of our own aspiration and our capacity to learn. God has given us many books of spiritual wisdom to teach and inspire us to make inner progress. The **New Testament** says, "For, behold, the days are coming, in the which they shall say, Blessed *are* the barren, and the wombs that never bare, and the paps which never gave suck" (Luke 23:29). Someday we will be able to think completely in terms of the Kingdom of God and realize that true nurturing only comes from God and not from human relationships. We must always recall that we easily misdirect ourselves. For example, Jesus notes we often think that our own birth and motherly nurturing instincts are of supreme importance. However, in our inner reality, they are really nothing compared to the Word of God. Because we live in the Kingdom of Man, we are keenly aware of our own existence and those who physically or emotionally nurture our existence. Not surprisingly, therefore, we often lose our perspective, but through spiritual wisdom, we can comprehend that the Word of God and not a mother's milk is what is truly significant to us.

◆

TRUE PERCEPTION

Question:

If we can see with a true perception on the Kingdom of God, will we discover a greater spiritual wisdom?

Brief Answer:

Yes, the more clearly we can see the more that is revealed to us.

from the *Gospel of Thomas*

80. Jesus said, "Whoever has come to know the world has discovered the body, and whoever has discovered the body, of that person the world is not worthy."

Longer Answer:

Human problems are usually false perspectives built on false values. The **Upanishad** says, "What is commonly called sacrifice is really the chaste life of a student of sacred knowledge, for only by leading such a life can a wise man find the [Brahman-world]" (Chandogya Upanishad 8,5:1). With an earthly perception, we would call a life of discipline a serious sacrifice, even if we understood intellectually that it made learning easier and increased our spiritual wisdom. How can an action be a sacrifice when we benefit greatly from it? The **Hebrew Bible** says, "And the Lord God formed man *of* the dust of the ground, and breathed into his nostrils the breath of life; and man became a living soul" (Genesis 2:7). When God first gave us a soul and the breath of life, He formed us but we had no knowledge. Buddha teaches, "The Noble Truth of the origin of suffering is this: It is this thirst (craving) which produces re-existence and re-becoming, bound up with passionate greed. It finds fresh delight now here and now there, namely, thirst for sense-pleasures; thirst for existence and becoming; and thirst for non-existence (self-annihilation)" (The First Sermon of the Buddha 5).

Because of the values of the Kingdom of Man, we became bound up with its passion and greed. We thirst insatiably for pleasures of the senses and remain fixed on the Kingdom of Man perspective which limits and debilitates us. The **Dhammapada** says, "This body, alas, will soon lie on the ground, without consciousness, abandoned like a useless piece of rotten wood" (Dhammapada 3:8). All worldly things, including our bodies, are temporary and transient. The **New Testament** says, "Ye adulterers and adulteresses, know ye not that the friendship of the world is enmity with God? whosoever therefore will be a friend of the world is the enemy of God" (James 4:4). We should not cultivate these false perceptions because they detain and divert us by being the enemy of God's eternal reality. The **Koran** says, "Their wealth and children shall in no way protect them from God. They are the inmates of the Fire, and there they shall abide for ever" (Koran 58:17). Wealth and children are part of the detraction that leads us to a false perception. The **Koran** says:

> Enjoin believing men to turn their eyes
> away from temptation and to restrain their carnal desires.
> This will make their lives purer.
> God has knowledge of all their actions.
>
> Enjoin believing women to turn their eyes
> away from temptation and to preserve their chastity;
> to cover their adornments (except such as are normally displayed);
> to draw their veils over their bosoms
> and not to reveal their finery except to their husbands,
> their fathers,
> their husbands' fathers,
> their sons,
> their step-sons,
> their brothers,
> their brothers' sons
> their sisters' sons,
> their women-servants,
> and their slave-girls;
> male attendants lacking in natural vigor,
> and children who have no carnal knowledge of women.

And let them not stamp their feet when walking
so as to reveal their hidden trinkets.
(Koran 24:30)

We must always try to discipline the mind to not focus on the temptations of the world. God understands and wants us to have purer lives, although denying our human condition with its worldly flaws is equally wrong. In ignoring our current human realities, we would not be facing the test properly. We need to minimize our limitations by using the mind to fully identify our serious limitations and faults. For example, if we simply do not think about sex outside marriage and do not encourage others to think about sex outside marriage, we will have purer and infinitely better lives. But this does not mean that sex urges do not exist nor that we should deny they exist. Such thinking leads to a false perception and ultimately failure to transcend the physical desire, because simply suppressing our human urges only postpones them. We must do the harder work required to truly transcend the desires before we can defeat them.

DROP THE FETTERS

Question:

Once we understand the implications of these false values, then what should we do?

Brief Answer:

Realize that you are free at last.

from the Gospel of Thomas

81. Jesus said, "Let one who has become wealthy rule, and let one who has power renounce (it)."

Longer Answer:

When we drop our attachments to the world, we are free. The **Upanishad** says,

> What is here conjoined together, —
> Perishable and imperishable,
> Manifest and unmanifest, —
> All this doth the Lord sustain;
> But for lack of mastery the SELF is bound,
> Its [very] nature to enjoy experience:
> [But] once it knows [its] God,
> From all fetters is it freed!
> (Svetasvatara Upanishad 1:8)

God created the infinite and the finite, heaven and earth, the imperishable and perishable, the manifested and the unmanifested, the Kingdom of Man and the Kingdom of God. God sustains all this for us. He waits for us to mature spiritually through experiencing the world as we learn about Him and His Kingdom. As we mature, our false perceptions that result from false values are broken. At last, we are free.

We should not be fooled by the tempting offers of the world and its finite existence. The **Hebrew Bible** says, "Trust not in oppression, and become not vain in robbery: if riches increase, set not your heart *upon them*" (Psalms 62:10). Our daily existence in life includes opposition, contradictions and changes in material fortune. The illusions are powerful and our vanity can distort our vision from seeing past them. The **Dhammapada** says, "Whatever knowledge a fool acquires tends to be harmful; it destroys the fool's virtue, going to his head: He may wish for undeserved honor, precedence among mendicants, rulership among settled populations, and homage among other groups" (Dhammapada 5:13-14). If our knowledge comes to us through false perceptions, then it will harm us by distorting our ability to comprehend and make sound choices and decisions. This may cause us to want unnecessary and perhaps undeserved rewards. The following **New Testament** parable may clarify for us how false perception can mislead a person:

> For *the kingdom of heaven is* as a man travelling into a far country,
> *who* called his own servants,
> and delivered unto them his goods.

And unto one he gave five talents,
to another two,
and to another one;
to every one according to his several ability (sic);
and straightway took his journey.

Then he that had received the five talents went
and traded with the same,
and made *them* other five talents.

And likewise he that *had received* two,
he also gained other two.

But he that had received one went and digged in the earth,
and hid his lord's money.

After a long time the lord of those servants cometh,
and reckoneth with them.

And so he that had received five talents came
and brought other five talents,
saying,
Lord,
thou deliveredst unto me five talents:
behold,
I have gained beside them five talents more.

His lord said unto him,
Well done,
thou good and faithful servant:
thou hast been faithful over a few things,
I will make thee ruler over many things:
enter thou into the joy of thy lord.

He also that received two talents came and said,
Lord,
thou deliveredst unto me two talents:
behold,
I have gained two other talents beside them.

His lord said unto him,
Well done,
good and faithful servant;
thou hast been faithful over a few things,
I will make thee ruler over many things;
enter thou into the joy of thy lord.

Then he which had received the one talent came and said,
Lord,
I knew thee that thou art an (sic) hard man,
reaping where thou hast not sown,
and gathering here thou hast not strawed:
And I was afraid,
and went and hid thy talent in the earth:
lo,
there thou hast *that is* thine.

His lord answered and said unto him,
Thou wicked and slothful servant,
thou knewest that I read where I sowed not,
and gather where I have not strawed:
Thou oughtest therefore to have put my money to the exchangers,
and *then* at my coming
I should have received mine own with usury.

Take therefore the talent from him,
and give *it* unto him which hath ten talents.

For unto every one that hath shall be given,
and he shall have abundance:
but from him that hath not shall be taken away
even that which he hath.

And cast ye the unprofitable servant into outer darkness:
there shall be weeping and gnashing of teeth.
(Matthew 25:14-30)

In this long parable, the metaphor of currency denotes spiritual wisdom. We are to take the spiritual wisdom given us by God and "grow" it within us as much as we possibly can. Our honor and joy is to cherish the gifts of inner knowledge given to us by God. If we are good and faithful students, we will be rewarded proportionately to the growth we have achieved with more spiritual wisdom. Eventually, God will fully enlighten us and we will become One with Him. If we fail to accept the gift that is given us, or we fail to tend it properly to make it grow, then we will lose even the little amount of light we had. In defining a good student, the **New Testament** says, "But [they] have renounced the hidden things of dishonesty, not walking in craftiness, nor handling the word of God deceitfully; but by manifestation of the truth commending ourselves to every man's conscience in the sight of God" (Corinthians 2,4:2). We learn to renounce the false perceptions of the finite world and be childlike in learning the simple lessons from God. Happy and eager to learn more, we are shown how to manifest the spiritual wisdom within ourselves by our actions.

The **Koran** says, "Your wealth and your children are but a temptation. God's reward is great. Therefore fear God with all your hearts, and be attentive, obedient, and charitable. That will be best for you" (Koran 64:15). When we gain spiritual wisdom, we can focus on God in our hearts, become more attentive, and give of ourselves unconditionally to others. True spiritual wealth is not defined in terms of money, possessions, or power but rather in terms of faith in God and the fullness of enlightenment. Real wealth is Oneness with the Supreme. In the **Gospel of Thomas** quote, Jesus recommends that power should be given to the truly wealthy. However, in the context of spiritual wisdom, the truly wealthy are the enlightened ones, because their wealth is Oneness. In recognition that worldly power corrupts, Jesus says that a wise person should renounce that kind of power. This is not saying that we should immediately drop all connections in the world, but only that in terms of our spiritual progress we would make faster progress if we renounce worldly wealth as our goal and as what is important to us.

EMBRACE GOD'S CHALLENGES AND GROW

Question:

Once we are no longer fooled by the false perception of the world, will we have complete spiritual wisdom?

Brief Answer:

No, for now we must embrace His challenges and grow with a clear vision.

from the *Gospel of Thomas*

82. Jesus said, "Whoever is near me is near the fire, and whoever is far from me is far from the kingdom."

Longer Answer:

The more barriers and distance we put between ourselves and God's Word, the further we are from Oneness with God. The **Upanishad** says, "As clouds of smoke surge up in all directions from a fire kindled from damp fuel, so too, I say, was this [whole universe] breathed forth from the great being, — Rig-Veda, Yajur-Veda, Sama-Veda, the Atharva-Veda, [the hymns of] the Angirases, the collections of stories, the ancient tales, wisdom, the secret doctrines, the verses, aphorisms, commentaries and commentaries on commentaries, — all these were breathed forth from It" (Brihadaranyaka Upanishad 2,4:10). God gave us His Word that He would challenge and encourage us to make a conscious choice between accepting or rejecting our spiritual path. The **Hebrew Bible** says:

> And the Lord spake unto you out of the midst of the fire:
> ye heard the voice of the words,
> but saw no similitude; only *ye heard* a voice.

> And he declared unto you his covenant,
> which he commanded you to perform,
> *even* ten commandments;
> and he wrote them upon two tables of stone.

And the Lord commanded me at that time
to teach you statutes and judgments,
that ye might do them in the land whither ye go over to possess it.

Take ye therefore good heed unto yourselves;
for ye saw no manner of similitude on the day
that the Lord spake unto you in Horeb out of the midst of the fire:
(Deuteronomy 4:12-15)

Spiritual wisdom is particularly powerful but also demanding. The **Hebrew Bible** says, "Then I said, I will not make mention of him, nor speak any more in his name. But *his word* was in mine heart as a burning fire shut up on my bones, and I was weary with forebearing, and I could not *stay*" (Jeremiah 20:9). We may try to put God out of our mind, but if God's spiritual wisdom is in our heart, we will still hear Him. The **Hebrew Bible** says, "*Is* not my word like as a fire? saith the Lord; and like a hammer *that* breaketh the rock in pieces?" (Jeremiah 23:29).

God's light opens our minds to see past our false perceptions from the limited Kingdom of Man. The **Dhammapada** says, "Life is easy to live for the shameless, for the impudent, for the spoiler, for the braggart, for the reckless, for the impure. But life is hard to live for the modest always seeking purity, for the independent, for the circumspect, for the seer who lives in purity" (Dhammapada 18:10-11). The Kingdom of God apprenticeship is difficult to complete. The **New Testament** says, "For our God *is* a consuming fire" (Hebrews 12:29). God is constantly confronting us with His lessons and causing us to examine and reflect on our actions, thoughts, and beliefs. The **New Testament** says, "Keep yourselves in the love of God, looking for the mercy of our Lord Jesus Christ unto eternal life. And of some have compassion, making a difference: And others save with fear, pulling *them* out of the fire; hating even the garment spotted by the flesh" (Jude 21-23). We must always remain in the heart, love unconditionally, seek God relentlessly, and have a compassionate heart for all of God's creation. We can gain an inner knowledge even from fear, doubt, and introspection that can help us reject those false perceptions and delusions of the transient physical world that are so difficult to avoid.

The **Koran** says, "Observe the fire which you light. Is it you that create its wood, or We? We have made it a reminder for man, and for the traveller a comfort" (Koran 56:73). As we increase our spiritual knowledge, our lessons become more challenging and more subtle as we move along our paths of life. Like many students who are challenged by their teacher, we may be frustrated and even resent the teacher because of the lessons' discomforts. However, God is the master teacher. The **Koran** says, "Whenever We sent a prophet to a city We afflicted its people with calamities and misfortunes so that they might abase themselves. Then We changed adversity to good fortune, so that in the hour of prosperity they said: 'Our fathers also had their sorrows and their joys.' And in their heedlessness We suddenly smote them" (Koran 7:95). When we comprehend that God has a strategy or plan for each of us, we can regard our so-called calamities and misfortunes as aids that can help us learn and grow.

These lessons are often not easy but they provide us the necessary insights for us to see the truth. The more distance we put between ourselves and God's challenges, the further we are from Oneness with Him. He is our guide. Jesus, Buddha, Mohammed, and others are our beloved messengers. Because Jesus and the others are One with God, they bring His light that illuminates our paths and permits us to grow into His Oneness. Jesus and the others help us to see, grow, and move faster along our paths to the goal of Oneness. In contrast, by distancing ourselves from His messengers, we move further away from God. If we achieve Oneness with the Supreme, then we have also consummate Oneness with Christ and all the others God has sent to communicate His spiritual wisdom to humankind.

———————◆———————

GOD'S TEACHING METHOD

Question:
Is there a method to God's teaching?

Brief Answer:
Yes, there is a very specific method to His teaching.

from the *Gospel of Thomas*

83. Jesus said, "Images are visible to human beings. And the light within these (images) is hidden by the image of the father's light: it will be disclosed. And his image is hidden by his light."
(See Layton, p. 394.)

Longer Answer:

Spiritual wisdom shows us that God has a specific method in teaching His wisdom — revealing His lessons one at a time. The **Upanishad** says, "He who, abiding in light, is other than light, whom light does not know, whose body is light, who controls light from within, — he is the SELF within you, the Inner Controller, the Immortal" (Brihadaranyaka Upanishad 3,7:14). God revels Himself to us by shedding light on all the dark corners of our lives, thus providing flashes of light that illuminate that which we were unable to see before. The SELF is the key that unlocks the spiritual wisdom within us.

The **Upanishad** also tells us, "Never on earth can a man bring back one close to him once he has departed this life so that he can see him. Yet whatever he may long for among the living and the dead, or whatever else he may long for and cannot obtain, all that will he find if he will but go to that [city of Brahman within the heart]; for there it is that his real desires are, [though now they are] covered over with unreality" (Chandogya Upanishad 8,3:1). We will find all that we long for if we go to the spiritual wisdom that is within our own hearts, because God's eternal light will illuminate the darkness and the deceit of the illusion of the "real" or bounded world. The **Hebrew Bible** says:

> They shall be abundantly satisfied with the fatness of thy house;
> and thou shalt make them drink of the river of thy pleasures.
> For with thee *is* the fountain of life:
> in thy light shall we see light.
> O continue thy loving kindness unto them that know thee;
> and thy righteousness to the upright in heart.
> (Psalms 36:8-10)

We are to use our spiritual wisdom to gain more wisdom through our loving hearts as we live out our lives, because God will continue this incremental learning process until we complete our apprenticeship with Him. God's teaching method is to have us learn by internalizing our lessons, because God does not want us to simply know spiritual wisdom. We must also live it, because spiritual wisdom is the image of God. He wants us to attain that wisdom. When we do, our new abilities will permit us to learn even more from our life experiences, because every moment, sight, sound, and thought is an opportunity for us to grasp some new lesson from Him. The **Dhammapada** says, "I have gone through many repeated beginnings seeking without finding the maker of this house; it is miserable to start over again and again" (Dhammapada 11:8). Like having to submit a report repeatedly until we get it right, God's method of teaching is to repeat the assigned lessons until we at long last succeed in piercing the veil of our ignorance.

Spiritual wisdom teaches us that God has a reason for us to experience the physical world before we fully realize the Kingdom of God. Everything has a correct maturation process. No step can be missed or taken out of order. First comes the natural or gross physical so that we can evolve into the spiritual. The **New Testament** says, "But we all, with open face beholding as in a glass the glory of the Lord, are changed into the same image from glory to glory, *even* as by the Spirit of the Lord" (Corinthians 2,3:18). With our increased light, we can see His full wisdom and become merged in His Oneness. The **New Testament** also says, "But if our gospel be hid, it is hid to them that are lost: In whom the god of this world hath blinded the minds of them which believe not, lest the light of the glorious gospel of Christ, who is the image of God, should shine unto them" (Corinthians 2,4:3-4).

Spiritual wisdom is hidden only to those who are lost or remain in the darkness by virtue of their own free choice not to learn. The **Koran** says, "No mortal eyes can see Him, through He sees all eyes. He is benignant and all-knowing" (Koran 6:103). God is all and knows all, but we cannot fully see Him until we have reached Oneness with Him. Although we can not fully comprehend God until we have reached Oneness, we can begin to see His images that are revealed to us through spiritual wisdom. They will eventually lead us to the Oneness we long for and seek. We see His light every day, but our minds prevent our senses from perceiving what is really there. Those who have not progressed along their path to Oneness are as handicapped as any unsighted person, because they have consciously chosen to remain in the darkness. One of God's ironies is that we are all handicapped. We can see only when our hearts cry for Him and He discloses or reveals His gifts of knowledge to us. Because of God's Grace, we are gradually able to remove our handicaps. Our minds see in earthly terms called images, impressions, and scenes. For example, the mind understands divine love and infinite peace in terms of humanity's physical and possessive love and world peace. The mind acts as a filter for interpretation. God reveals Himself to us constantly but in His own way and not in our preconceived way. We must learn to accommodate to God's style and method of teaching. Our challenge is to recognize it, love it, and cherish it.

◆

SLOW LEARNERS

Question:
If we do not learn our spiritual lessons, will God repeat the lessons?

Brief Answer:
Yes, even if it takes many lifetimes, because He wants us to succeed.

from the Gospel of Thomas

84. Jesus said, "When you see your resemblance you are happy. But when you see your images that came into existence before you and are neither mortal nor visible, how much you have to bear!"
(See Layton, p. 395.)

Longer Answer:

There is a maturation process in both our physical and inner development. We must learn each lesson from God in its proper order before we can go on to the next lesson. The **Upanishad** says:

[He said:] "There is indeed another, different [self]: it is known as the 'elemental'; [or 'individual'] self which [really] is affected by the fruits of [his own] works, be they white or black, and who must [ever again] enter into the wombs of good or evil [women], thus ascending or descending [in the order of existence], wandering around at the mercy of [all manner of] dualities.

"Let us define it further. The five 'subtle elements' are classified as bhutas, '[individual contingent] beings,' and the five gross elements are classified under the same head. The combination of the two is called the body. Now, when we speak [of a self as being] 'within the body,' we most certainly mean this '[elemental or] individual self.' Now this [self itself] has [another] *immortal* self which is [unaffected by the body] 'like a drop of water on a lotus petal.' That [other] one, however, is subject to the 'constituents' of Nature.

"Because it is subjected [to them], it becomes confused; and because it is confused, it does not see [that] the Lord God who indwells the SELF [is the sole] cause of agency. Swept away by the currents of Nature's constituents and made turbid by them, unstable, fickle, mutilated, full of desire, restless, it becomes conscious of itself as a separate individual. Thinking, 'This am I, this is mine,' it of its own accord binds [it]self like a bird [entangled] in a net. Accordingly, overcome by the fruits of [its own] works, it must [ever again] enter into the wombs of good and evil [women], thus ascending or descending [in the order of existence], wandering around at the mercy of [all manner of] dualities." (Maitri Upanishad 3:2)

Although we physically exist in the world because to avoid it is impossible, our goal in life should be to make inner progress. Because we have life, we can inwardly learn the lessons of spiritual wisdom, which we should translate into actions that define our lives. In each life, we have a body that we identify with as "our self" that we call it our identity, individuality or personality. It is the part of us influenced by the false perceptions we call our senses, which can and does mislead us into negative choices and slows our progress toward spiritual development. Fortunately, God has also provided us with what the Hindus call SELF and what some others call the Holy Spirit, because only through SELF can we achieve inner progress.

Each time we die, the spiritual wisdom we garnered in that lifetime perishes too and is not transferred to the next life. The **Upanishad** tell us that, "As here on earth the worldly station that is won by work must perish, so too must the [heavenly] state won by merit perish in the next world (Chandogya Upanishad 8,1:6). We cannot take our earthly treasure into our next life. Not surprisingly, we cannot take our heavenly treasures either. The **Hebrew Bible** says, "So God created man in his *own* image, in the image of God created he him: male and female created he them" (Genesis 1:27). We are only mere images of God that need the substance of spiritual wisdom. The **Hebrew Bible** says, "Then Job arose, and rent his mantle, and shaved his head, and fell down upon the ground, and worshipped. And said, Naked came I out of my mother's womb, and naked shall I return thither: the Lord gave, and the Lord hath taken away: blessed be the name of the Lord. In all this Job sinned not, nor charged God foolishly" (Job 1:20-22). Job was correct. In each life, we start with and end with an absolutely clean slate.

Realizing how many times we have failed is difficult for an aspiring seeker, especially because it is discouraging to have to learn the same lessons over and over again. The **Hebrew Bible** says, "As a dream when *one* awaketh; *so* O Lord, when thou awakest, thou shall despise their image. Thus my heart was grieved, and I was pricked in my reins (Psalms 73:20-21). God has blessed us with forgetfulness. We carry with us from lifetime to lifetime only the essence of our learning, but not the specific experiences associated with the lesson. The **Dhammapada** says, "Death carries off someone absorbed in picking flowers, just as a flood sweeps away a sleeping village. Death overpowers one absorbed in picking flowers, before one has attained one's aim" (Dhammapada 4:4-5). What is important is focusing on how much progress we can make in this lifetime, in this body, and in this set of life circumstances.

Often instead of learning our spiritual lessons, we let our earthbound senses distract us and before we realize it, our life is over, we die, and we have wasted a whole lifetime of opportunities in which we could have made spiritual progress. The **Dhammapada** also says, "Just as a tree will regrow even if cut, as long as its root has not been destroyed and is firm, so will this misery regrow again and again as long as the tendency to craving is not rooted out" (Dhammapada 24:5). As long as we keep faith in our covenant with God, we will continue to grow. However, we will experience the same misery again and again unless we are able to transcend our ignorance and move closer to the Kingdom of God.

The **New Testament** says, "And not as Moses, *which* put a veil over his face, that the children of Israel could not stedfastly look to the end of that which is abolished: But their minds were blinded: for until this day remaineth the same veil untaken away in the reading of the old testament; which *veil* is done away in Christ. But even this day, where Moses is read, the veil is upon their heart. Nevertheless when it shall turn to the Lord, the veil shall be taken away" (Corinthians 2,3:13-16). When we reach full realization, the veil of ignorance is removed from our eyes.

God sets our path and all we have to do is walk it. The **New Testament** says, "But let every man prove his own work, and then shall he have rejoicing in himself alone, and not in another. For every man shall bear his own burden" (Galatians 6:4-5). We need not concern ourselves with past lives but only with the matters of this life. The **Koran** says, "The fate of each man We have bound about his neck. On the Day of Resurrection We shall confront him with a book spread wide open, saying: 'Here is your book; read it. Enough for you this day that your own soul should call you to account'" (Koran 17:13). Our karma from past lives carries over to determine our fate in this life. By the choices we make in this lifetime, our next life or lives will be made more or less difficult. The **Koran** says, "No man before you (Muhammad) have We made immortal. If you yourself are doomed to die, will they live for ever? Every soul shall taste death. We will prove you all with evil and good. To Us you shall return" (Koran 21:34). We must not feel sad or happy about the number of times we have repeated the life-death-rebirth cycle, for we are simply given as many opportunities as we need to learn the lesson and proceed.

WE CAN SUCCEED

Question:
If fate is set, can we succeed?

Brief Answer:
We can always succeed.

from the *Gospel of Thomas*

85. Jesus said, "Adam came from great power and great wealth, but he was not worthy of you. For had he been worthy, [he would] not [have tasted] death."

Longer Answer:

The only way to overcome the cycle of being reborn again and again is by building up our inner wealth. The **Upanishad** says, "But Maitreyi said: 'If, sir, this whole earth, filled as it is with riches, were to belong to me, would I be immortal thereby?' 'No,' said Yajnavalkya. 'As is the life of the rich, so would your life be. For there is no hope of immortality in riches'" (Brihadaranyaka Upanishad 2,4:2). As we learned before, earthly wealth is not spiritual wealth. The **Hebrew Bible** says, "And thou say in thine heart, My power and the might of *mine* hand hath gotten me this wealth. But thou shalt remember the Lord thy God: for *it is* he that giveth thee power to get wealth, that he may establish his covenant which he sware unto thy fathers, as *it is* this day" (Deuteronomy 8:17-18). God gives us the power to gain spiritual wealth. We are often quite unaware of how He is moving in and about our lives, as His presence is without sound or form. The **Diamond Sutra** says:

> "Subhuti, what do you think? May the Tathagata be perceived by the thirty-two marks [of a great man]?"
>
> Subhuti answered: "Yes, certainly the Tathagata may be perceived thereby."
>
> Then Buddha said: "Subhuti, if the Tathagata may be perceived by such marks, any great imperial ruler is the same as the Tathagata."
>
> Subhuti then said to Buddha: "World-Honored One, as I understand the meaning of Buddha's words the Tathagata may not be perceived by the thirty-two marks."
>
> Whereupon the World-Honored One uttered this verse:
> "Who sees me by form,
> Who seeks me in sound,
> Perverted are his footsteps upon the way;
> For he cannot perceive the Tathagata."
> (The Diamond Sutra 26)

God's gift to us is unlimited opportunity. The **New Testament** says:

> (For until the law sin was in the world:
> but sin is not imputed when there is no law.
> Nevertheless death reigned from Adam to Moses,
> even over them
> that had not sinned after the similitude of Adam's transgression,
> who is the figure of him that was to come.
> But not as the offense,
> so also *is* the free gift.
> For if through the offence of one many be dead,

much more the grace of God, and the gift by grace,
which is by one man,
Jesus Christ,
hath abounded unto many.
And not as *it was* by one that sinned,
so is the gift:
for the judgment *was* by one to condemnation,
but the free gift *is* of many offenses unto justification.
For if by one man's offence death reigned by one;
much more they which receive abundance of grace
and of the gift of righteousness shall reign in life by one,
Jesus Christ.)

Therefore as by the offence of one *judgment*
came upon all men to condemnation;
even so by the righteousness of one *the free gift*
came upon all men unto justification of life.
(Romans 5:13-18)

God's gifts are Grace and righteousness as demonstrated by His messengers. For example, even the life and death of Jesus are spiritual lessons. Jesus was the first or best fruit of God's harvest. Christ demonstrated what we must do with our lives, including how we must live them. First, we must learn spiritual wisdom and then reach full realization. Next, we must live spiritual wisdom. In this way, we can be God's helper. In this way, we can also be His ideal harvest. Through our many lives we are now maturing as part of God's crop. When the crop is fully mature, God will harvest it and end the cycle of death and rebirth. We must be constantly aware of the challenges, distractions, and temptations that confront us through life. The **Koran** says, "Do they think that, in giving them wealth and children, We are solicitous for their welfare? By no means! They cannot see. Those who walk in fear of their Lord; who believe in the revelations of their Lord; who worship none beside their Lord; who give alms with hearts filled with awe, knowing that they will return to their Lord: These vie with each other for salvation and shall be the first to attain it" (Koran 23:58).

NO PLACE TO REST

Question:

Is there ever a time to rest from the task of learning God's spiritual lessons from life?

Brief Answer:

No. There is no such place or time.

from the *Gospel of Thomas*

86. Jesus said, "[Foxes have] their dens and birds have their nests. But a child of humankind has no place to lay his head and gain repose." (See Layton, p. 395.)

Longer Answer:

The **Bhagavad-Gita** says:

> Not for a moment can a man
> Stand still and do no work;
> For every man is powerless and forced to work
> By the 'constituents' born of Nature.
> (Bhagavad-Gita 3:5)

According to spiritual wisdom, there is no rest for the living. The **Upanishad** says, "This 'person,' on being born and on being embodied, is conjoined with evil things. When he departs and dies he leaves evil things behind" (Brihadaranyaka Upanishad 4,3:8). When we are born, part of the Kingdom of Man is born with us. The good news is that when we die, that impermanent part dies with us because it is an inescapable aspect of the human condition. Our spiritual work, meaning learning and living, is never done. Our spiritual work is the very purpose of our lives. The **Hebrew Bible** says, "For ye are not as yet come to the rest and to the inheritance, which the Lord your God giveth you" (Deuteronomy 12:9). The progress earned from our efforts comes at our rest but not before. The **Hebrew Bible** also says, "Arise ye, and depart; for this *is* not *your* rest: because it is polluted, it shall destroy *you*, even with a sore destruction" (Micah 2:10). Grace touches us in order to begin our spiritual journey, therefore we can embrace the lessons with gusto and enthusiasm so that life's challenges do not become overwhelming. We can celebrate being alive. The **Hebrew Bible** also says, "Unto whom I sware in my wrath that they should not enter into my rest" (Psalms 95:11).

Until we reach our goal of complete Oneness, there is no rest. The **Dhammapada** says, "There is nowhere in the world — not in the sky, nor in the sea, nor in the depths of the earth — where one can escape evil deeds. There is nowhere in the world — not in the sky, nor in the sea, nor in the depths of the earth — where death will not overcome you" (Dhammapada 9:12-13). Because we exist in the finite world, living in a finite human condition, we are constantly subjected to all manner of temptations and diversions. At any moment, we can succumb to them because there is no escaping them; however, we can transcend them. The **Dhammapada** says, "People compelled by fear go to many a refuge — mountains, forests, resorts, trees, and shrines. That is not a safe refuge, that is not the ultimate refuge; one is not freed of all miseries by going to that refuge" (Dhammapada 14:10-11). We may think there is a place of refuge, such as a convent or a monastery. We may even feel we must escape when life is overwhelming, but there is no such place — it is all an illusion. Even if we move to a distant and remote retreat our thoughts and desires will still tempt us.

The **New Testament** says, "And Jesus saith unto him, The foxes have holes, and the birds of the air *have* nests; but the Son of man hath not where to lay *his* head" (Matthew 8:20 and Luke 9:58). There is no place of rest even if we have reached the Kingdom of God, because we are still in the living, finite world. Therefore, we still have to grapple with our human condition. The **Koran** says:

Men,
it is your own souls that you are corrupting.
Take your enjoyment in this life:
to Us you shall in the end return,
and We will declare to you all that you have done.

This present life is like the rich garment
with which the earth adorns itself
when watered by the rain We send down from the sky.

Crops,
sustaining man and beast grow luxuriantly:
but,
as its tenants begin to think themselves its masters,
down comes Our scourge upon it,
by night or in broad day,
laying it waste,
as though it did not blossom but yesterday.
Thus do We make plain Our revelations to thoughtful men.
(Koran 10:23-24)

Why is there no rest for the living? Often we are weak, seek shortcuts that do not exist, and allow ourselves to slip back into the Kingdom of Man, thus corrupting our progress. These are the hard lessons that we all must learn. Because God sends us these rich spiritual lessons called life experiences, we are challenged, sustained, and assisted in our inner growth. Sometimes when our experiences run too smoothly, we start believing that we are self-made or in total control of our own lives, and, because we thus fool ourselves, we stop asking for God's guidance. Whether the lessons are easy or hard, God gives them to us, with His love, for our individual spiritual growth. We must not avoid them, try to circumvent them, or take them for granted. Instead, we must embrace them with our heartfelt gratitude and do our best to recognize and master the lessons, because we cannot escape life's continual challenges. The tests are relentless, happening with or without our active involvement or permission. Our quest for inner growth is always moving forward like a river flowing to the sea, because the moment we stop rowing we are carried away by the force of the river's current. Progress is often slow and the work engages our life forever because the challenges are endless and do not permit us to stand still. Rest can only come when we are One with the Supreme. We are sadly mistaken if we think that we are masters of our lives and in control of our own destiny.

FALSE PATHS TO GOD

Question:

Can inner growth be achieved with and through the physical body?

Brief Answer:

No, we achieve inner growth by transcending the physical.

from the *Gospel of Thomas*

87. Jesus said, "How miserable is the body that depends on a body, and how miserable is the soul that depends on these two."

Longer Answer:

Spiritual wisdom explains there are two false paths: (1) allowing ourselves to be driven by the appetites and desires of the body, and (2) becoming dependent on those appetites and desires experienced through the body. Those paths are false because they both only lead to sorrow and frustration. An example of the first false path is being overly concerned with physical appearances in the worldly lifestyle: fashion, cosmetics, appearances, and entertainment. When we live for our bodies or what we put on our bodies, we are diverting our attention from the real purpose of life — inner growth. The **Upanishad** says, "But Indra, even before he had rejoined the Gods, saw this danger. ['True,' he thought,] 'when this body is gorgeously attired, clad in fine raiment and [richly] adorned, so too will that [SELF] be gorgeously attired, clad in fine raiment and [richly] adorned; but should this [body] be blind or lame or maimed then that [SELF] too will be blind or lame or maimed; and when once this body is destroyed, it too must follow it in its destruction. I see nothing enjoyable in this'" (Chandogya Upanishad 8,9:1). Undue focus on the body leads to vanity and desire for a temporal existence. When the finery fades and the beauty ages, we are left empty and still searching for fulfillment.

Examples of the second false path include addictions that feed our desires, such as money, drugs, sex, gambling, and food. They only feed our temporary physical appetites and desires and create permanent physical dependency without fulfillment or happiness. By definition an appetite recurs at regular intervals and we must continually attend it. Such actions divert people from their inner growth, thus preventing permanent joy and satisfaction. The **Upanishad** also says, "Bountiful one! For sure this body is mortal, held in the grip of death. Yet it is the dwelling-place of the immortal, incorporeal SELF. [And this SELF,] while still in the body, is held in the grip of pleasure and pain; and so long as it remains in the body there is no means of ridding it of pleasure and pain. But once it is freed from the body, pleasure and pain cannot [so much as] touch it" (Chandogya Upanishad 8, 12:1). Although the body is the house of the SELF, it is not a place of rest but rather the place for dynamic action and inner progress for the soul.

We need to consciously seek out our own correct path. The **Hebrew Bible** says, "Treasures of wickedness profit nothing: but righteousness delivereth from death. The Lord will not suffer the soul of the righteous to famish: but he casteth away the substance of the wicked" (Proverbs 10:2-3). Like a good teacher, God rewards His good students with "good grades" but He also gives "bad grades" to those who earned them. In our hearts, we always know the grade we have earned. What makes a good student? Buddha says, "The Noble Truth of the Path leading to the Cessation of suffering is this: It is simply the Noble Eightfold Path, namely right view; right thought; right speech, right action; right livelihood; right effort; right mindfulness; right concentration" (The First Sermon of the Buddha 7). By being good students, we can avoid the false paths.

We have many aids in becoming good students. The Holy Spirit helps us learn and preserve our righteousness, and the soul speaks to and inspires our hearts. Grace from God descends to provide ample opportunities and insights. For example, Jesus, Buddha, Mohammed, and all of God's messengers teach us and help us avoid the pitfalls of the Kingdom of Man. The **New Testament** says, "For if ye live after the flesh, ye shall die: but if ye through the Spirit do mortify the deeds of the body, ye shall live" (Romans 8:13). The SELF teaches us righteousness so that we can exist in the body and not be of the body — in other words: be in the world but not of the world. The **Koran** says, "Restrain yourself, together with those who pray to their Lord morning and evening, seeking His pleasure. Do not turn your eyes away from them in quest of the allurements of this life, nor obey him whose heart We have made heedless of Our remembrance; who follows his appetite and gives a loose rein to his desires" (Koran 18:28). We also can and should take strength from group meditation and prayer. The force of the collective aspiration can easily propel the individual seeker along his or her path.

Warnings

◆

GOD'S MESSENGERS

Question:
What should we look for from God's messengers?

Brief Answer:
We should look for spiritual wisdom, but we also need to return their gifts in kind.

from the *Gospel of Thomas*

88. Jesus said, "The messengers and the prophets are coming to you, and they will give you the things that you possess. And you, too — give them the things that you have, and say among yourselves, 'When are they coming to take their own?'" (See Layton, p. 395.)

Longer Answer:

The messengers and prophets prepare our way to Oneness with God. They illuminate the path so that we can run quickly toward our goal without stumbling and falling. They guide us, inspire us, and catch us when we do fall. The **Diamond Sutra** warns us:

> "Subhuti, do not say that the Tathagata conceives the idea 'I must set forth a teaching.' For if anyone says that the Tathagata sets forth a teaching he really slanders Buddha and is unable to explain what I teach. As to any truth-declaring system, truth is undeclarable; so 'an enunciation of truth' is just the name given to it.'
>
> Thereupon, Subhuti spoke these worlds to Buddha: "World-Honored One, in the ages of the future will there be men coming to hear a declaration of this teaching who will be inspired with belief?"
>
> And Buddha answered: "Subhuti, those to whom you refer are neither living beings nor not-living beings. Wherefore? Because, Subhuti, these 'living beings' are not really such; they are just called by that name." (The Diamond Sutra 21)

Although the messengers and prophets such as Buddha prepare the way for us, they can not declare in words God's full spiritual wisdom, because that is infinite and beyond any bounded language. God's spiritual wisdom can only be fully communicated from the heart of the messenger to the hearts of the seekers. Because people cannot see past the illusions of the Kingdom of Man, they are prevented from being inspired by spiritual wisdom. We can only acquire truth through our own enlightenment. The **New Testament** says, "Many will say to me that day, Lord, Lord, have we not prophesied in thy name? and in thy name have cast out devils? and in thy name done many wonderful works? And then will I profess unto them, I never knew you: depart from me, ye that work iniquity" (Matthew 7:22-23).

In terms of reaching Oneness, God is always looking for seekers. A good teacher appreciates excellent and dedicated students. They sometimes become the "teacher's pet" because such students wish to please the teacher and the teacher appreciates their interest and dedication. However, this situation can be a problem because such students sometimes feel their attention warrants a high grade in spite of the fact that they did not earn the grade. Regardless of the students' attitude, the teacher's goal remains the same for all students, that is, helping the student to learn the necessary lessons. A good teacher awards grades based only on what the students have actually learned contrasted to what the students should have learned. The **Koran** says, "We have sent you only to proclaim good news and to give warning. Say: 'I demand of you no recompense for this. Let him who will take the right path to his Lord'" (Koran 25:57).

Saying 88 asks what will the messengers and prophets take from us that is theirs? The **Koran** says, "Mankind were once one nation. Then God sent forth prophets to give them good news and to warn them, and with these He sent down the Book with the Truth, that it might judge the disputes of men. (None disputed it save those to whom it was given, and that was through envy of one another, after veritable signs had been vouchsafed them.) So God guides by His will those who believed in the truth which had been disputed. God guides whom He will to a straight path" (Koran 2:213). We need to give the messengers back our Oneness, our unconditional love, and to cease our fragmentation and divisiveness.

Why has God allowed division to exist, especially among his believers? "They say: 'Why does he not bring us a sign from his Lord? Have they not been given sufficient proof in previous scriptures?' Had We destroyed them before his (Muhammad's) coming they would have said: 'Lord, if only You had sent us an apostle! We would have followed Your revelations before we were humbled and disgraced.' Say: 'All are waiting: so wait if you will. You shall know who has followed the right path and who has been rightly guided'" (Koran 20:131-135). God has waited and cried for us to mature enough to realize that our Oneness must be our loving gift back to Him and to His messengers and prophets.

What else can we give to the messengers and prophets of God? We can also give up our ignorance. The **Hebrew Bible** says, "Behold, I will send my messenger, and he shall prepare the way before me; and the Lord, whom ye seek, shall suddenly come to his temple, even the messenger of the covenant, whom ye delight in: behold, he shall come, saith the Lord of hosts" (Malachi 3:1). The **New Testament** says, "But what went ye out for to see? A prophet? yea, I say unto you, and more than a prophet. For this is *he*, of whom it is written, Behold, I send my messenger before thy face, which shall prepare thy way before thee" (Matthew 11:9-10).

Prophets and messengers have three purposes: giving good news, warning people, and transmitting spiritual wisdom. The **Upanishad** says, "When one has faith, then one thinks. No one thinks until he has faith. Only by having faith does one think. So [you] should really want to understand faith" (Chandogya Upanishad 7,19). To understand faith and its importance, the **Bhagavad-Gita** says:

> For,
> so sustained by sacrifice,
> the gods
> Will give you the food of your desire.
> Whoso enjoys their gift,
> yet gives nothing [in return],
> Is a thief,
> no more nor less.
> (Bhagavad-Gita 3:12)

According to our ever-growing capacity, we must return His gifts in kind or we are thieves. If we enjoy those gifts, we must return the good news, warning, and spiritual wisdom by passing it on to others. To do otherwise, we are hoarding God's gifts which are really meant for all of us. In our ignorance, many of us fail to recognize them, learn from them, and act according to what we might learn from God's messengers. We should embrace and embody what they offer us: true knowledge and eternal Oneness with God. In return, we should give up our ignorance, limitations, and bondage to the Kingdom of Man. This exchange should be a mutual act constituting and reflecting our devotion and surrender to God. Appropriately, we should also return God's unconditional love as reflected in the words and deeds of His messengers and prophets, because they have prepared our path to Oneness with Him. They prepare us, guide us, and help us remain steady on our path. They inspire us, give us strength when we are weak, pick us up when we fall, and speak to our hearts so that we can understand His message.

◆

PAY ATTENTION TO THE INSIDE

Question:

Do we need to pay attention to God's messengers?

Brief Answer:

Yes, but we must also pay attention to our inner being.

from the *Gospel of Thomas*

89. Jesus said, "Why do you wash the outside of the cup? Do you not understand that the one who made the inside is also the one who made the outside?"

Longer Answer:

When attempting to gain spiritual wisdom, most people tend to pay inappropriate attention to external matters and insufficient attention to the internal ones. The **Upanishad** says, "What is called Brahman, that is what this space outside a man is; and what that space outside a man is, that is what this space within a man is; and what that space within a man is, that is what this space within the heart is. That is the 'full,' — inactive, undeveloped. Whoso knows this wins good fortune, full inactive, undeveloping" (Chandogya Upanishad 3,12:7). God is everywhere but He especially wants us to develop the space within our own hearts. We can do this through His guidance, but we must make a good effort to do the hard work.

The **Hebrew Bible** says, "The Lord *is* the portion of mine inheritance and of my cup: thou maintainest my lot" (Psalms 16:5). We shall inherit or join Him because Oneness is the true nature of His creation. The **Dhammapada** says, "Those in whom the mind is correctly cultivated in the limbs of perfect enlightenment, who have no attachments and enjoy being free from grasping, and who have stopped all compulsion, attain perfect nirvana here in this world" (Dhammapada 6:14). We develop the space within our hearts through our gradual enlightenment and diligent practice of the discipline of nonattachment.

As humans, we tend to focus on what we look like to others, rather than on what we are like to God. God's eternal relationship is with our souls. He knows us by our inner being and not by the temporary outer appearances of our faces or bodies. The **Dhammapada** says, "What good is matted hair to you, idiot? What good is hide clothing? While your inward state is a tangle, you polish your exterior" (Dhammapada 26:12). We must not be so foolish as to believe that what we wear is important. Our dress only demonstrates how we wish others to perceive us. What is of paramount importance is to make sure our "souls" are "properly attired." That is, we need to make sure our inner light is growing with God's spiritual wisdom.

The **New Testament** says, "Woe unto you, scribes and Pharisees, hypocrites! for ye make clean the outside of the cup and of the platter, but within they are full of extortion and excess. *Thou* blind Pharisee, cleanse first that *which is* within the cup and platter, that the outside of them may be clean also" (Matthew 23:25-26; similar Luke 11:39-41). Our actions reflect our inner state. We must not be hypocritical to God. If we have "dressed" our inner being in peace, spiritual wisdom, and love, then our outer actions will be properly reflected. The **Koran** says, "Do not treat men with scorn, nor walk proudly on the earth: God does not love the arrogant and the vainglorious (sic). Rather let your gait be modest and your voice low: the harshest of voices is the braying of the ass" (Koran 31:18).

Paying attention to appearances and external matters is often easier than developing the inner person. We choose to focus on external matters and to forget about our spiritual growth because it is convenient and easy for us. We see clothes, houses, wealth, sunsets, flowers, other people, but we do not see the beauty within us. Certainly, external matters such as beautiful sunsets or the vastness of the ocean touching the horizon are inspiring. Man is proud of his scientific discoveries, technological advances, and accumulated wealth. Yet our creator also gave us a soul that is infinitely more beautiful and amazing. How many of us notice a noble soul, a compassionate heart, a person who can transcend anger, jealousy, or pride? We take time to dress well, eat well, improve our bodies, enjoy our sports, and engage in our business and politics. Do we take sufficient time to look inward and foster our inner growth? God tells us clearly that there are separate inner and outer lives. God is outside and He is inside us; but we often choose to ignore that space within us. Our only eternal responsibility is to reach enlightenment. In other words, we must focus our attention on matters of the heart and soul.

REST AND REPOSE

Question:
Is this as difficult as it appears?

Brief Answer:
Actually, this is restful work with a gentle teacher.

from the *Gospel of Thomas*
90. Jesus said, "Come to me, for my yoke is easy (to use) and my lordship is mild, and you will find repose for yourselves."
(See Layton, p. 395.)

Longer Answer:
Our apprenticeship in the Kingdom of God is not a hardship at all; rather it is restful and satisfying work. We are encouraged and guided every step of the way along our path by the most gentle and loving teacher. The **Bhagavad-Gita** says:

> Right soon will his SELF be filled with righteousness
> And win eternal rest.
> Arjuna,
> of this be sure:
> None who pays me worship of loyalty and love is ever lost.
> (Bhagavad-Gita 9:31)

In the above, God tells His loyal and devoted helper, Arjuna, that he will not be lost and that he will succeed. God tells all of us the same thing. The **Hebrew Bible** says, "The Lord redeemeth the soul of his servants: and none of them that trust in him shall be desolate" (Psalms 34:22). None that trust in the Lord shall lose. The **Dhammapada** says, "The mendicant who lives in kindness, with clear-minded faith in the teaching of the Enlightened, will go to the state of peace, the bliss where conditioning has ceased" (Dhammapada 25:9). No matter our station in life, God is with us every step of the way. Even beggars will not be lost if they are faithful, loving, and trusting in God.

We will find satisfaction and fulfillment in our spiritual achievements. The **New Testament** says, "Come unto me, all *ye* that labour and are heavy laden, and I will give you rest. Take my yoke upon you, and learn of me; for I am meek and lowly in heart: and ye shall find rest unto your souls. For my yoke *is* easy, and my burden is light" (Matthew 11:28-30). God is a remarkable teacher. The **Koran** says, "We charge no soul with more than it can bear. Our Book records the truth: none shall be wronged" (Koran 23:62). God will not ask us to do more than we can. However, He knows that often we cannot see our own strength and capability because, too often, we sell ourselves short by not even trying. The **Koran** also says, "The life of this world is but a sport and a pastime. He will reward you if you believe in Him and guard yourselves against evil. He does not ask for all your wealth. If He demanded all and strongly pressed you, you would grow niggardly, and this would show your malice" (Koran 47:37). God knows the pace at which we can learn. He will protect us, but He will also challenge us as does any good teacher.

Oneness with God is not a hardship but a sublime joy. Once we surrender our lives, including our actions, to God, He becomes the musician and we become His devoted instrument. As the master musician draws His bow across the well-built violin, the instrument plays the most beautiful music. In a similar manner, He draws His bow across our soul, made strong by our spiritual efforts. The result is celestial music, as the actions of our lives become easier and our accomplishments greater. God wishes each of us to take our remarkable talents and use them to their utmost. However, we must surrender the results of our actions to Him. As His willing instruments, our actions are directed inwardly, our tasks are made easier, and our accomplishments are not ours but His. Thus our actions become our loving gifts to God and no gift to God goes unnoticed or unappreciated.

DIFFICULT TO SEE GOD

Question:
Can we see God?

Brief Answer:
Certainly, since we need only look about us.

from the *Gospel of Thomas*

91. They said to him, "Tell us who you are, so that we may believe in you."
    He said to them, "You are testing the face of heaven and earth, and you have not recognized the one who is in your presence! And you do not recognize how to test this time of crisis."
    (See Layton, p. 396.)

Longer Answer:

As we move closer toward enlightenment, we literally see God everywhere around us. We become more sensitive to and aware of His presence. The **Upanishad** says:

> Know by an awakening It is seized upon by thought,
> And so a man finds immortality:
> By the SELF one valor wins,
> By wisdom immortality.
>
> If one has known [It] here,
> then is there truth;
> If one has here not known [It],
> great is the destruction:
> Discerning It in each single contingent being,
> Wise men,
> departing from this world,
> become immortal.
> (Kena Upanishad 2:4-5)

The increasing spiritual wisdom within awakens us just as God awakened Jacob. The **Hebrew Bible** says:

And Jacob awaked out of his sleep,
and he said,
Surely the Lord is in this place;
and I knew *it* not.

And he was afraid,
and said,
How dreadful *is* this place!
this *is* none other but the house of God,
and this *is* the gate of heaven.

And Jacob rose up early in the morning,
and took the stone that he had put *for* his pillows,
and set it up *for* a pillar,
and poured oil upon the top of it.

And he called the name of that place Beth-el:
but the name of that city *was called* Luz at the first.

And Jacob vowed a vow,
saying,
If God will be with me,
and will keep me in this way that I go,
and will give me bread to eat,
and raiment to put on,
So that I come again to my father's house in peace;
then shall the Lord be my God.

And this stone,
which I have set for a pillar,
shall be God's house:
and of all that thou shalt give me I will surely give the tenth unto thee.
(Genesis 28:16-22)

Because we are limited and flawed human bodies, we understand God primarily in terms of the Kingdom of Man and only secondarily in terms of the Kingdom of God. The **Diamond Sutra** says:

"Subhuti, what do you think? Is the Tathagata to be recognized by some material characteristic?"

"No, World-Honored One; the Tathagata cannot be recognized by any material characteristic. Wherefore? Because the Tathagata has said that material characteristics are not, in fact, material characteristics."

Buddha said: "Subhuti, wheresoever are material characteristics there is delusion; but whoso perceives that all characteristics are in fact no-characteristics, perceives the Tathagata." (The Diamond Sutra 5)

If we think in terms of the Kingdom of Man, our minds filter our understanding in terms of the world's material characteristics. We cannot truly understand God that way. The true image of God is all around us if we know how to look for Him. The **New Testament** says:

> And he said also to the people,
> When ye see a cloud rise out of the west,
> straightway ye say,
> There cometh a shower;
> and so it is.

> And when *ye see* the south wind blow,
> ye say,
> There will be heat;
> and it cometh to pass.

> *Ye* hypocrites,
> ye can discern the face of the sky and of the earth;
> but how is it that ye do not discern this time?

> Yea,
> and why even of yourselves judge ye not what is right?
> (Luke 12:54-57)

If we are so perceptive that we can see and understand signs that forecast the weather, we should also be able to read the everyday signs from God that foretell His presence in our lives. The **New Testament** says:

> Then said they unto him,
> Who art thou?
> And Jesus saith unto them
> Even *the same* that I said unto you from the beginning.

> I have many things to say and to judge of you:
> but he that sent me is true;
> and I speak to the world those things which I have heard of him.

> They understood not that he spake to them of the Father.

Then said Jesus unto them,
When ye have lifted up the Son of man,
then shall ye know that I am *he,*
and *that* I do nothing of myself;
but as my Father hath taught me,
I speak these things.

And he that sent me is with me:
the father halt not left me along;
for I do always those things that please him.
(John 8:25-29)

Some turn their back on God by choosing not to live His message and thus they cannot see Him. The **Koran** says:

We have sent down revelations demonstrating the Truth.
God guides whom He will to a straight path.

They declare:
"'We believe in God and the Apostle and obey."

But no sooner do they utter these words
than some among them turn their backs.
Surely these are no believers.

And when they are called to God and His apostle
that he may judge between them
some turn away.
Had justice been on their side
they would have come to him in all obedience.

Is there a sickness in their hearts,
or are they full of doubt?
Do they fear that God and His apostles may deny them justice?
Surely they are themselves the wrong doers.

But when true believers are called to God and His apostle
that he may pass judgment upon them,
their only apostle that he may pass judgement upon them,
their only reply is:

"We hear and obey."

Such men will surely prosper.
(Koran 24:46)

Their problem is they let doubt cloud their minds. If we cultivate our hearts to become aspiring seekers, He will guide us out of darkness and lift our veils of ignorance.

CONTINUALLY SEEK

Question:

If we continually seek, then will we find Oneness?

Brief Answer:

Yes, but never stop seeking even when you are well along your path towards enlightenment, as there is no end to what you will discover.

from the *Gospel of Thomas*

92. Jesus said, "Seek and you will find. In the past, however, I did not tell you the things about which you asked me then. Now I am willing to tell them, but you are not seeking them."

Longer Answer:

As a good teacher knows that students learn incrementally, God knows we need to evolve slowly and gradually to be able to comprehend the more advanced lessons that will occur at later stages on our spiritual path. The **Upanishad** says:

Understanding is greater than meditation.

For it is with the understanding that one understands the Rig-Veda,
the Yajur-Veda and the Sama-Veda,
the Atharva-Veda and the ancient collections of stories
as fourth and fifth,
grammar,
the funeral rites of the dead,
arithmetic,
divination,
chronometry,
logic,
politics,
the etymological and semantic interpretations of the scriptures,
the way to approach disembodied spirits,
archery,
astronomy,
the art of dealing with snakes,
and the fine arts.

It is with the understanding too that one understands heaven and earth,
wind and space,
water and fire,
gods and men,
beasts and birds,
grasses and trees,
animals right down to worms,
moths and ants,
right and wrong,
truth and falsehood,
good and evil,
pleasant and unpleasant,
food and taste,
this world and the next.

Revere the understanding.

Whoso reveres the understanding as Brahman,
attains to states of being characterized by understanding and wisdom.
He gains freedom of movement in the whole sphere of understanding,
— whoso reveres understanding as Brahman.
(Chandogya Upanishad 7,7)

We need to grow in understanding in order to comprehend the truth. We cannot comprehend God's strategy without understanding "understanding" itself. The **Hebrew Bible** says, "Incline your ear, and come unto me: hear, and your soul shall live; and I will make an everlasting covenant with you, *even* the sure mercies of David" (Isaiah 55:3). As a teacher, God is always assessing our capacity to understand His lessons and determining if we are really making an effort to learn more. Regardless of the length of our apprenticeship, we must always seek to know more, for when we stop seeking, we stop learning.

The **Diamond Sutra** says, "Then Subhuti asked Buddha: 'World-Honored One, in the attainment of the consummation of incomparable enlightenment did Buddha make no acquisition whatsoever?' Buddha replied: 'Just so, Subhuti. Through the consummation of incomparable enlightenment, I acquired not even the least thing; wherefore it is called "consummation of incomparable enlightenment"'" (The Diamond Sutra 22). We do not *acquire* spiritual wisdom. Instead, we complete or perfect our spiritual wisdom. A good teacher wants inquiring students who are always trying to perfect their understanding. The **New Testament** says:

> And I say unto you,
> Ask,
> and it shall be given you;
> seek,
> and ye shall find;
> knock,
> and it shall be opened unto you.
>
> For every one that asketh receiveth;
> and he that seeketh findeth;
> and to him that knocketh it shall be opened.
>
> If a son shall ask bread of any of you that is a father,
> will he give him a stone?
> or if *he ask* a fish,
> will he for a fish give him a serpent?

Or if he shall ask an egg,
will he offer him a scorpion?

If ye then,
being evil,
know how to give good gifts unto your children:
how much more shall *your* heavenly Father give the Holy Spirit to them that ask
him?
(Luke 11:9-13)

God is the perfect teacher. He will not confuse or mislead us with His teachings because He knows when we are or are not ready for some lessons. The **New Testament** also says, "But these things have I told you, that when the time shall come, ye may remember that I told you of them. And these things I said not unto you at the beginning, because I was with you. But now I go my way to him that sent me; and none of you asketh me, Whither goest thou?" (John 16:4-5). We must never stop being inquiring students, because God's knowledge is infinite and therefore so is our learning. The **Koran** says, "Do not be quick to recite the Koran before its revelations are completed, but rather say: 'Lord, increase my knowledge'" (Koran 20:114). As we read this, God has given us not only good news but also a warning. Part of that warning is in the context of God's method in teaching by incremental steps. The **Koran** also says, "People of the Book! Our apostle has come to you with revelations after an interval during which there were no apostles, lest you say: 'No one has come to give us good news or to warn us.' Now someone has come to give you good news and to warn you. God has power over all things" (Koran 5:19).

The **Gospel of Thomas** stresses God's desire for us to seek Him eternally, because learning spiritual wisdom is not merely a single experience or realization. Our only responsibility in life is to seek Oneness, but Oneness includes a knowledge of our own soul and its union with the Supreme. Achieving that goal for each of us takes time, because we must be able to accept and receive the full measure of God's light. As we increasingly receive His light, we are astounded because, no matter how much we thought we were prepared for it, such knowledge is always outside our previous level of awareness. As we change due to that increased understanding, we grow closer to God. With our new inner knowledge, we gain an inner satisfaction that provides comfort and allows us to feel that all is indeed good because this sense of joy surrounds us. Because God grants us this understanding, we need only seek and we will receive it. However, God decides when and even how to reveal His spiritual wisdom. Therefore, we must be patient and not give up on God, as He will never give up on us. We must communicate by listening to Him in our meditations and speaking to Him in our prayers. Because He loves us and His answers reflect the depth of His love for us, we need to be quick to ask and slow to listen to Him. We must always have the patience to let Him increase the knowledge within us in His own time. Once learned in the heart, these lessons give us an even greater ability to understand our relationship with the Supreme, His truth, and even the nature of understanding itself.

GIVE APPROPRIATELY TO OTHERS

Question:
Once we have God's knowledge, what should we do with it?

Brief Answer:
We must never proselytize, but we must give willingly to those who are ready to receive spiritual wisdom.

from the *Gospel of Thomas*

93. "Do not give what is holy to dogs, or they might throw them upon a manure pile. Do not throw pearls [to] swine, or they might . . . it [. . .]."
(Note: The manuscript was damaged here and a full translation was impossible as indicated.)

Longer Answer:
Spiritual wisdom recognizes that not all people are at the same point on their paths to enlightenment. The **Bhagavad-Gita** says:

> Never must thou tell this [Word] to one
> Whose life is not austere,
> to one devoid of love and loyalty,
> To one who refuses to obey,
> Or one who envies Me.
> (Bhagavad-Gita 18:67)

Although sharing spiritual wisdom is important, not all people are ready to receive it. We must never force spiritual wisdom on someone who is not interested in God. Attempting to fill a very small cup with a very large amount of nectar is foolish and wasteful. The **Hebrew Bible** says, "So foolish *was* I, and ignorant: I was as a beast before thee" (Psalms 73:22). If people are content in the Kingdom of Man, they will not be capable of holding or retaining very much. We are wiser to leave them until God has awakened them. Although we should share God's wisdom, we should give it only to those who genuinely want it. The **Dhammapada** says, "Even if a fool associates with someone wise all his life, he will never know the truth, just as a spoon cannot discern the taste of the soup" (Dhammapada 5:5). A person must first know the value of seeking before they can be interested in becoming a seeker. An ignorant person can never know the inner spiritual truth.

The **New Testament** says, "Give not that which is holy unto the dogs, neither cast ye your pearls before swine, lest they trample them under their feet, and turn again and rend you" (Matthew 7:6). There is little point wasting God's precious light until such time as God has guided them to the point that they want to seek His presence. Then we can be a part of God's plan for them.

The **Koran** says,"You cannot make the dead hear you, nor can you make the deaf hear your call when they turn their backs and pay no heed. It is not for you to guide the blind out of their error. None shall hear you except those who believe in Our revelations and surrender themselves to Us" (Koran 27:80). We must have the self-discipline to leave God's work to God. We can help Him the most by helping and encouraging new seekers so that they might grow faster. The **Koran** also says, "Call men to the path of your Lord with wisdom and kindly exhortation. Reason with them in the most courteous manner. Your Lord best knows those who stray from His path and those who are rightly guided" (Koran 16:125). We can use our acquired wisdom and address any seeker with kindness, especially by being nonjudgmental. We can reason, but should never argue, because words rarely change a person's heart or mind. As we are God's helpers, being courteous and accepting are a part of living the Kingdom of God. God knows best and He alone will be their guide just as He is our own guide. The **Diamond Sutra** reflects this point:

> "Subhuti, if anyone should say that Buddha declares any conception of egoity, do you consider he would understand my teaching alright?"
>
> "No, World-Honored One, such a man would not have any sound understanding of the Tathagata's teaching, because the World-Honored One declares that notions of selfhood, personality, entity, and separate individuality, as really existing, are erroneous — these terms are merely figures of speech."
>
> [Thereupon Buddha said:] "Subhuti, those who aspire to the consummation of incomparable enlightenment should recognize and understand all varieties of things in the same way and cut off the arising of [views that are mere] aspects. Subhuti, as regards aspects, the Tathagata declares that in reality they are not such. They are [merely] called "aspects." (The Diamond Sutra 31)

Buddha tells us that we need to see the same truth in many ways, which is why spiritual wisdom uses metaphors, parables, dialogues, and stories. The truth can be told in infinite ways as God is infinite.

◆

WE MUST KNOCK AND WALK IN

Question:

What responsibilities must we assume?

Brief Answer:

We must become responsible for our own inner growth and progress.

from the *Gospel of Thomas*

94. Jesus [said], "One who seeks will find; for [one who knocks] it will be opened."

Longer Answer:

Will power is an important element of spiritual growth. The **Upanishad** says, "On whatever end a man set his heart, whatever [object of] desire he desires, by a mere act of will the same [end and object] rises up before him and, possessed of it, he is [duly] magnified" (Chandogya Upanishad 8,2:10). We must apply will power to the heart with diligence and desire. When we do this we will grow. The **Hebrew Bible** says:

> But if from thence thou shalt seek the Lord thy God,
> thou shalt find *him*,
> if thou seek him with all thy heart and with all thy soul.

> When thou art in tribulation,
> and all these things are come upon thee,
> *even* in the latter days,
> if thou turn to the Lord thy God,
> and shalt be obedient unto his voice:

> (For the Lord thy God *is* a merciful God:)
> he will not forsake thee,
> neither destroy thee,
> nor forget the covenant of thy fathers which he sware unto them
> (Deuteronomy 4:29-31).

We must seek with our hearts as we turn toward God. We must follow His guidance, but we will not be able to hear that guidance without the proper inner knowledge. God will never forsake our quest for spiritual wisdom. The **Dhammapada** says, "Cut off the flow, O priestly one; make effort, dispel desire. Knowing the extinction of conditioning, you know the uncreated" (Dhammapada 26:1). Will power is needed to diminish and eventually eliminate earthly desires, thus releasing us from being their hostage. The goal is Oneness with God and God's righteousness. The **New Testament** says, "But seek ye first the kingdom of God, and his righteousness; and all these things shall be added unto you" (Matthew 6:33). We must first seek the mind-set called the Kingdom of God by kindling the flame of aspiration in our hearts. Then we must seek righteousness. With God's guidance, He will give all the spiritual wisdom we need during our apprenticeship with Him. The **New Testament** also says, "If ye then be risen with Christ, seek those things which are above, where Christ sitteth on the right hand of God. Set your affection on things above, not on things on the earth" (Colossians 3:1-2). If we set our hearts on the rich rewards of the Kingdom of God, then earthly riches pale in importance and even begin to look tacky and tarnished.

Living in the Kingdom of God includes being God's helper. The **Hebrew Bible** says, "And the LORD came, and stood, and called as at other times, 'Samuel, Samuel.' Then Samuel answered, 'Speak, for thy servant heareth'" (Samuel 1,3:10). When we are called to serve God, we should respond eagerly with, "Speak, for your servant is listening. My honor and privilege is to serve you." The **Koran** says, "When My servants question you about Me, tell them that I am near. I answer the prayer of the suppliant when he calls to Me; therefore let them answer My call and put their trust in Me, that they may be rightly guided" (Koran 2:186). If we are questioned by others about God, we must tell them what we know, being truthful about our experiences. God will answer their prayers for spiritual wisdom individually. All they need to do is trust in Him and ask.

We can only be One with the Supreme through God's Grace. But if we seek, God will give us His Grace in abundant measure. However, when the door is opened for us, we must choose to walk through the door and continue on the journey with God as our guide. If we sincerely seek inner knowledge, we will grow inwardly. By our actions, we give an outer voice to our heart's inner cry. In time God will reveal more and more to us. The process continues, and we grow more spiritual as long as we are seeking. The path to Oneness includes our growing in our capacity to understand and know.

GIVE WITHOUT EXPECTATION

Question:

What should we expect in return from those we give that knowledge to?

Brief Answer:

We should never expect anything from anyone except God.

from the *Gospel of Thomas*

95. [Jesus said], "If you have money, do not lend it at interest. Rather, give [it] to someone from whom you will not get it back."

Longer Answer:

In many sacred texts, wealth is often a metaphor for spiritual wisdom for those with the Kingdom of God mind-set. In the metaphor, money becomes a specific aspect of knowledge and the interest on monies is the return on the inner investment. As God's helper, we will likely often be asked about spiritual wisdom. The **Upanishad** says, "Give with faith: do not give without faith. Give with grace: give modestly; give with awe; give conscientiously" (Taittiriya Upanishad 1:11). We should always happily share what knowledge and wisdom God has given us with our faith and His Grace. We should not preach spiritual wisdom, but rather freely share the knowledge with our love and our gratitude to God. If that is done, our sincerity is obvious. The **Hebrew Bible** says, "Ho, every one that thirsteth, come ye to the waters, and he that hath no money; come ye, buy, and eat; yea, come buy wine and milk without money and without price" (Isaiah 55:1). We should give all sincere seekers the nourishment of what we possess. In the Kingdom of God, the medium of exchange is not money but spiritual wisdom. Buddha tells us not to be concerned about achieving merit, as it is only an illusion. The **Diamond Sutra** says:

> "Subhuti, if one bodhisattva bestows in charity sufficient of the seven treasures to fill as many worlds as there be sand grains in the river Ganges, and another, realizing that all things are egoless, attains perfection through patient forbearance, the merit of the latter will far exceed that of the former. Why is this, Subhuti? It is because all bodhisattvas

are insentient as to the rewards of merit."

Then Subhuti said to Buddha: "What is this saying, World- Honored One, that bodhisattvas are insentient as to rewards of merit?"

[And Buddha answered:] "Subhuti, bodhisattvas who achieve merit should not be fettered with desire for rewards. Thus it is said that the rewards of merit are not received." (The Diamond Sutra 28)

Spiritual wisdom gives specific advice for helpers. The **New Testament** says, "Give to him that asketh thee, and from him that would borrow of thee turn not thou away" (Matthew 5:42). Spiritually, we should give to all those who ask and give each of them everything we have. We should not turn any- one away who is a sincere seeker nor try to hide anything that they can grasp. The **New Testament** also says, "Give to every man that asketh of thee; and of him that taketh away thy goods ask *them* not again" (Luke 6:30). The **Koran** says, "If your debtor be in straits, grant him a delay until he can dis- charge his debt; but if you waive the sum as alms it will be better for you, if you but knew it" (Koran 2:280). God gives His wisdom and love uncondi- tionally to us. Therefore, by example, we must also give those gifts uncondi- tionally to others. There is never a profit made by God nor a debt owed Him. Neither should there be one paid to or owed us. The **New Testament** says:

> And if ye lend *to them* of whom ye hope to receive,
> what thank have ye?
> for sinners also lend to sinners,
> to receive as much again.
>
> But love ye your enemies,
> and do good,
> and lend,
> hoping for nothing again;
> and your reward shall be great,
> and ye shall be the children of the Highest:
> for he is kind unto the unthankful and to the evil.
>
> Be ye therefore merciful, as your Father also is merciful.
> (Luke 6:34-36)

We must love all of God's creation and expect nothing from anyone. Through our faith, God provides for us as He inspires our actions. Giving is an integral part of spirituality, but we can only give that which God has given us. In our very temporally oriented world, our minds think of giving money and charity. Instead, we should think of the gifts God has given us and share them with others to complete His circle of Oneness.

THE KINGDOM OF GOD IS GROWING

Question:
If we share unconditionally, will the Kingdom of God grow?

Brief Answer:
Yes, the Kingdom of God grows from every small act of kindness into a kingdom of infinite kindness.

from the *Gospel of Thomas*

96. Jesus [said], "The father's kingdom is like [a] woman. She took a little yeast, [hid] it in dough, and made it into large loaves of bread. Whoever has ears should hear!"

Longer Answer:
Spiritual wisdom tells us that the Kingdom of God depends on each of us individually. Our apprenticeship in the Kingdom of God begins as something tiny and blossoms into something much larger and quite beautiful. The **Upanishad** says:

He who consists of mind, whose body is the breath of life, whose form is light, whose idea is the real, whose self is space, through whom are all works, all desires, all scents, all tastes, who encompasses all this universe, who does not speak and has no care, — he is my SELF within the heart, smaller than a grain of rice or barley-corn, or a mustard-seed, or a grain of millet, or the kernel of a grain of millet; this is my SELF within my heart, greater than the earth, greater than the atmosphere, greater than the sky, greater than all these worlds.

All works, all desires, all scents, all tastes belong to it: it encompasses all this universe, does not speak and has no care. This my SELF within the heart is that Brahman. When I depart from hence I shall merge into it. He who believes this will never doubt. (Chandogya Upanishad 3,14:3-5)

We must always try to be righteous. The **Hebrew Bible** says, "The righteous shall flourish like the palm tree: he shall grow like a cedar in Lebanon. Those that be planted in the house of the Lord shall flourish in the courts of our God. They shall still bring forth fruit in old age; they shall be fat and flourishing" (Psalms 92:12-14). If we are righteous, we will grow in outer capacity and inner strength. In this way, our lives become an example to others. The **Dhammapada** says, "Even if one talks a lot about what is beneficial, if one does not put it into practice, one is negligent, like a herder counting the livestock of others; one has no share in spirituality" (Dhammapada 1:19). Being an apprentice in the Kingdom of God means nothing unless we practice the Kingdom of God consciously in our everyday lives. The **New Testament** says:

> Then Jesus sent the multitude away,
> and went into the house:
> and his disciples came unto him,
> saying,
> Declare unto us the parable of the tare of the field.
>
> He answered and said unto them,
> He that soweth the good seed is the Son of man;
> The field is the world;
> the good seed are the children of the kingdom;
> but the tares are the children of the wicked *one*;
> The enemy that sowed them is the devil;
> the harvest is the end of the world;
> and the reapers are the angels.
>
> As therefore the tares are gathered and burned in the fire;
> so shall it be in the end of the world.

The Son of man shall send forth his angels,
and they shall gather out of his kingdom all things that offend,
and them which do iniquity;
And shall cast them into a furnace of fire:
there shall be wailing and gnashing of teeth.

Then shall the righteous shine forth
as the sun in the kingdom of Their Father.
How hath ears to hear,
let him hear.
(Matthew 13:36-43)

The explanation of this parable clarifies the key points of spiritual wisdom. The good seeds are seekers that consciously seek God. If we exist in the Kingdom of God, we are among the good seeds. The bad seeds are those who remain firmly in darkness and attached to the desires of the world. The harvest comes when we are fully matured and we have reached enlightenment and Oneness with God. The **Koran** says, "God will strengthen the faithful with the steadfast Word, both in this life and in the hereafter. He leads the wrong doers astray. God accomplishes what He pleases" (Koran 14:28). Spiritual wisdom tells us that the importance of His Word shall continue well past the point of our apprenticeship. His mysteries continue, but as we evolve even more, we will continue to grow in capacity and God will reveal more and more of His mysteries.

The smallest light within us starts our spiritual life. Like yeast and a mustard seed, spiritual wisdom can grow with proper care, love, stimulation, and diligence because God provides us with the right conditions, understandings, and continued life opportunities. His light reveals His mysteries and helps us see more and more until we reach the goal of Oneness with Him. That Oneness is a shelter for all. We participate with God with the proper preparation of our heart and soul through discipline and devotion. With that preparation and God's love and guidance, the vastness of the universe is revealed. God has told us that He starts with the smallest and creates the most magnificent. The tiny seed of God that is within us is infinite, and everything is concentrated in this little space inside our hearts. He carefully cultivates our seed; and as it grows, we repattern our lives by first seeing the SELF inside ourselves and next revisiting our experiences with a new awareness that nourishes and grows our little seed until it is a huge tree.

LOSING OPPORTUNITIES

Question:
Can we lose our opportunities?

Brief Answer:
Yes, and we do so when we are foolishly unaware of them.

from the *Gospel of Thomas*

97. Jesus said, "[What] the kingdom of the [father] resembles [is] a woman who was conveying a [jar] full of meal. When she had traveled far [along] the road, the handle of the jar broke and the meal spilled out after her [along] the road. She was not aware of the fact; she had not understood how to toil. When she reached home she put down the jar and found it empty."
(See Layton, p. 396.)

Longer Answer:

This parable of the spilled jar of meal is only found in the **Gospel of Thomas**, but the quotes from other sacred scriptures can help us understand its lesson. The **Upanishad** says:

> Fools pursue desires outside themselves,
> Fall into the snares of widespread death:
> But wise men,
> discerning immortality,
> Seek not the stable here among unstable things.
> (Katha Upanishad 4:2)

If we are wise, we will seek the permanence of the spiritual wisdom of God among our daily life experiences as they define our opportunities. The **Hebrew Bible** says, "The foolishness of man perventeth his way: and his heart fretteth against the Lord" (Proverbs 19:3). The foolish fret and agitate against God and some even argue against His existence. They allow their intuitive understanding to be overpowered by the divisiveness of the mind and the sensations of the body. The **Dhammapada** says, "Fools, unintelligent people, indulge in heedlessness. The wise one, however, guards vigilance as the best of riches" (Dhammapada 2:6). We need to heed our lessons and be ever watchful, cautious, and circumspect about what is truly of value to us. This often requires a force of will to slow down and contemplate our lives, using meditation and thoughtful reflection.

Also, we can learn much more from the scriptures. For example, the **New Testament** says, "Casting all your care upon him; for he careth for you. Be sober, be vigilant; because your adversary the devil, as a roaring lion, walketh about, seeking whom he may devour: Whom resist steadfast in the faith, knowing that the same affections are accomplished in your brethren that are in the world" (Peter 1,5:7-9). We must be ever careful and alert as we can easily lose opportunities especially when our faith is challenged or somehow damaged. We may not always understand His ways, but He is always with and for us. The **Koran** says, "'Lord,' he will say, 'why have You brought me blind before You when in my life I was clear-sighted?' He will answer: 'Just as Our revelations were declared to you and you forgot them, so on this day you are yourself forgotten'" (Koran 20:125). We must try very hard to recognize and understand God's messages and revelations to us by trusting and listening to Him. In turn, He will fulfill His duty to us. The **Koran** tells us:

Say:
"Obey God and obey the Apostle.
If you do not,
he is still bound to fulfil his duty,
as you yourselves are bound to fulfil yours.

If you obey him,
you shall be rightly guided.

The duty of an apostle is only to give plain warning."

God has promised those of you who believe and do good works
to make them masters in the land as He had made their ancestors before them,
to strengthen the Faith He chose for them,
and to change their fears to safety.
Let them worship Me and serve none besides Me.

Wicked indeed are they who after this deny Me.
(Koran 24:54)

In this **Gospel of Thomas** parable, the *road* is our path in life that we travel. The *house* is our goal or the *final destination*, and the *end of the path* is death. The woman is traveling down the path of life. However, she is unaware that she is losing meal as she walks along her path of life. The *meal* represents the opportunities for learning spiritual wisdom given to her by God. Life for each of us has a limited set of opportunities, like the sands in an hour glass. They stop at journey's end. Like the woman in the parable, we need to become aware and start using our gifts from God rather than losing them. We must be alert to the opportunities we are forfeiting, because the "meal" is our inner nourishment. The more nourishment we lose, the weaker we become, and we place ourselves more at risk of not succeeding on our spiritual journey. Unfortunately, most of us are unaware of the presence and importance of those opportunities and the necessity for the spiritual nourishment that we are losing.

Why are we so unconscious of our opportunities and the importance of spiritual nourishment? *Maybe* because the everyday desires of the Kingdom of Man trap us in the long cycles of birth and rebirth, and we forget to seek Oneness with God. *Maybe* it is because we argue with and even against God and in the process cloud our understanding of Him. *Maybe* we do not learn and apply our spiritual lessons. *Maybe* it is because we are simply not careful about with whom we associate and allow to influence our thinking. *Maybe* we just do not care for God. Those *maybes* and a thousand more represent the **broken handle of the jar** as we move down the path of life. For any one of those reasons, we may not reach our goal. No matter how much inner knowledge we may have accumulated, we can fail to see the wonderful gifts we are given and waste them unless we remain conscious of them and open up our minds fully to receive them. Unless we train ourselves to be aware, we lose ground from attacks of the vital sensations including desire, fear, jealousy, and anger. We lose our light and in turn lose more opportunities to grow. We must become more and more aware of the possible threats to our inner life—and where possible, turn them into learning experiences.

BE READY

Question:

How do we prepare properly?

Brief Answer:

We strengthen our faith and ready ourselves constantly.

from the *Gospel of Thomas*

98. Jesus said, "What the kingdom of the father resembles is a man who wanted to assassinate a member of court. At home, he drew the dagger and stabbed it into the wall in order to know whether his hand would be firm. Next, he murdered the member of court."
(See Layton, p. 397.)

Longer Answer:

Reaching Oneness with God requires preparation. We must practice in private and be resolute in purpose. How do we prepare? The **Upanishad** says:

> Once he has given instruction in the Veda,
> the teacher should proceed to instruct his pupils [as follows]:
> Speak the truth.
> Do what is right.
> Do not neglect study [of the Veda].
> After you have given your teacher an acceptable sum,
> Do not let your family line die out.

Do not be careless about truth.
Do not be careless about what is right.
Do not be careless about welfare.
Do not be careless about prosperity
Do not be negligent in the study and recitation [of the Veda].
Do not neglect your duties to the gods and ancestors.
Let your mother be a god to you.
Let your father be a god to you.
Let a guest be a god to you.
Perform only deeds to which no blame attaches,
no others.
Respect such deeds of ours as have been well done,
no others.
Offer the comfort of a seat to whatever Brahmans may be better than we.
(Taittiriya Upanishad 1:11)

The metaphor of a fight is useful in understanding the importance of preparation. The **Hebrew Bible** says, "Thou therefore, son of man, prophesy, and smite, *thine* hands together, and let the sword be doubled the third time, the sword of the slain: it *is* the sword of the great *men that are* slain, which entereth into their privy chambers" (Ezekiel 21:14). We need to be able to anticipate the future and be prepared for anything. The **Dhammapada** says, "As a frontier city is guarded inside and out, so should you guard yourself. Do not let even a moment slip by, for those who let the moments slip by grieve when they have been consigned to hell" (Dhammapada 22:10). When we become complacent and let our guard down, we lose ground and become vulnerable from all sorts of attacks.

The **New Testament** says, "And I say unto you my friends, Be not afraid of them that kill the body, and after that have no more that they can do. But I will forewarn you whom ye shall fear: Fear him, which after he hath killed hath power to cast into hell; yea, I say unto you, Fear him" (Luke 12:4-5). We should not be afraid of confrontation. We must be prepared so that we are not caught off guard by those who would hurt us. The **New Testament** also says, "For the word of God *is* quick, and powerful, and sharper than any two-edged sword, piercing even to the dividing asunder of soul and spirit, and of the joints and marrow, and *is* a discerner of the thoughts and intents of the heart" (Hebrews 4:12). God's word is quick, powerful, and sharper than any weapon. God is our mightiest defense, but we must know how to use Him. God loves His helpers. He is pleased when His children proudly claim Him as their own. The **Koran** says, "God loves those who fight for His cause in ranks as firm as a mighty edifice" (Koran 61:3). We can stand firm and confident always knowing that conflict may come but it will not defeat us.

The **Gospel of Thomas** acknowledges that we live in the Kingdom of Man with all its dangers. Preparing ourselves inwardly readies us for trying times. The true battle we must fight is on the spiritual rather than the physical plain. Attacks of desire even defeated the strength of Samson, the strongest man in the world. Prayer, mediation, and studying prepare us for the battles we face against our own weaknesses.

KNOW OUR FRIENDS

Question:
Who can we judge to be our friends?

Brief Answer:
Our friends are the ones who do the will of God.

from the *Gospel of Thomas*

99. The followers said to him, "Your brothers and your mother are standing outside."

He said to them, "Those here who do the will of my father are my brothers and my mother. They are the ones who will enter my father's kingdom."

Longer Answer:

We must prepare for our battles, but we must also be able to recognize and know our true friends. We cannot be foolish enough to think that by definition family members are automatically counted among our friends and supporters. The **Hebrew Bible** says, "For the son dishonoureth the father, the daughter riseth up against her mother, the daughter-in-law against her mother-in- law; a man's enemies *are* the men of his own house. Therefore I will look unto the Lord; I will wait for the God of my salvation; my God will hear me" (Micah 7:6-7). Our spiritual enemies are often found in our own homes. We must shut out our spiritual enemies regardless of who they might be. Although this might be a difficult and painful task, this is one area where being weak willed is particularly foolish. The **Dhammapada** says, "Killing mother and father, and two warrior kings, killing a kingdom with all its subjects, the priestly one goes untroubled" (Dhammapada 21:5). Metaphorically, we need to "kill" or treat our spiritual enemies as if they were dead so that they cannot influence our lives and environments. We must remove them from our lives and reject anyone who would stand against our spiritual growth.

We should not think that just because people are from different religious traditions that we should consider them to be our enemies. On the contrary, formal religion is just how we choose to demonstrate our faith; it should not be the be-all and end-all of anyone's spirituality. The **Koran** says, "If the People of the Book accept the true faith and keep from evil, We will pardon them their sins and admit them to the gardens of delight. If they observe the Torah and the Gospel and what is revealed to them from their Lord, they shall enjoy abundance from above and from beneath" (Koran 5:65). Belonging to or even not belonging to any particular religious tradition does not define our friends or our enemies. What is in a person's heart, including their attitude toward God and His entire creation, defines a person's spiritual life. A religious tradition is a comfortable and familiar way to celebrate one's individual relationship with God. Spiritual wisdom tells us to look past the seemingly obvious and ask ourselves: who are our *true* family members? Our spiritual family is made up of those who are seekers and live spiritual wisdom in their daily lives. The **New Testament** says:

> While he yet talked to the people,
> behold,
> *his* mother,
> and his brethren stood without,
> desiring to speak with him.

Then one said unto him,
Behold,
thy mother and thy brethren stand without,
desiring to speak with thee.

But he answered and said unto him that told him,
Who is my mother?
and who are my brethren?

And he stretched forth his hand toward his disciples,
and said,
Behold my mother and my brethren!

For whosoever shall do the will of my Father which is in heaven,
the same is my brother,
and sister, and mother.
(Matthew 12: 46-50; similar Mark 3:31-35 and Luke 8:19-21)

Proceeding along the path to Oneness is not an easy task, and we need to know who our true supporters are. Certainly, support provided by family and friends is important, but we must recognize that those who do God's will are truly the ones that support us. The **Upanishad** says:

> This did Brahma tell to Prajapati, Prajapati to Manu, and Manu to his descendants.
> The man who has studied the Veda in his teacher's family in accordance with the prescribed ordinances and in the time left over after he has performed his duties for his teacher; and who, after returning home, has continued his Vedic studies in his house and in a clean place; who has produced virtuous [sons]; and who has concentrated all his faculties on the SELF, taking care to hurt no living thing except in sacrifice, — such a man, if he perseveres in this throughout life, will reach the Brahman-world and will not return again, — he will not return again. (Chandogya Upanishad 8,15)

Clarifications

◆

GIVE TO THE OTHER DEMANDS OF LIFE THEIR RELATIVE DUE

Question:

How should we treat the physical world and those in it?

Brief Answer:

Treat the world and those in it with an importance relative to that given to God.

from the *Gospel of Thomas*

100. They showed Jesus a gold coin and said to him, "Caesar's people demand taxes from us."

He said to them, "Give Caesar the things that are Caesar's, give God the things that are God's, and give me what is mine."

Longer Answer:

Although we live in the temporal world, our challenge is to transcend it — not to reject it. God expects our participation in the material world because it is part of His creation. The physical world is God's "teaching laboratory" for us to learn and grow. For example, when honor and duty for righteousness's sake are required, we may even have to engage in physical battle. The key to discerning how we should live and behave in the temporal world is relative to our own conscious engagement in it. An action in one situation may be totally wrong but in another could be absolutely divine. The **Bhagavad-Gita** says:

> But if thou wilt not wage this war
> Prescribed by thy (caste-)duty,
> Then,
> by casting off both honor and (caste-)duty,
> Thou wilt bring evil on thyself.
>
> Yes,
> this thy dishonor will become a byword
> In the mouths of men in ages yet to come;
> And dishonor in a man well-trained to honor
> [Is an ill] surpassing death.
> (Bhagavad-Gita 2:33-34)

In important situations, we must go deep within our hearts to know the right action to take because it must always be based on our correct consciousness, which includes our surrendering the results to God. The **Hebrew Bible** says, "And Jehoiakim gave the silver and the gold to Pharaoh; but he taxed the land to give the money according to the commandment of Pharaoh: he exacted the silver and the gold of the people of the land, of every one according to his taxation, to give *it* unto Pharaoh-nechoh" (Kings 2,23:35). Every society and community has laws and customs that it follows in keeping order, including paying taxes. We must pay taxes even though we may not approve of how the governing body uses our money. This does not mean we simply accept what we believe to be wrong, but we must address it in the correct way. If a law is unjust or otherwise incorrect, we need to find the proper ways and channels to change it. We cannot simply walk away from a civic responsibility because we want to do so.

Spiritual wisdom provides guidance for these kind of circumstances. The **Dhammapada** says, "Speak the truth, do not become angered, and give when asked, even be it a little. By these three conditions one goes to the presence of the gods" (Dhammapada 17:4). There are three simple rules: (1) Always speak the truth; (2) Be detached and objective; (3) Be generous. If we always keep our priorities grounded in the Kingdom of God, we will direct our actions according to the needs of God's entire creation. The **Koran** says, "When We made a covenant with the Israelites We said: 'Serve none but God. Show kindness to your parents, to your kinsfolk, to the orphans, and to the destitute. Exhort men to righteousness. Attend to your prayers and render the alms levy.' But you all broke your covenant except a few, and gave no heed" (Koran 2:83). We should always show kindness and compassion to all of God's creation. We cannot love one without the other. In loving God, we also love all of His creations and in loving His creations we are also loving Him. The **Koran** also says, "Eat of the good and lawful things which God bestowed on you, and give thanks for His favors if you truly serve Him" (Koran 16:114). God wants us to enjoy and participate in all the good and lawful things that the world has to offer.

There is a difference between the above **Gospel of Thomas** quote and the following **New Testament** quote:

> Then went the Pharisees,
> and took counsel how they might entangle him in *his* talk.

> And they sent out unto him their disciples with the Herodians,
> saying,
> Master,
> we know that thou art true,
> and teachest the way of God in truth,
> neither carest thou for any *man:*
> for thou regardest not the person of men.

> Tell us therefore,
> What thinkest thou?
> Is it lawful to give tribute unto Caesar,
> or not?

But Jesus perceived their wickedness,
and said,
Why tempt ye me,
ye hypocrites?

Shew me the tribute money.
And they brought unto him a penny.

And he saith unto them,
Whose *is* this image and superscription?

They say unto him,
Caesar's.

Then saith he unto them,
Render therefore unto Caesar the things which are Caesar's;
and unto God the things that are God's.

When they had heard *these words*,
they marvelled,
and left him,
and went their way.
(Matthew 22:15-22; similar Mark 12:13-17 and Luke 20:21-26)

The key phrase to note in the above quote involves rendering to Caesar or the governing body of the society the things of that society. In other words, we are to render unto man those things that are of the Kingdom of Man. Conversely, we are to render unto God the things that are of the Kingdom of God. The **Gospel of Thomas** adds that we should also render unto Jesus what is His. Christ is One with God and He brought God's word to humankind. Therefore, we should render to Jesus all the love, respect, and manifestations that reveal our love and surrender to God.

LOVE SPIRITUALLY

Question:

How is spiritual love different from human love?

Brief Answer:

Spiritual love is like the love of a teacher for her students. She wants them to learn and eventually to be successful based on their earned merit.

from the *Gospel of Thomas*

101. "Whoever does not hate [father] and mother as I do cannot be a [follower] of me, and whoever does [not] love [father and] mother as I do cannot be a [follower of] me. For my mother [...], but my true [mother] gave me life."
(Note: The omission is due to missing material in the only text available.)

Longer Answer:

Saying 101 seems to be an impossible conundrum but the illusion of inconsistency disappears when we reflect on the difference between the Kingdom of God's and the Kingdom of Man's interpretation of love. Spiritual love means making God our highest goal and seeing God in all His creation. Spiritual love means being loyal to God, and consciously trying to transcend all other attachments and conditions. The **Bhagavad-Gita** says:

> Do works for Me,
> make Me thy highest goal,
> Be loyal in love to Me,
> Cast off [all other] attachments,
> Have no hatred for any being at all:
> For all who do thus shall come to Me.
> (Bhagavad-Gita 11:55)

The **Hebrew Bible** says, "Whoso curseth his father or his mother, his lamp shall be put out in obscure darkness" (Proverbs 20:20). We are to curse no one and certainly not our mothers and fathers. The **Hebrew Bible** also says, "Honor thy father and thy mother: that thy days may be long upon the land which the Lord thy God giveth thee" (Exodus 20:12). We should give our parents our heart-felt love for providing life for our souls so that we can continue our work and progress.

However, in the Kingdom of God, love means caring for our inner development. The **Dhammapada** says, "What not even a mother, a father, or any other relative will do, a rightly directed mind does do, even better" (Dhammapada 3:10). Naturally, a mother, father, and other relatives care for a child, but we need to go much further and assume the responsibility for the care for our own progress. We need to direct our minds pointedly toward the Kingdom of God and not the passions and illusions of the world. Our parents and children are given to us by God for a purpose as they are part of His plan to teach us spiritual wisdom. A particular set of life experiences including family relationships, nationality, and economic circumstances become God's learning laboratory that He has tailored specifically for us. Those life experiences provide each of us with a wealth of learning opportunities to glean His wisdom from them. In the Kingdom of God, love means that we hold God as our highest value and truth. The **New Testament** says:

> And he said unto them,
> Full well ye reject the commandment of God,
> that ye may keep your own tradition.
>
> For Moses said,
> Honor thy father and thy mother;
> and,
> Whoso curseth father or mother,
> let him die the death:
> But ye say,
> If a man shall say to his father or mother,
> *It is* Corban,
> that is to say,
> a gift,
> by whatsoever thou mightest be profited by me;
> *he shall be free.*
>
> And ye suffer him no more to do ought for his father or his mother;
> Making the word of God of none effect through your tradition,
> which ye have delivered:
> and many such like things do ye.
> (Mark 7:9-13)

The common misunderstanding in the Kingdom of Man is that we should value our families at the same level or even higher than God. Perhaps because of this the **Hebrew Bible** says, "Honor thy Father and thy Mother: that thy days may be long upon the land which the LORD thy God giveth thee" (Exodus 20:12). Yes, we must honor and respect them because God chose them to provide us with specific lessons in our early spiritual education. We should not ignore the lessons God provides, but we must realize that those lessons need to be appreciated within the larger context of our ultimate goals. The **New Testament** clarifies this even further: "And the brother shall deliver up the brother to death, and the father the child: and the children shall rise up against *their* parents, and cause them to be put to death. And ye shall be hated of all *men* for my name's sake: but he that endureth to the end shall be saved" (Matthew 10:21-22; similar Mark 13:12-13). All such family passions are misplaced and we need to understand those passions in the larger perspective of holding God as our highest value. The **Koran** says, "Your wealth and your children are but a temptation. God's reward is great. Therefore fear God with all your hearts, and be attentive, obedient, and charitable. That will be best for you" (Koran 64:14).

The illusions of the physical world with its tempting promise of wealth and children try to fool us. Therefore, we need to look past the illusions of the Kingdom of Man and find God. In the Kingdom of Man, love is born out of desire, attachment, and conditionality. We manipulate others emotionally with favors and threats, and we mislabel it "love." In the Kingdom of God, a loving relationship exists when all parties care first and foremost about God, secondly, about their own spiritual development, and thirdly, about the spiritual growth of others when they are ready. We must love ourselves enough to want to grow, and we must also love to see others grow as well. This concern for inner mutual growth must always be unconditional.

RELIGIOUS LEADERS
CONFUSE AND DISTRACT

Question:
Can religious leaders be relied upon to help us?

Brief Answer:
No, we should only rely on God.

from the *Gospel of Thomas*

102. Jesus said, "Damn the Pharisees, for they are like a dog sleeping in the cattle manger, for it does not eat or [let] the cattle eat."

Longer Answer:

Spiritual wisdom warns us that the very people who make their living bringing us the Word can also mislead us. How? The **Bhagavad-Gita** answers:

> The essence of the soul is will, —
> [The soul] of men who cling to pleasure and to power,
> Their minds seduced by flowery worlds,
> Are not equipped for ecstasy.

> Such men give vent to flowery words,
> The fools,
> Delighting in the Veda's lore,
> Saying there is naught else.
> (Bhagavad-Gita 2:42-43)

Today's and yesterday's religious leaders, such as the Pharisees at the time of Christ, focus on ceremonies, "correct" manners, flowery words, and myths associated with a limited man-made religion, rather than on God's vast authentic spiritual wisdom. Many have made a lucrative business out of religion and exploited the faith of others to make themselves rich in the Kingdom of Man. Some have used religion for political reasons, such as creating an elite class of rulers or controlling a population. A useful metaphor for this type of religious leader is the watchman. The **Hebrew Bible** says, "His watchmen *are* blind: they *are* all ignorant, they are all dumb dogs, they cannot bark; sleeping lying low, loving to slumber. Yea, *they are* greedy dogs *which* can never have enough, and they are shepherds *that* cannot understand: they all look to their own way, every one for his gain, from his quarter" (Isaiah 56:10-11).

Unfortunately, sometimes these leaders do not seek spiritual wisdom either for themselves or for their congregations, because they prefer the illusion of the Kingdom of Man. They use religion to advance their worldly desires, including wealth and power. The **Dhammapada** says, "One who would wear the saffron robe while not free from impurity is lacking in self-control and is not genuine, thus unworthy of the saffron robe" (Dhammapada 1:9). (As a note of explanation, the saffron robe is the traditional religious garb of Buddhist leaders.) Certainly not all religious leaders are impure or misleading. In fact, many genuinely live in the Kingdom of God. The question becomes, How can we identify the impostors from the genuinely righteous ones? The answer is not in what the leader does or does not wear. Neither is the answer that the leaders are always free from impurity. Instead, the answer lies in their actions, sincerity, and genuineness. The **Diamond Sutra** says:

> "Subhuti, what do you think? Does a disciple who has entered the stream of the holy life say within himself, 'I obtain the fruit of a stream entrant?'"
>
> Subhuti said: "No, World-Honored One. Wherefore? Because 'stream entrant' is merely a name. There is no stream entering. The disciple who pays no regard to form, sound, odor, taste, touch, or any quality is called a stream entrant."
>
> "Subhuti, what do you think? Does an adept who is subject to only one more rebirth say within himself, 'I obtain the fruit of a once-to-be reborn' is merely a name. There is no passing away nor coming into existence. [The adept who realizes] this is called 'once-to-be-reborn.'
>
> "Subhuti, what do you think? Does a venerable one who will never more be reborn as a mortal say within himself, 'I obtain the fruit of a nonreturner?'"
>
> Subhuti said: "No, World-Honored One. Wherefore? Because 'nonreturner' is merely a name. There is no nonreturning; hence the designation 'nonreturner.'"
>
> "Subhuti, what do you think? Does a holy one say within himself, 'I have obtained perfective enlightenment?'"

> Subhuti said: "No, World-Honored One. Wherefore? Because there is no such condition as that called 'perfective enlightenment.' World-Honored One, if a holy one of perfective enlightenment said to himself, 'Such am I,' he would necessarily partake of the idea of an ego entity, a personality, a being, or a separated individuality. World-Honored One, when the Buddha declares that I excel among holy men in the yoga of perfect quiescence, in dwelling in seclusion, and in freedom from passions, I do not say within myself, 'I am a holy one of perfective enlightenment, free from passions.' World-Honored One, if I said within myself, 'Such am I,' you would not declare, 'Subhuti finds happiness abiding in peace, in seclusion in the midst of the forest.' This is because Subhuti abides nowhere; therefore he is called 'Subhuti, Joyful Abider in Peace, Dweller in Seclusion in the Forest.'" (The Diamond Sutra 9)

If the leader claims and boasts that they *are* holy, this indicates that the person is a fraud. A holy person would not aggrandize their individual ego. We should beware of such persons. Spiritual wisdom is very disapproving of fraudulent leaders, because the trust they command from their followers gives them the potential to hurt a large number of sincere seekers. The **New Testament** says, "But woe unto you, scribes and Pharisees, hypocrites! for ye shut up the kingdom of heaven against men: for ye neither go in *yourselves*, neither suffer ye them that are entering to go in" (Matthew 23:13). Scholars, reporters, and religious leaders are often hypocrites because their very actions and words lead people away from the Kingdom of God, away from Oneness, and into doubt and division. Sometimes when we realize that our religious leaders are wrong, we become angry, disillusioned, and cynical because we feel foolish and gullible for having trusted and believed so easily. Subsequently, we fail to seek further; however, ultimately, each of us is responsible for being a seeker for ourselves. What anyone else does or does not do is unimportant because our relationship is directly with God.

Although not seeking because of what someone else has done is a mistake for anyone to make, a much more serious mistake is to deliberately keep others from seeking. The **Koran** says, "Believers, many are the clerics and the monks who defraud men of their possessions and debar them from the path of God. To those that hoard up gold and silver and do not spend it in God's cause, proclaim a woeful punishment. The day will surely come when their treasures shall be heated in the fire of Hell, and their foreheads, sides, and backs branded with them. They will be told: 'These are the riches which you hoarded. Taste then what you were hoarding'" (Koran 9:35). They may dupe and mislead us; however, karma will determine their fate. True leaders of God consider themselves helpers or assistants because they wish to only assist others to continually discover God's wisdom messages sometimes even by challenging our beliefs. In contrast, Kingdom of Man religious leaders have rigid belief systems rooted in distrust, hate, and discord. They do not seek reconciliation or divine evolution; rather, they insist on blind obedience. Religious leaders should not advocate their versions of faith nor champion particular points of view. Instead, they should only provide seekers with a viewing place to increase our own awareness, potential, and ultimately our Oneness with God.

BE FOREWARNED AND FOREARMED

Question:

Do people resent seekers of the Kingdom of God?

Brief Answer:

Yes, there is often resentment. Therefore, we need to be equipped to deal with the assaults.

from the *Gospel of Thomas*

103. Jesus said, "Fortunate is the person who knows where the robbers are going to enter, so that [he] may arise, bring together his estate, and arm himself before they enter."

Longer Answer:

Spiritual wisdom tells us that to be forewarned is to be forearmed. As spiritual seekers, we know the enemy is the Kingdom of Man and that the enemy will eventually attack us. How can we prepare for such

inevitabilities? One answer is through meditation, using the mantra or chant
AUM to bring us closer to the SELF. The **Upanishad** says,

[Now,]

this is the SELF in its relationship to syllables:

it is Om.

As to the letters,

the quarters [enumerated above] are the letters;

and the letters are the quarters,

— A + U + M.

The waking state,

common to all men,

is A,

the first letter,

signifying *apti*,

"obtaining,"

or *adimattva*,

"'what is in the beginning".

For he who knows this obtains all his desires and becomes the beginning.

The state of dream,

composed of light,

is U,

the second letter,

signifying *utkarsa*,

"'exaltation,"

or *ubhayatva*,

"'partaking of both."

He who knows this exalts the continuum of knowledge

and becomes like a [Brahman].

In his family there is none who does not know Brahman.

The state of deep sleep,

the wise,

is M,

the third letter,

signifying *miti*,

"building up" [or measuring],

or *apiti*,

"'absorption."

He who knows this builds up [or measures]
the whole universe in very deed and is absorbed [into it].

The fourth it beyond [all] letters:
there can be no commerce with it;
it brings [all] development to an end;
it is mild and devoid of duality.
Such is Om,
the very SELF indeed.
He who knows this merges of his own accord into the SELF,
— yes,
he who knows this.
(Mandukya Upanishad 8-12)

Another way to prepare is by growing closer to God by deliberately avoiding harmful things. The **Hebrew Bible** says, "Blessed *is* the man *that* doeth this, and the son of man *that* layeth hold on it; and keepeth the sabbath from polluting it, and keepeth his hand from doing any evil. Neither let the son of the stranger, that hath joined himself to the Lord, speak, saying, The Lord hath utterly separated me from his people: neither let the eunuch say, Behold, I *am* a dry tree" (Isaiah 56:2-3). If we stay focused on doing God's work, there is no time for earthly desires to distract us. Being prepared requires a great deal of advance thought and preparation on our part. The **Diamond Sutra** says:

"Subhuti, the Tathagata teaches likewise that the perfection of patience is not the perfection of patience: such is merely a name. Why so? It is shown thus, Subhuti: When the Raja of Kalinga mutilated my body, I was at that time free from the idea of an ego entity, a personality, a being, and a separated individuality. Wherefore? Because then, when my limbs were cut away piece by piece, had I been bound by the distinctions aforesaid, feelings of anger and hatred would have been aroused within me. Subhuti, I remember that long ago, sometime during by last five hundred mortal lives, I was an ascetic practicing patience. Even then was I free from those distinctions of separated selfhood. Therefore, Subhuti, bodhisattvas should leave behind all phenomenal distinctions and awaken the thought of the consummation of incomparable enlightenment by not allowing the mind to depend upon notions evoked by the sensible world — by not allowing the mind to depend upon notions evoked by sounds, odors, flavors, touch contracts, or any qualities. The mind should be kept independent of any thoughts that arise within it. If the mind depends upon anything, it has no sure haven. This is why Buddha teaches that the mind of a bodhisattva should not accept the appearances of things as a basis when exercising charity. Subhuti, as bodhisattvas practice charity for the welfare of all living beings, they should do it in this manner. Just as the Tathagata declares that characteristics are not characteristics, so he declares that all living beings are not, in fact, living beings.

"Subhuti, the Tathagata is he who declares that which is true, he who declares that which is fundamental, he who declares that which is ultimate. He does not declare that which is deceitful nor that which is monstrous. Subhuti, that truth to which the Tathagata has attained is neither real nor unreal.

"Subhuti, if a bodhisattva practices charity with mind attached to formal notions he is like a man groping sightless in the gloom; but a bodhisattva who practices charity with mind detached from any formal notions is like a man with open eyes in the radiant glory of the morning, to whom all kinds of objects are clearly visible.

"Subhuti, if there be a good men and good women in future ages, able to receive, read, and recite this discourse in its entirety, the Tathagata will clearly perceive and recognize them by means of his buddha-knowledge; and each one of them will bring immeasurable and incalculable merit to fruition." (The Diamond Sutra 14)

Being forearmed also takes great practice and discipline because it includes being free from ego, the idea of personality, and the idea of a separate individuality. In other words, the closer we move towards Oneness the stronger and more prepared we are to deal with the hostilities of the outer world. While the exterior is in turmoil and conflict, our inner existence will remain untouched, tranquil, and at peace. The **Dhammapada** says, "As rain leaks into a poorly roofed house, so does passion invade an uncultivated mind. As no rain leaks into a well-roofed house, passion does not invade a cultivated mind" (Dhammapada 1:13-14). Preparation cultivates the mind so that passion cannot invade our consciousness. Without preparation, we risk losing our centered Oneness.

The **Koran** says, "Exalted and throned on high, He lets the Spirit descend at His behest on those of His servants whom He chooses, that He may warn them of the day when they shall meet Him; the day when they shall rise up from their graves with nothing hidden from God. And who shall reign supreme on that day? God, the One, the Almighty" (Koran 40:16). Because of God's love, He will always warn us but we need to have enough inner peace to be able to hear the warning. The **New Testament** says, "Watch therefore: for ye know not what hour your Lord doth come. But know this, that if the goodman of the house had known in what watch the thief would come, he would have watched, and would not have suffered his house to be broken up. Therefore be ye also ready: for in such an hour as ye think not the Son of man cometh" (Matthew 24:42-44; similar Luke 12:39). We must always be on guard and listen for His warning, because the attacks will come from unexpected sources, unanticipated directions, and at unpredictable times. If we are forewarned, then we can be forearmed. This saying tells us that we are very fortunate if we know where and when the enemy will attack. With that knowledge we can prepare and defeat those who would rob us of our inner light.

◆

MAINTAINING THE KINGDOM OF GOD

Question:
What happens if those who attack are successful?

Brief Answer:
Pray for God's help and guidance.

from the *Gospel of Thomas*
104. They said to Jesus, "Come, let us pray today and let us fast."
Jesus said, "What sin have I committed, or how have I been undone? Rather, when the bridegroom leaves the wedding chamber, then let people fast and pray."

Longer Answer:

Being in the wedding chamber is a metaphor for union or Oneness. If we falter and lose our Oneness with God, we need to pray very hard for God's help and guidance to lead us back to Him. When we are truly in the Kingdom of God, everything we do is a gift of our spiritual love to God. Our very actions and thoughts are a continuous prayer to Him. There is no separation between the individual and God as we reach Oneness. In spiritual wisdom, there is a difference between theory and practice. We can learn it in theory, and we can comprehend the lessons in the mind. However, the theory is not real until we can live it continuously and we identify with it through the heart. In other words, we must become the theory ourselves. If it becomes too difficult to live it, then we have lost our Oneness. The **Bhagavad-Gita** says:

> This wisdom has been revealed to thee in theory;
> Listen now to how it should be practiced:
> If by this wisdom thou art exercised,
> Thou wilt put off the bondage inherent in [all] works.
> (Bhagavad-Gita 2:39)

The **Hebrew Bible** says, "Behold, ye fast for strife and debate, and to smite with the fist of wickedness: ye shall not fast as *ye do this* day, to make your voice to he heard on high" (Isaiah 58:4). When we use prayer and fasting for entirely the wrong reasons, we cannot find our Oneness with God. Only the sincere aspiration of our hearts motivating our actions can bring us into union with Him.

Although spiritually loving everyone is important, praying for everyone's success is foolish, as God has granted each of us the liberty of free choice. Such prayers are asking God to negate the expression of love He made to us when He granted us free choice. Instead, we should pray for His will to be done; and once we pray in this manner, we must then detach ourselves from any expected outcome. The fact that He wants all of us to reach Oneness with Him, and that everyone of us has the opportunity to be successful, should comfort us. The **Diamond Sutra** says:

> "Subhuti, what do you think? Let no one say the Tathagata cherishes the idea 'I must liberate all living beings.' Allow no such thought, Subhuti. Wherefore? Because in reality there are no living

beings to be liberated by the Tathagata. If there were living beings for the Tathagata to liberate, he would partake in the idea of self-hood, personality, ego entity, and separate individuality.

"Subhuti, though the common people accept egoity as real, the Tathagata declares that ego is not different from nonego. Subhuti, those whom the Tathagata referred to as 'common people' are not really common people; such is merely a name." (The Diamond Sutra 25)

God wants each of us to choose the Kingdom of God ourselves with our free choice. The **Dhammapada** says, "Just as rust eats away the iron from which it is produced, so do their own deeds lead the overindulgent into a miserable state" (Dhammapada 18:6). We are our own worst enemies, in that our own overindulgent deeds are the choices that create the karma that influences the likelihood of our success in this and following lifetimes. In granting us free choice, God expects that we will sometimes choose wisely and sometimes foolishly. The **New Testament** says, "Then came to him the disciples of John, saying, Why do we and the Pharisees fast oft, but thy disciples fast not? And Jesus said unto them, Can the children of the bridechamber mourn, as long as the bridegroom is with them? but the days will come, when the bridegroom shall be taken from them, and then shall they fast" (Matthew 9:14-15; similar Mark 2:18-20 and 5:33-35). When we are One with God, extreme demonstrations of devotion and faith-like fasting are not essential or even necessary, because we have direct and instant access to Him. However, there will be times in our lives when we will not be able to maintain our Oneness with God. When we feel distant and remote from Him, fasting and other sincere spiritually uplifting actions are essential and necessary to rekindle our aspiration and reinspire our determination, because they help remind us of our cherished goal.

The **Koran** says, "They think they have conferred on you a favor by embracing Islam. Say: 'In accepting Islam you have conferred on me no favor. It was God who bestowed a favor on you in guiding you to the true Faith...'" (Koran 49:18). His gift to us is His gentle guidance; and grasping this subtle truth is difficult but essential because His message is never forceful. The true place of worship is inside ourselves. This temple is not a physical building nor is it to be found in any man-made institutions we

call religion. God is everywhere, including inside all of us. Because God
has given us spiritual wisdom, our true form of worship is to practice it.

EXPECT CONDEMNATION

Question:
What should a spiritually developed person expect from others?

Brief Answer:
Never expect anything, but be prepared for everything.

from the *Gospel of Thomas*
105. Jesus said, "Whoever knows the father and the mother will be called the child of
a whore."

Longer Answer:
The simple action of trying to move forward spiritually often generates
a reflex action in others that tries to hold us in the place where they
are standing. They do not want us, or anyone, to proceed beyond
them. Thus, we can anticipate ridicule and condemnation when we seek our
spiritual development. The **Bhagavad-Gita** says:

> The Blessed Lord said:
> Where comes this faintness on thee?
> [Now] at this crisis-hour?
> This is ill beseems a noble,
> wins none a heavenly state,
> But brings dishonor,
> Arjuna.
> (Bhagavad-Gita 2,2)

God wants us to be strong in our faith at the moment of crisis. The **Hebrew Bible** says, "They gather themselves together against the soul of the righteous, and condemn the innocent blood. But the Lord is my defence; and my God *is* the rock of my refuge" (Psalms 94:21-22). Although righteousness is vital to our spiritual growth, righteousness often brings condemnation from peers. No matter how good or gentle we are, we can anticipate hostility as one of life's unpleasant characteristics. The **Dhammapada** says, "It is an old saying, not a new one: 'They disparage one who remains silent, they disparage one who talks a lot, and they even disparage one who speaks in moderation.' There is no one in the world who is not disparaged" (Dhammapada 17:7).

We should try to consider condemnation from others as a positive rather than a negative sign. The **New Testament** says, "Blessed *are* they which are persecuted for righteousness's sake; for theirs is the kingdom of heaven. Blessed are ye, when *men* shall revile you, and persecute *you*, and shall say all manner of evil against you falsely, for my sake" (Matthew 5:10-11). We can anticipate that friends and foes alike will direct all manner of criticism at us because of our life's choices, given that fear leads them to rail against what they cannot fathom. We should not become discouraged at these actions; rather we need to feel compassion for their fear and love them all the more. The **Koran** provides an example:

> Carrying the child,
> she came to her people,
> who said to her:
> "Mary,
> this is indeed a strange thing!
> Sister of Aaron,
> your father was never a whore-monger,
> nor was your mother a harlot."
>
> She made a sign to them,
> pointing to the child.
> But they replied:
> "How can we speak with a babe in the cradle?"
>
> Whereupon he spoke and said:
> "I am the servant of God.

He has given me the Book and ordained me a prophet.
His blessing is upon me wherever I go,
and He was commanded me to be steadfast in prayer
and to give alms to the poor as long as I shall live.
He has exhorted me to honor my mother
and has purged me of vanity and wickedness.
I was blessed on the day I was born,
and blessed I shall be on the day of my death;
and may peace be upon me on the day I shall be raised to life."

Such was Jesus, the son of Mary.

That is the whole truth, which they still doubt.

God forbid that He Himself should beget a son!

When He decrees a thing He need only say:
"Be,"
and it is.
(Koran 19:28)

Mary, the mother of Jesus Christ, was condemned. She did God's will and for that she was called a whore-monger and a harlot. Yet, she bore that resentment with grace and dignity because of the joy she had in doing God's will far surpassed anything anyone could say or do to her.

CHILDREN OF HUMANITY

Question:

How do we reach Oneness with God?

Brief Answer:

We get there by making the two into One.

from the *Gospel of Thomas*

106. Jesus said, "When you make the two into one and you will become children of humanity, and when you say, 'Mountain, move from here,' it will move."

Longer Answer:

How can we make two into one? In the context of spiritual wisdom, the expression is calling us to reach Oneness with God. The **Bhagavad-Gita** says:

> But he who roves among the things of sense,
> His senses subdued to SELF, from hate and passion free,
> And is self-possessed [himself],
> Is not far off from calm serenity.
>
> And from him thus becalmed
> All sorrows flee away:
> For once his thoughts are calmed,
> then soon
> Will his soul stand firmly [in its ground].
> (Bhagavad-Gita 2:64-65)

In order to be successful at making the two into one, we must control our senses, let God be our guide, and remain detached from the Kingdom of Man. What will happen when we decide to do that? The **Hebrew Bible** says:

> Multitudes,
> multitudes in the valley of decision:
> for the day of the Lord is near in the valley of decision.

The sun and the moon shall be darkened,
and the stars shall withdraw their shining.

The Lord also shall roar out of Zion,
and utter his voice from Jerusalem;
and the heavens and the earth shall shake:
but the Lord *will be* the hope of his people,
and the strength of the children of Israel.

So shall ye know that I *am* the Lord your God dwelling in Zion,
my holy mountain:
then shall Jerusalem be holy,
and there shall no strangers pass through her any more.

And it shall come to pass in that day,
that the mountains shall drop down new wine,
and the hills shall flow with milk,
and all the rivers of Judah shall flow with waters,
and a fountain shall come forth of the house of the Lord,
and shall after the valley of Shittim.
(Joel 3:14-18)

By consciously deciding to become One with God, we draw Him into our decisions; and He brings us hope and strength because we feel His presence grow within us. The **Dhammapada** says, "Dispassionate, unassuming, well versed in language and expression, knowing the assemblage of letters and their order, one in the final body with great insight is called a great person" (Dhammapada 24:19). When we recognize and comprehend the value of Oneness, we achieve great wisdom. The **Gospel of Thomas** says that when you make two into one you are a child of humanity. The **New Testament** clarifies that spiritual message as follows:

And Jesus answering saith unto them,
Have faith in God.
For verily I say unto you,
That whosoever shall say unto this mountain,
Be thou removed,

and be thou cast into the sea;
and shall not doubt in his heart,
but shall believe that those things which he saith shall come to pass;
he shall have whatsoever he saith.

Therefore I say unto you,
What things soever ye desire,
when ye pray,
believe that ye receive *them,*
and ye shall have *them.*

And when ye stand praying,
forgive,
if ye have ought against any:
that your Father also which is in heaven may forgive your trespasses.

But if ye do not forgive,
neither will your Father which is in heaven forgive your trespasses.
(Mark 11:22-26)

Spiritual wisdom teaches us that our actions reveal what we really are to everyone including ourselves. When we realize that and act accordingly, we become a child of humanity concerned chiefly or wholly with furthering others and being completely surrendered to God. If we earnestly try and we believe wholeheartedly in our God-given capacity, He becomes the source of our energy and our strength, because *He* is the doer of all our actions; there are thus no limits to what we can achieve. The **Koran** says, "Your religion is but one religion, and I am your only Lord. Therefore serve Me. Men have divided themselves into factions, but to Us they shall all return. He that does good works in the fullness of his faith, his endeavors shall not be lost: We record them all" (Koran 21:94). In the **Gospel of Thomas** quote, telling a mountain to move is a metaphor expressing that we *can* do the impossible. Certainly, having humankind realize that only one spiritual reality exists is an impossibility, but we can accomplish that impossibility when we comprehend His Oneness. Because we are what our actions are, with Oneness we will finally come to discern that there is no sense to having factions and divisions.

◆

SPECIAL CHILD

Question:
Does God really want me?

Brief Answer:
Yes, He wants every one of us. That was His plan from the beginning.

from the *Gospel of Thomas*

107. Jesus said, "The kingdom is like a shepherd who had a hundred sheep. One of them, the largest, went astray. He left the ninety-nine and sought the one until he found it. After he had gone to this trouble, he said to the sheep, 'I love you more than the ninety-nine.'"

Longer Answer:

The parable of the one lost sheep indicates God's special love for each of us. He particularly cares for the ones that He has nurtured and guided over time in spite of the fact that we may have wandered away from Him. The **New Testament** says:

> What man of you,
> having an hundred sheep,
> if he lose one of them,
> doth not leave the ninety and nine in the wilderness,
> and go after that which is lost,
> until he find it?
>
> And when he hath found *it*,
> he layeth *it* on his shoulders,
> rejoicing.

And when he cometh home,
he calleth together *his* friends and neighbours,
saying unto them,
Rejoice with me;
for I have found my sheep which was lost.

I say unto you,
that likewise joy shall be in heaven over one sinner,
that repenteth,
more than over ninety and nine just persons,
which need no repentance.
(Luke 15:4-7)

Each of us is a rare individual, because we are seekers trying to understand the subtle meaning of our lives, the greatest of all mysteries, the hidden truth within us, and the Grace of God Himself. The **Upanishad** says:

More subtle than the subtle,
greater than the great,
The SELF is hidden in the heart of creatures [here]:
The man without desire,
[all] sorrow spent,
beholds It,
The majesty of the SELF,
by the grace of the Ordainer.
(Katha Upanishad 2:20)

The rare person begins to strive for the perfection of Oneness, but the rarer person finds Oneness. The **Bhagavad-Gita** says:

Among thousands of men but one,
maybe,
Will strive for self-perfection;
And even among these [athletes] who have won perfection['s crown]
But one,
maybe,
will come to know Me as I really am.
(Bhagavad-Gita 7:3)

God feeds us spiritual wisdom. The **Hebrew Bible** says:

> I will feed my flock,
> and I will cause them to lie down,
> saith the Lord God.

> I will seek that which was lost,
> and bring again that which was driven away,
> and will bind up *that which was* broken,
> and will strengthen that which was sick:
> but I will destroy the fat and the strong;
> I will feed them with judgment.

> Therefore thus saith the Lord God unto them;
> Behold,
> I *even* I,
> will judge between the fat cattle and between the lean cattle.
> (Ezekiel 34:15-16,20)

God can cause us to do whatever He wants, but He chooses to give us free choice. He wants us to yearn to join Him in Oneness. Because of His remarkable concern for us, He mends and strengthens us but He has no similar interest in the "fat and strong" of the Kingdom of Man. The wise person transcends the Kingdom of Man by looking past its illusions. The **Dhammapada** says, "Swans travel the path of the sun, magical powers travel through space; the wise are led out of the world, having conquered all bedevilments" (Dhammapada 13:9). God does not want to lose any of us. The **New Testament** says:

> For the Son of man is come to save that which was lost.

> How think ye?
> if a man have an hundred sheep,
> and one of them be gone astray,
> doth he not leave the ninety and nine,
> and goeth into the mountains,
> and seeketh that which is gone astray?

> And if so be that he find it,
> verily I say unto you,
> he rejoiceth more of that *sheep*,
> than of the ninety and nine which went not astray.

> Even so it is not the will of your Father which is in heaven,
> that one of these little ones should perish.
> (Matthew 18:12-14)

God sent Jesus to be one of His messengers so that we could find our path. The **Koran** says, "God invites you to the Home of Peace. He guides whom He will to a straight path. Those that do good works shall have a good reward, and more besides. Neither blackness nor misery shall overcast their faces. They are the heirs of Paradise: in it they shall abide for ever" (Koran 10:26). We are all invited into God's Home of Peace because we are His students; and if we are good students, our lessons will lead us straight to His Home of Peace. In the Thomas parable of the shepherd, God cares for all of us, but He particularly cares for the largest or those most filled with light. This preference is in response to those who have sought diligently and have come the closest to Oneness with Him. When we show that we are receptive to both His presence and His gifts in our lives, the Oneness works two ways: not only do we grow closer to Him but He grows closer to us. If we falter and stray from the path, He will especially seek us out again and again with infinite patience to guide us back to our path so that we can resume our journey. His love for us individually is endless.

ACHIEVING ONENESS

Question:

Does God want me to achieve Oneness?

Brief Answer:

Yes, but you have already achieved Oneness. You just have not realized it yet.

from the *Gospel of Thomas*

108. Jesus said, "Whoever drinks from my mouth will become like me; I myself shall become that person, and the hidden things will be revealed to that person."

Longer Answer:

True nurturing comes from God's spiritual wisdom. The **Upanishad** says: "The SELF is exempt from evil, untouched by age or death or sorrow, untouched by hunger or thirst: its desire is the real, its idea is the real. This is what [you] must want to understand. Whoso has found this SELF and understands it, wins all states of being and all [objects of] desire" (Chandogya Upanishad 8,7:1). SELF or the Holy Spirit nurtures us; and we seek to understand the SELF by listening to the heart. The **Hebrew Bible** says, "Hear this, all *ye* people; give ear, all *ye* inhabitants of the world: Both low and high, rich and poor, together. My mouth shall speak of wisdom; and the meditation of my heart *shall be* of understanding" (Psalms 49:1-3). God gives us spiritual wisdom, but we must meditate on the heart in order to understand that wisdom. The **Dhammapada** says, "When truth is correctly explained, those who follow truth will go beyond the domain of death, which is so hard to cross over" (Dhammapada 6:11). If spiritual wisdom is correctly understood and followed, it is our bridge to Oneness. God recognizes that we are already One with Him, but we need to realize that fact ourselves. The **New Testament** says, "Verily, verily, I say unto you, The servant is not greater than his lord; neither he that is sent greater than he that sent him" (John 13:16). The **New Testament** also says, "So we, being many are one body in Christ, and every one members one of another" (Romans 12:5). Christ and the Father are One, just as we are One with Christ. All are One.

We can only realize our Oneness through spiritual wisdom. The **Koran** says, "God will strengthen the faithful with His steadfast Word, both in this life and in the hereafter. He leads the wrongdoers astray. God accomplishes what He pleases" (Koran 14:28). God will continue to strengthen us as we move closer towards Him. The **Koran** also says, "Blessed be He who has revealed Al-Furqan to His servant, that he may warn the nations; Sovereign of the heavens and the earth, who has begotten no children and has no partner in His sovereignty; who has created all things and ordained them in due proportion" (Koran 25:1).

EVER-PRESENT TREASURE

Question:
Has God been within us all this time?

Brief Answer:
Yes, but we lacked an awareness of His presence.

from the *Gospel of Thomas*

109. Jesus said, "The kingdom is like a person who had a treasure hidden in his field but did not know it. And [when] he died, he left it to his [son]. The son [did] not know (about it). He took over the field and sold it. The buyer went plowing, [discovered] the treasure, and began to lend money at interest to whomever he wished."

Longer Answer:

Spiritual wisdom tells us that we have always been One with God and that our greatest treasure is the SELF. Our challenges are always to see past the veil of ignorance and know that the whole universe is within us. We must comprehend spiritual wisdom in our hearts to recognize the Oneness and let God ultimately enlighten us. The **Upanishad** says:

For the man who sees and thinks and understands in this way, life [wells up] from the SELF; hope and memory [well up] from the SELF; space, heat and water [well up] from the SELF; appearance and disappearance, food and strength [well up] from the SELF; understanding, meditation, thought, will, mind, speech and name [well up] from the SELF; sacred formulas and [sacred] actions, nay, this whole universe [wells up] from the SELF. On this there are the following verses:

> The seer does not see death,
> Nor sickness nor yet sorrow:
> Seeing the All,
> the seer
> Attains the All in every way.
> Onefold,
> threefold it becomes,
> Fivefold,
> sevenfold,
> nine,
> — Again they say elevenfold,
> One hundred-and-elevenfold,
> And twenty-thousandfold.
> (Chandogya Upanishad 7,26)

How do we discover this? We pray, serve others spiritually, love others, and live our faith. We realize that God has gathered us together from all sorts of places solely because we are seekers. We need to associate with other seekers to learn from them and let them inspire us. The **Hebrew Bible** says:

> Also the sons of the stranger,
> that join themselves to the Lord,
> to serve him,
> and to love the name of the Lord,
> to be his servants.
> every (sic) one that keepeth the sabbath from polluting it,
> and taketh hold of my covenant;

> Even them will I bring to my holy mountain,
> and make them joyful in my house of prayer:
> their burnt offerings and their sacrifices *shall be* accepted upon mine alter:
> for mine house shall be called an house of prayer for all people.

> The Lord God which gathereth the outcasts of Israel saith,
> Yet will I gather *others* to him,
> beside those that are gathered unto him.
> (Isaiah 56:6-8)

The **New Testament** says, "Again, the kingdom of heaven is like unto treasure hid in a field; the (sic) which when a man hath found, he hideth, and for joy thereof goeth and selleth all that he hath, and buyeth that field" (Matthew 13:44). Now, with joy, we realize, first, that the so-called wealth of the Kingdom of Man is worthless; second, the treasure is hidden within us; third, that we are God's treasure. The **Dhammapada** says, "Who will conquer this earth, and this world of death, with its gods? Who will gather well-expressed words of truth, as an expert gathers flowers?" (Dhammapada 4:1-2). Who, indeed, if not us?

Our gift from God is life and that is an opportunity beyond description. We can use this life to realize the ultimate treasure — Oneness. The **Koran** says, "Serve none but God. I am sent to you from Him to warn you and to give you good tidings. Seek forgiveness of your Lord and turn to Him in repentance. A goodly provision He will make for you till an appointed day, and will bestow His grace on those that have merit. But if you give no heed, then beware the torment of a fateful day. To God you shall all return. He has power over all things" (Koran 11:2). Spiritual wisdom tells us to spend our lives serving no one but God and seeking His love and compassion. We need to listen carefully and hear His messages and directions. We must appreciate that we have always been One with Him.

Most of us go through life and do not recognize the treasure that we have buried within us. We die. With reincarnation, we return with a new body but the gift is still buried within us. Eventually we not only discover it but we learn to appreciate its worth. In the parable, the treasure is revealed when the new owner works the field of life just as we discover the treasure when our reincarnated being learns to appreciate God's spiritual wisdom. Once we have discovered our treasure, we are rich enough to lend it out to others. This act of sharing will return us interest from God in joy and light, because every person who seeks to serve God discovers even more of God's treasure. Often cited as a children's story, Aesop Fable 42 is a parallel parable to Thomas 109. (Meyer, p. 107). As a farmer lay dying he told his sons a treasure is hidden in the farmer's vineyard. After the death of the farmer and a great search in the vineyard, the treasure was not found. However, the vineyard repaid them with a harvest many times greater than the treasure they sought. Eventually, they came to realize that their work in their father's vineyard brought them their father's treasure. As in the parable, the treasure buried within us must be worked so that through our efforts we help harvest God's ultimate treasure — His love and our eternal happiness.

What Is Next

◆

AFTER ENLIGHTENMENT

Question:

What should we do once we are awakened?

Brief Answer:

We must renounce the desires of the Kingdom of Man.

from the *Gospel of Thomas*

110. Jesus said, "The one who has found the world and has become wealthy should renounce the world."

Longer Answer:

Once we accept God's presence within us and awaken to the realization that we are already One with Him, our interests and desires change. We begin the slow and steady march toward transcending

worldly desires. While we are living in the physical world, we need to participate in it on God's own terms. Small children love to play in the dirt and
sometimes even eat dirt. As they grow, they may still play in the dirt, but they
do not eat it any longer. Just like children, we need to mature continually, and
when we do, we will eventually transcend our physical desires, not so much
through the power of our minds but through the power of our hearts. We
reach a point where physical desire no longer has any meaning, because we
realize what we truly want and need is not of this world. In order to grasp the
infinite, we must let go of what we previously held dear. We know that it is
only through life and through experiencing the Kingdom of Man that we can
reach the true goal of the infinite, the permanent, and the stable. Oneness is
found in the act of recognition that occurs as God helps us remove the layers
of ignorance from our lives. The poetry of the **Upanishad** says:

> I know that what's called treasure is impermanent,
> For by things unstable the Stable cannot be obtained.
> Have I,
> them,
> builded up the Naciketa fire, -
> By things impermanent have I the Permanent attained?
> (Katha Upanishad 2:10)

Although vital to our enlightenment, eventually we must outgrow and transcend the Kingdom of Man. The **Hebrew Bible** is particularly helpful in
giving us insight into this aspect of spiritual wisdom. It says, "The Lord God
hath sworn by himself, saith the Lord the God of hosts, I abhor the excellen-
cy of Jacob, and hate his palaces: therefore will I deliver up the city with all
that is therein" (Amos 6:8). As we have said, the Kingdom of Man has and
does provide us with God's valuable lessons although God paradoxically
abhors its illusion of power and wealth and He is saddened when we are
fooled by it. The **Hebrew Bible** says, "For when he dieth he shall carry
nothing away: his glory shall not descend after him" (Psalms 49:17). This does
not mean that the earth will disappear when we have reached this major mile-
stone of SELF realization or that the world of desires is not necessary because
God does not like the illusion. The **Hebrew Bible** says, "And all their
wealth, and all their little ones, and their wives took them captive, and spoiled
even all that *was* in the house" (Genesis 34:29). The world does not disappear

with SELF realization. What is gone is the power that illusion had over us. No longer can the illusion spoil or cloud our understanding of God.

Renouncing the Kingdom of Man gives us freedom to grow. The **Dhammapada** says, " 'I have sons, I have wealth' — the fool suffers thinking thus. Even one's self is not one's own; how then sons, how then wealth?" (Dhammapada 5:3). If we understand fully that we belong to God, then logically everything we thought belonged to us really belongs to God. We discern and comprehend that we cannot live separately from Him. We grasp that everything is interconnected and exists as the Oneness of God. The **New Testament** says:

> But woe unto you that are rich!
> for ye have received your consolation.

> Woe unto you that are full!
> for ye shall hunger.

> Woe unto you that laugh now!
> for ye shall mourn and weep.

> Woe unto you,
> when all men shall speak well of you!
> for so did their fathers to the false prophets.
> (Luke 6:24-26)

The illusions of the Kingdom of Man are all part of God's larger plan. The **Koran** says, "Every misfortune that befalls the earth, or your own person, is ordained before We bring it into being. That is easy enough for God; so that you may not grieve for the good things you miss, or be overjoyed at what you gain. God does not love the haughty, the vainglorious; nor those who, being niggardly themselves, enjoin others to be niggardly also. He that gives no heed should know that God alone is self-sufficient and worthy of praise" (Koran 57:22). God executes His plan for us as we live out our lives, including all our joys, misfortunes, and calamities. We must neither grieve nor become overjoyed by the effects of the illusions themselves, because through spiritual wisdom we learn the importance of detachment and the great comfort of knowing God alone is the architect of our lives.

AFTER ONE HAS FOUND ONESELF

Question:

In what ways are we now different?

Brief Answer:

We now see and understand everything differently.

from the *Gospel of Thomas*

111. Jesus said, "The heavens and the earth will roll up in your presence. And the one who is alive out of the one who is alive will not see death."
(See Layton, p. 399. According to Layton, the following comment was added to saying 111 by an ancient reader and later erroneously incorporated in the text: "Doesn't Jesus mean that the world is not worthy of a person who found the self?" The comment itself reflects the query of a true seeker.)

Longer Answer:

Spiritual wisdom says that once we are awake, everything is radically different because we now see, feel, and experience everything from a dissimilar perspective. Literally, we understand and know everything differently because we have found ourselves in God. The **Upanishad** says:

> Now,
> the SELF is a bridge
> which hold these worlds apart lest they should split asunder.
>
> On this bridge there passes neither day nor night,
> neither old age nor death nor sorrow,
> neither deeds well done nor deeds ill done.
> All evils recoil from it,
> for in this Brahman-world evil has ever been laid low.
>
> And so,
> let the blind pass along this bridge and he will regain his sight;
> let the wounded [pass along it] and he will be healed;
> let the fevered [pass along it] and his fever will be calmed.
> And so it is that once a man has passed along this bridge,
> night will reveal itself as day indeed,
> for this Brahman-world is once and for all light [by its own light].

> To them alone belongs this Brahman-world
> who discover it by living the Brahman-life.
> In all the worlds they have [full] freedom of movement.
> (Chandogya Upanishad 8,4)

Our bridge to Oneness is the SELF or Holy Spirit. Only seekers pass over that bridge when freed from the attachment to the illusions of the world, because from this vantage point everything in the world looks and feels different. For example, we can now grasp the significance of human suffering because it no longer affects us. Physical space ceases to have the same reality. We can now view the Kingdom of Man as a story or lesson on paper that we take out and study, or roll up and put it aside when we are finished with the lesson. The **Upanishad** says:

> When men shall roll up space
> As though it were a piece of leather,
> Then will there be an end of suffering
> For him who is apart from knowing God!
> (Svetasvatara Upanishad 6:20)

Now, we comprehend that we must always turn to God. The **Hebrew Bible** says, "Stand in awe, and sin not: commune with your own heart upon your bed, and be still" (Psalms 4:4). The implications of the Kingdom of Man being created solely as a teaching device instills awe in us in terms of both God's remarkable love for us and His remarkable power. Once we begin to grasp the implications of what God has done, how can we deviate from our paths to Him? We must still all the other interferences in our lives and listen to our hearts, which are filled with love and gratitude for Him. The **Hebrew Bible** says, "Let us search and try our ways, and turn again to the Lord" (Lamentations 3:40). Our paths will not always be easy, because we sometimes have great difficulty letting go of our desires and emotions. Sometimes we surrender something to God only to take it back again. However, as long as our love of Him is strong and our spiritual thirst sincere, we will try and try again until we succeed, because we must always search for spiritual wisdom from God and try our best to live His ways. We must always turn again and again to God for strength and guidance.

The **Hebrew Bible** says, "And all the host of heaven shall be dissolved, and the heavens shall be rolled together as a scroll: and all their host shall fall down, as the leaf falleth off from the vine, and as a falling *fig* from the fig tree" (Isaiah 34:4). All the myths, ceremonies, and rituals become stories on paper that we can pull out and use to enjoy, entertain, inform, and comfort ourselves; and then we can fold them up and put them aside. We can establish them in proper perspective by judging them in the full context of spiritual wisdom. Now that we have found ourselves, we can proceed with certainty. The **Dhammapada** says, "Meditative, persevering, always striving diligently, the wise attain nirvana, supreme peace" (Dhammapada 2:3). We need to continue to meditate, persevere, and always strive diligently toward greater spiritual wisdom. We must never become complacent or overconfident that we are knowledgeable enough, because there is always more to understand. The **New Testament** says:

> Thou hast loved righteousness,
> and hated iniquity;
> therefore God,
> *even* thy God,
> hath anointed thee with the oil of gladness above thy fellows:
> And,
> Thou,
> Lord,
> in the beginning hast laid the foundation of the earth;
> and the heavens are the works of thine hands:
> They shall perish;
> but thou remainest;
> and they all shall wax old as doth a garment;
>
> And as a vesture shalt thou fold them up,
> and they shall be changed;
> but thou are the same,
> and thy years shall not fail.
> (Hebrews 1:9-12)

The **New Testament** also says:

> And the heaven departed as a scroll when it is rolled together;
> and every mountain and island were moved out of their places.

And the kings of the earth,
and the great men,
and the rich men,
and the chief captains,
and the mighty men,
and every bondman,
and every free man,
hid themselves in the dens and in the rocks of the mountains;

And said to the mountains and rocks,
Fall on us,
and hide us from the face of the him that sitteth on the throne,
and from the wrath of the Lamb:

For the great day of his wrath is come;
and who shall be able to stand?
(Revelations 6:14-17)

Spiritual wisdom tells us we no longer exist with the same understanding about heaven and earth, because our new perspective has changed everything. The **Koran** says, "On that day We shall roll up the heaven like a scroll of parchment. Just as We brought the First Creation into being, so will We restore it. This is a promise We shall assuredly fulfil" (Koran 21:104).

◆

OUR SOUL'S FUTURE DEPENDENCY

Question:
How else are we different?

Brief Answer:
We can also recognize the nonrelationship of desire and our eternal self.

from the *Gospel of Thomas*
112. Jesus said, "Damn the flesh that depends on the soul. Damn the soul that depends on the flesh."

Longer Answer:

Prior to understanding spiritual wisdom, we thought that our soul and the body were contingent upon each other. The **Upanishad** says, "He who transcends hunger and thirst, sorrow, confusion, old age and death [sic]. Once Brahmans have come to know this SELF, they rise above their desire for sons, their desire for riches, their desire for [exalted] states of being, and wander forth to lead a beggar's life. For there is no difference between a desire for riches and a desire for [exalted] states of being: all of them are nothing more than desire" (Brihadaranyaka Upanishad 3,5). Once we are aware of the SELF or God within us, the desires that drove us in the world are no longer important to us, because they lack any relevance to our new perspectives.

The **Hebrew Bible** says, "With my soul have I desired thee in the night; yea, with my spirit within me will I seek thee early: for when thy judgments *are* in the earth, the inhabitants of the world will learn righteousness" (Isaiah 26:9). We want God to lighten our lives in moments of darkness, but once we comprehend Oneness, we quickly realize that we need to seek God not only in time of darkness but always. More and more people awakening to spiritual wisdom raises the collective consciousness of the world so that His whole creation can better comprehend Oneness. Buddha says, "The Noble Truth of the Cessation of suffering is this: It is the complete cessation of that very thirst, giving it up, renouncing it, emancipating oneself from it, detaching oneself from it" (The First Sermon of the Buddha 6). Eventually, the world will perceive the critical need to follow the Noble Truth of Cessation of Suffering. The **Dhammapada** says, "Others do not know we must pass away here; but for those who know this, contention thereby ceases" (Dhammapada 1:6). As more awaken, strife, disputes, and controversy will diminish and eventually fade away.

Our future progress depends on us maintaining this relationship. The **New Testament** says, "Are ye so foolish? having begun in the Spirit, are ye now made perfect by the flesh?" (Galatians 3:3). Now, we grasp that our future progress does not depend on physical desires but on the aspiration of the heart. The **New Testament** also says, "For the flesh lusteth against the Spirit, and Spirit against the flesh: and these are contrary the one to the other: so that ye cannot do the things that ye would" (Galatians 5:17). We understand desires of the flesh to be incompatible with our continued spiritual growth. In time, we will simply outgrow them. The **New Testament** also says, "For he that soweth to his flesh shall of the flesh reap corruption: but he that soweth to the Spirit shall of the Spirit reap life everlasting" (Galatians 6:8). If we stubbornly bind ourselves to the desires of life, we will become entrapped by them. Instead, we can look to the Spirit within ourselves for continued growth and inspiration. The **Koran** says, "Those that preserve themselves from their own greed will surely prosper. If you give a generous loan to God, He will pay you back twofold and will forgive you. Gracious is God, and benignant" (Koran 64:17). When we give of ourselves unconditionally, the greater spiritual wealth is ours.

THE NEW KINGDOM OF GOD

Question:

When will the new Kingdom of God come?

Brief Answer:

It has already begun.

from the *Gospel of Thomas*

113. His followers said to him, "When will the kingdom come?"

"It will not come by watching for it. It will not be said, 'Look, here it is,' or 'Look, there it is.' Rather, the father's kingdom is spread out upon the earth, and people do not see it."

Longer Answer:

The new Kingdom of God has already come, yet most do not see it. God is everywhere, but few people take the trouble to see Him. As spiritual wisdom is everywhere, including within each of us, we must merely recognize it and grow with it. As we learned earlier from spiritual wisdom, a metaphor for knowledge is light. We can sense the presence of God's light everyplace. The **Upanishad** says:

Now,
the light which shines beyond the heavens,
on to the back of all things,
on to the back of very single thing,
in the highest and most exalted worlds,
that is indeed the same as the light within man.

When a man feels the heat in the body [of another] by touching it,
he sees that [light].
When he stops up his ears and hears something like a rumbling or the crackling of
a blazing fire,
he hears that [light].
So it should be revered as something seen and heard.
Whoso knows this will be [well-]seen and [his name will be] noised abroad,
— whoso knows this.
(Chandogya Upanishad 3,8)

Time is an invention of humankind, but God is as infinite as His use of time. For us, the past is now dust because it did not offer us the fulfillment called Oneness and the future has not yet arrived. The only moment that is useful to us is NOW. God is constantly establishing His Kingdom in this moment. The **Hebrew Bible** says, "Thy kingdom *is* an everlasting kingdom, and thy dominion *endureth* throughout all generations" (Psalms 145:13). Unlike the Kingdom of Man, the new kingdom is everlasting. The **Hebrew Bible** also says, "And in the days of these kings shall the God of heaven set up a kingdom, which shall never be destroyed: and the kingdom shall not be left to other people, *but* it shall break in pieces and consume all these kingdoms, and it shall stand for ever" (Daniel 2:44). Step by step, God is and has always been establishing His kingdom. As more and more awake to their Oneness with God, His kingdom will eventually grow within each of us, and, in time, it will consume the Kingdom of Man.

The **Dhammapada** says, "If you can make yourself as still as a broken gong, you have attained nirvana; there is no agitation in you" (Dhammapada 10:6). We must be still to hear our hearts without agitation by meditating calmly and quietly. The **New Testament** says, "But the righteousness which is of faith speaketh on this wise, Say not in thine heart. Who shall ascend into heaven? [that is, to bring Christ down *from above*:] Or, Who shall descend into the deep? [that is, to bring up Christ again from the dead]" (Romans 10:6-7). With righteousness based on faith, we are *not* to judge others as being good or bad or as being a part of or not a part of this Kingdom. God alone judges us. The **Koran** says, "Each apostle We have sent has spoken in the language of his own people, so that he might make his meaning clear to them. But God leaves in error whom He will and guides whom He pleases. He is the Mighty, the Wise One" (Koran 14:3). God has sent His messengers to speak to all peoples in ways they can appreciate. Ultimately, God decides who is really to be guided and who is not. We are only responsible for our own soul's progress. We must do our best for that for which we are responsible and let God do the rest.

IMPLICATIONS OF FREE CHOICE

Question:
What characteristic indicates a person is achieving Oneness?

Brief Answer:
There are no external characteristics from the Kingdom of Man that indicate whether a person will or will not achieve Oneness. The internal characteristic from the Kingdom of God is freely choosing Oneness with God.

from the *Gospel of Thomas*

114. Simon Peter said to them, "Mary should leave us, for females are not worthy of life." Jesus said, "Look, I shall guide her to make her male, so that she too may become a living spirit resembling you males. For every female who makes herself male will enter heaven's kingdom."

Longer Answer:

Free *conscious* choice is critical to spiritual wisdom because it is essential at the beginning of our journey, during every critical moment on our path, and at the end of our quest. The **Upanishad** says, "Now whoever departs this world without having caught a glimpse of the state of being appropriate to himself will have not part in it because it will have no knowledge of

him, — just like the Veda if it is not recited, or any other work left undone.
Yes, even if a man were to perform a great and holy work without knowing
this, — this, in the end, would be lost for him indeed" (Brihadaranyaka
Upanishad 1,4:15). Spiritual gains must derive from a conscious steady
progress rather than an accidental windfall. The **Upanishad** also says:

> The better part is one thing,
> the agreeable another;
> Though different their goals both restrict a man:
> For him who takes the better of the two all's well,
> But he who chooses the agreeable fails to attain his goal.
> (Katha Upanishad 2:1)

> Not he who has not ceased from doing wrong,
> Nor he who knows no peace,
> no concentration,
> Nor he whose mind is filled with restlessness,
> Can grasp Him,
> wise and clever though he be.
> (Katha Upanishad 2:24)

Our spiritual gains come for reasons that we may not understand. For
example, inner progress does not occur because we are wise or intelligent. We
cannot achieve inner peace by being agreeable to others. Instead, we must
make our inner progress through having our life choices predicated on spiritual wisdom. We must make those choices using our conscience and concentration, because the right mind-set is critical to successfully reaching the goal.
The **Bhagavad-Gita** says:

> For whosever makes Me his haven,
> Base-born though he may be,
> Yes,
> women too,
> and artisans,
> even serfs, —
> Theirs it is to tread the highest Way.
> (Bhagavad-Gita 9:32)

Concern about what God wants is very important. Economic well-being, social status, gender, occupation, or other ways to create status and division in the Kingdom of Man mean nothing in terms of our ability to reach Oneness. The **Hebrew Bible** says, "Favor *is* deceitful, and beauty *is* vain: *but* a woman *that* feareth the Lord, she shall be praised" (Proverbs 31:30). Buddha suggests, "THE THIRD REALIZATION is that the human mind is always searching for possessions and never feels fulfilled. This causes impure actions to ever increase. Bodhisattvas however, always remember the principle of having few desires. They live a simple life in peace in order to practice the Way, and consider the realization of perfect understanding as their only career" (The Sutra on the Eight Realizations of the Great Beings 3). The wisest action to establish the correct attitude within us is to live a simple life with few desires. Once someone has freely chosen to gain spiritual wisdom, no one should interfere with their spiritual growth process. In the following brief story, Martha tries to interfere with her sister's spiritual growth and path. The **New Testament** says:

<blockquote>
Now it came to pass,
as they went,
that he entered into a certain village;
and a certain woman named Martha received him into her house.

And she had a sister called Mary,
which also sat at Jesus's feet,
and heard his word.

But Martha was cumbered about much serving,
and came to him,
and said,
Lord,
dost thou not care that my sister hath left me to serve alone?
bid her therefore that she help me.

And Jesus answered and said unto her,
Martha,
Martha,
thou are careful and troubled about many things:

But one thing is needful:
and Mary hath chosen that good part,
which shall not be taken away from her.
(Luke 10:38-42)
</blockquote>

In contrast, if someone has freely chosen not to gain spiritual wisdom, no one should seek to intercede. God has given each of us our own free choice and we need to respect God's decision. The **Koran** says:

> But when a man's soul is about to leave him and those around him cry:
> Will no one save him?
> When he knows it is the final parting and the pangs of death assail him
> — on that day to your Lord he shall be driven.
> For in this life he neither believed nor prayed;
> he denied the truth and,
> turning his back,
> went to his kinsfolk elated with pride.
>
> Well have you deserved this door;
> well have you deserved it.
>
> Well have you deserved this doom;
> too well have you deserved it!"
> (Koran 75:24)

God's greatest gift to each of us is free choice and no one should attempt to disturb that gift. For example, for anyone such as Peter in the Thomas saying to not let a woman exercise her *free will* in regards to her spiritual development is disturbing God's will. Each person must exercise his or her individual free will to be on his or her own path to Oneness with the Supreme as long as others including the environment are not harmed. God selects and presents spiritual learning opportunities to all of us according to our circumstances and abilities. Within those constraints, we should be free to follow our own path as defined by God and accept or reject God's direction. Each of us must live out the consequences of our choices. No government should compel a particular religious practice and no one should exclude one person or a segment of society from being fully free to learn spiritual wisdom or any part of spiritual wisdom. Freedom of choice is essential and we must exercise it in our own lives and respect it fully in the lives of all others.

References

Bloom, Harold. "A Reading" in Marvin Meyer, *The Gospel of Thomas*. New York: Harper Collins, 1992.

Cleary, Thomas (translator). *Dhammapada*. New York: Bantam Books, 1994.

Conze, Edward. "Buddhism and Gnosis" in *The Allure of Gnosticism* edited by Robert A. Segal. Chicago: Open Court, 1995.

Dawood, N. J.(translator). *Koran*. New York: Penguin Books, 1993.

deHaven-Smith, Lance. *The Hidden Teaching of Jesus*. Grand Rapids, Michigan: Phane Press, 1994.

Friedman, Richard Elliott. *Who Wrote the Bible?* New York: Harper and Row, 1987, 1989.

Grenz, Stanley J. *A Primer on Postmodernism* Grand Rapids, Michigan: Wm. B. Eerdmans Publishing Co., 1969.

Holy Bible (King James version). Cleveland, Ohio: The World Publishing Company, first published in 1611.

Kersten, Holger. *Jesus Lived in India*. Rockport, Massachusetts: Element, 1986, 1994.

Kloppenborg, John S., Marvin W. Meyer, Stephen J. Patterson, and Michael G. Steinhauser. *Q Thomas Reader*. Sonoma, California: Polebridge Press, 1990.

Koester, Helmut. "Introduction" to The Gospel of Thomas in *The Nag Hammadi Library* edited by James Robinson M. New York: Harper and Row, 1987.

Layton, Bentley. *The Gnostic Scriptures*. Garden City, New York: Doubleday and Company, 1987.

Mack, Burton L. *Who Wrote the New Testament?* New York: Harper San Francisco, 1994.

Mead, G. R. S. *Pistis Sophia*. Kila, Massachusetts: Kessinger Publishing Co., not dated.

Meinardus, Otto F. A. *Monks and Monasteries of the Egyptian Desert*. Cairo, Egypt: The American University Press, 1989.

Meyer, Marvin. *The Gospel of Thomas*. Harper San Francisco, 1992.

Price, A. F. and Wong Mou-lam (translators). *The Diamond Sutra and the Sutra of Hui-neng*. Boston: Shambhala, 1990.

Prophet, Elizabeth Clare. *The Lost Years of Jesus*. Livingson, Massachusetts: Summit University Press, 1984.

Rahula, Walpola (translator). *The Buddha Taught*. New York: Grove Weidenfeld, 1974.

Robinson, James M. (ed.). *The Nag Hammadi Library*. New York: Harper and Row, 1987.

Rudolph, Kurt. *Gnosis: The Nature and History of Gnosticism*. New York: Harper and Row, 1987.

Singer, June. "The Evolution of the Soul" in *The Allure of Gnosticism* edited by Robert A. Segal. Chicago: Open Court, 1995.

Thich, Nhat Hanh. *The Sutra on the Eight Realizations of the Great Being*. Berkeley, California: Parallax Press, 1987.

Winterhalter, Robert. *Fifth Gospel*. New York: Harper and Row, 1988.

Zaehner, R. C. (translator). *Hindu Scriptures*. London, England: J. M. Dent and Sons Ltd., 1992.

Index